D0782987

COLLECTED POEMS

David **Constantine** was born in 1944 in Salford, Lancashire. He read Modern Languages at Wadham College, Oxford, and lectured in German at Durham from 1969 to 1981 and at Oxford from 1981 to 2000. He is a freelance writer and translator, a Fellow of the Queen's College, Oxford, and co-editor with Helen Constantine of *Modern Poetry in Translation*. He lives in Oxford and Scilly.

His first book of poems, *A Brightness to Cast Shadows* (Bloodaxe Books, 1980), was widely acclaimed. His second collection, *Watching for Dolphins* (Bloodaxe Books, 1983), won the 1984 Alice Hunt Bartlett Prize, and his academic study, *Early Greek Travellers and the Hellenic Ideal* (Cambridge University Press, 1984), won the first Runciman Prize in 1985. His first novel, *Davies*, was published by Bloodaxe in 1985, and his first book of stories, *Back at the Spike* by Ryburn Publishing in 1994. *Fields of Fire*, his biography of Sir William Hamilton, was published by Weidenfeld & Nicolson in 2001.

His third collection, *Madder* (Bloodaxe Books, 1987), a Poetry Book Society Recommendation, won the Southern Arts Literature Prize. The French edition of *Madder*, translated by Yves Bichet as *Sorlingues* (Éditions La Dogana, 1992), won the Prix Rhône-Alpes du Livre. His *Selected Poems* (Bloodaxe Books, 1991) was a Poetry Book Society Recommendation. *Caspar Hauser: a poem in nine cantos* (Bloodaxe Books, 1994) was followed by *The Pelt of Wasps* (Bloodaxe Books, 1998), including his verse-play *Lady Hamilton and the Elephant Man*, first broadcast on BBC Radio 3 in 1997, and *Something for the Ghosts* (Bloodaxe Books, 2002), shortlisted for the Whitbread Poetry Award.

He has published translations of poetry and prose by German, French and Greek writers. He was joint winner of the European Translation Prize in 1998 for his translation of Friedrich Hölderlin's *Selected Poems* (Bloodaxe, 1990; new edition, 1996), published a critical introduction to the poetry of Hölderlin (OUP, 1988), and translated Hölderlin's versions of Sophocles' *Oedipus* and *Antigone* as *Hölderlin's Sophocles* (Bloodaxe, 2001). His translation of Hans Magnus Enzensberger's *Lighter Than Air* (Bloodaxe, 2002) won the Poetry Society's Corneliu M Popescu Prize for European Poetry Translation in 2003. He has also translated Goethe's novel *Elective Affinities* (OUP, World's Classics, 1994), Kleist's *Selected Writings* (Dent, 1997) and Goethe's *Faust* (forthcoming in Penguin Classics). The Bloodaxe Contemporary French Poets series includes his translations of (with Helen Constantine) *Spaced, Displaced* by Henri Michaux (1992) and (with Mark Treharne) *Under Clouded Skies / Beauregard* by Philippe Jaccottet (1994).

His *Collected Poems* is published by Bloodaxe Books in 2004 at the same time as *A Living Language: Bloodaxe/Newcastle Poetry Lectures*.

DAVID CONSTANTINE

Collected Poems

BLOODAXE BOOKS

ISBN: 1 85224 667 7

First published 2004 by
Bloodaxe Books Ltd,
Highgreen,
Tarset,
Northumberland NE48 1RP.

www.bloodaxebooks.com
For further information about Bloodaxe titles
please visit our website or write to
the above address for a catalogue.

Bloodaxe Books Ltd acknowledges
the financial assistance of
Arts Council England, North East.

Cover printing by J. Thomson Colour Printers Ltd, Glasgow.

Printed in Great Britain by
Bell & Bain Limited, Glasgow, Scotland

ACKNOWLEDGEMENTS

This book includes all the poems which David Constantine wishes to keep in print from his previous Bloodaxe collections *A Brightness to Cast Shadows* (1980), *Watching for Dolphins* (1983), *Madder* (1987), *Selected Poems* (1991), *Caspar Hauser: A Poem in Nine Cantos* (1994), *The Pelt of Wasps* (1998) and *Something for the Ghosts* (2002); together with the whole of two Delos Press limited editions, *Sleeper* (1995) and *A Poetry Primer* (2004); and a new collection.

Acknowledgements are due to the editors of the following publications in which some of the previously uncollected poems first appeared: *Babel*, *Being Alive* (Bloodaxe Books, 2004), *Black Lamb*, *Dream Catcher*, *Forward Book of Poetry 2003* and *2004* (Forward, 2002 & 2003), *Magma*, *Manhattan Review* (USA), *The New Republic* (USA), *New Welsh Review*, *The North*, *Oxford Magazine*, *Oxford Poetry*, *Poetry London* and *The Reader*.

CONTENTS

FROM **MADDER** (1987)

FROM **SELECTED POEMS** (1991)

SOMETHING FOR THE GHOSTS (2002)

FROM

A BRIGHTNESS
TO CAST SHADOWS

(1980)

'As our bloods separate'

As our bloods separate the clock resumes,
I hear the wind again as our hearts quieten.
We were a ring: the clock ticked round us
For that time and the wind was deflected.

The clock pecks everything to the bone.
The wind enters through the broken eyes
Of houses and through their wide mouths
And scatters the ashes from the hearth.

Sleep. Do not let go my hand.

Birdsong

Most are sleeping, some
Have waited hopelessly for mercy,
Others even by this will not be stayed.
But we who have not slept for quantity
Of happiness have heard
The dawn precipitate in song
Like dewfall.

We think our common road a choir of trees.

'Daffodils in vases'

Daffodils in vases, watch them daily
For the first touch of dying, even
The blossom you came carrying
Of cherry and almond I will raise
The fire with tonight to see
You naked by, only the tulips
Wider and wider leave them opening
Until their petals fall
In gouts on the marble hearth.

'But most you are like'

But most you are like
The helpless singing of birds
To whom the light happens
On whom it falls
And at whose purity of voice
The skies weep and there is a pause
In all the world before beginning
And before the ending.

A Brightness to Cast Shadows

And now among them these dark mornings yours
Ascendant and of a brightness to cast shadows.
Love the winter, fear
The earlier and earlier coming of the light
When in the mantle blue we turn our dead faces.

The Fool

Be still, only believe me, said the Fool
Love and with impartial pleasure
Touched her breasts and mine

Ignoring any history of lovers and children
But as a matter of sole beauty
Admired their present marks

On my breasts now and see, he said,
The lighter halo of hers. A while,
The dancers' above earth,

We did take hands she and I
And the Fool in a ring against
Outliving Time

Whom I saw sardonically looking
To enter the round between us
Facing the boy Love.

'Eyes wide with the moon'

Eyes wide with the moon
He speaks in a tangle of words
How cold her hair was

He would have me imagine the moon
The briars the bedded leaves
A place out of the cold

The cold shines into me
The bright face takes my breath
Withers my warm reply

He will have warmed her hands
A tree he says the branches her cold hair
Among the embracing roots

She will have been drawn into
The moon in his eyes her tongue
Into his mouth...

'You are distant, you are already leaving'

You are distant, you are already leaving
You will have seemed here only between trains
And we are met here in the time of waiting
And what you last want is our eyes on you.

We shall have said nothing, we shall have done
Nothing in all that meantime there will
Have been not one gift pleasing us
You will have looked away and only behind
The pane of glass taking your seat with strangers
Being conveyed from here and when there is
No stay of parting you will smile perhaps
And give your face then the small mercy of weeping.

'In the meantime, in the waiting time'

In the meantime, in the waiting time
There is no present stay, we are
Not capable of interlude, we seem
In talk attending to elsewhere
And that it wants a while yet to the sun's going
Will not warm us in the long shade of our own.
Giving nothing to time present how
We overburden time remaining
With what we have not said we know
And raise the burden to impossible. Remembering
How cold under this future promontory
We studied only to effect evasions
Love do not elsewhere think of death as mountains
Shutting out the sun even before midday.

Eurydice

He turned. Nor was she following. The god
Shrugged and departed – on such a fool's errand
He will in future be harder to engage.

She remained staring into the black pool
Transfixed
As though in love but without
Any pleasure in the beloved face.

Soon there were none among the living
Who could remember her
As living. For her recovery
She imagined one who should descend the interminable spirals
Never having seen her live and yet
Imagining she might, one who would climb
Confident of the daylight and of her following.

On the coming of such a one
She waited. And not
At a crossroads but
In Hell.

The Damned

I see the damned are like this:
Loquacious to no effect, for ever
Coming to the end of their poor abilities,
Words failing them, neither

Their blows nor their embraces
Serving them better,
Incapable of nakedness
They rasp their hands on one another

Like two dead trees' branches
They sound the skull with a long finger,
Their speech is a sort of trepanning, lidless
The eyes watch barrenly for ever.

Dawn: slow fall of song...The sky
I imagine white, streaming with mercy.

'All wraiths in Hell are single'

All wraiths in Hell are single though they keep
Company together and go in troops like sheep.
None meets a lover from the former world,
No souls go hand in hand, round each is curled
The river Acheron. They suffer most
Who violently joined the myriad host,
Who angrily to spite love in the face
Before their time intruded on that place,
Putting themselves by pride beyond recovery,
Beyond sight, beyond calling. They seem to be
Alive among the dead wishing the thing undone
By which they put themselves beyond Acheron.
Divested of anger, cold, without reprieve
Sine die along the riverbanks they grieve.
They hear one calling after love into the black
But cannot answer and cannot come back.

Streams

It was never enough only to trace their courses
Nor to follow alongside, and the best were pathless,
But I must be always in them straddling the waters,
Clawing among roots, fingers poked in the wet moss
And parting the long grasses for a grip of stone.
Best to be naked as well as possible to feel
The switch of birches, smooth trunks of rowan,
Sticks and fronds of fern and tassels of hazel.

Hand on either bank and foothold to embrace
The reclining falls and rainbowed round to sunder
The water like a tree for a breathless space...
And for the smell of mud there is in worming under
The grasses, the toppled boles are finger-soft
And the glimmering rock flakes like the bark of birches.
The eyes may be shut with moss in some such cleft,
Mouth and nose pressed to in a deep kiss.

One I remember climbing from the blue renowned
As deepest of all the lakes and verdant black
Among lawns and pines the enclosed garden ground
To where, between scented equal hills, my back
And praising arms brightly arrayed in sun,
Wet-lipped from a hoof of sedge the water grew.
You will have thought below I'd gone for heaven
When I stood there at the sky on the brink of all blue.

Lamb

A lamb lay under the thorn, the black
Thorn bending by the last broken wall
And grasping what it can.

The dead lamb picketed a ewe.
She cropped round, bleating
And chewing in that machinal way of sheep.
And although she backed to a safe distance,
When I climbed down towards her lamb
Through a gap in the wall,
It was as if painfully paying out the fastening cord.

The crow was there, also
At a safe distance, waiting for the ewe to finish;
And sidled off a further yard or so,
Waiting until I too should have finished.

In high relief the lamb
Lay leaping, the small hooves down-pointed at
The instant of spring, one foreleg already flexing
To step forward on the air.
The head like a new tennis ball
But stained; the mouth grim as a shark's.
For the eye had gone, and all
That swelled from the socket was a black bubble.

The ewe, chewing and mourning, and
The crow, that fathoms the convenient eye-hole,
Had approached on either hand. The bubble burst
And a hole sank such a depth into the skull
That not a sound returned.

I backed away, and again
The ewe could circle the navel of her earth;
But the crow, with a hunching of wings and a jump sideways,
Glanced over the raised cloak of one wing,
And trod, and grasped its feet into the ground,
And could wait
Until hunger stretched and parted
The cord, and the monotony
Of chewing deadened any pain.

Even from river level I knew the place
In the angle where the wall descends
And I thought I could make out the bush
And the white dot of the dead lamb under it.

And I thought in that place there is always an exit
From the light of the sun, an issue of darkness
Opened by the crow's black beak. I know the way
Into the hillside
Through the eye of a lamb.

That was in April, when
Snow still lies beyond the wall, before
The blackthorn flowers.

Near Zennor

Coming among the grazing boulders
They herded them into hedges
And tended their own cattle on the vacated ground.

They made houses of the stones skirting the carn
And beyond mounds for their dead
In a quiet herd, and paths from place to place.

It is not easy now to distinguish between
Their circles and the collars of the dead mines.
The hedges and paths are as they were.

And a stone riven by frost from the mother flank
Their feet have gone over across water,
Their heads bowed under daily into the house.

To go back unobtrusively under the moor
Is one grace of austerity, to flower
And be quarried for a successor's building.

The Lane

The lane's especial beauty, why especially
You are at home there, is the way it has
Of winding unhurriedly and for no remembered reason,
And this I have come to love more even than
The scent and the quiet between its hedges.

Even alone now, though by nature one
For landmarks on the horizon to be reached by dark,
As far as is possible I adopt your way
And walk in the lane's good time that never offers
More to our view than we should be content with;

And after the farm becomes impassable,
Under the vaulting of both hedges' trees,
In any season but of the hardest drought or frost:
Which ultimatum at the outset lends
Your dawdling its complacency.

For these your and the lane's own qualities
And that in special once, a moonless night
And close with honeysuckle,
The sea pausing between wave and wave,
You came to meet me down it,

Nowhere is more home. A certainty
Of love is that of taking hands
And elsewhere turning into this same lane,
Sending ahead the old precursors:
The fox, the cat, the finches.

The Journey

Leaving the watered villages
The ash and poplar cool in their appearances
We came the companionable stream and I
To the last farm by and by.

For the whitethorn there
That was in flower later than anywhere
The girl water would not continue with me
I left her under the last tree.

Then some days following
I cast the long shadows of morning and evening
At noon I rode the sun on my shoulder
I was without water.

The white sheep lay
Like the remaining snow in February
On the north side of walls, in holes they hid
In poor embraces of shade.

Beyond pasture, beyond enclosure
On the common land of rock how far below were
Any cwm, any cradled pool and the water-veined
Wide folds. There intervened

No cloud, no bough between
Myself and the sun, only a hawk was shone
Steadily upon me in the grip of noon
I trod my shadow down.

I dreamed of the girl Artemis
She wore the ash and the poplar in a green dress
She led three burning hounds and seeing me
She smiled and set them free.

'Pitiless wind'

Pitiless wind, the hedges
Queue for dole, there is
No warmth in line. More
Pitiless light, searching
From under snowclouds, level

Like the wind, discovering
Rags, cans and what
Have been hugged to the heart
Since May: nests, all
Empty but one or two

And these, harboured since there
Were leaves, containing small
Frail skeletons bent
Like embryos. The wind, the light
Show up our few belongings.

'The wind has bared the stars'

The wind has bared the stars,
The skeletons, the after-images.

The life of trees has flown,
Their swarm of leaves, their hail of birds, their bone-

Dry sticks tap-tap,
Their blades slant in the earth's cold lap,

And leafless we are shown
To be rooted apart, two trees not one.

The dust and hail belong
Nowhere particular, our leaves and song;

Disperse among the stars,
Our skeletons, our after-images.

'Trewernick'

1

House in the marsh, it was always at evening
   We saw you first, over reed-tops, through a haze
Of lichened willows, after twelve hours travelling.
   Beyond our terminus the daylight set
Slowly from off the remaining terra firma,
   But we retraced our passage through the reeds
To the gate and threshold among apple trees before
   The night came roosting in your cypresses.
House in the marsh, had you taught your children nothing
   But the reliable grace of such a welcome
Yet you'd have charged a family for generations
   So that they shone with the warm glow of gold.

2

Mounding the earth, facing it in with rusty stone,
   Raising upon the borders of culture
Fine distinctions in heather and broom, gently you made
   Your garden join the field, your tended plants
Confused their colours with a savage hedge behind
   Of gorse and bramble. Had I to indicate
Your tact with rooted lives I'd put my finger on
   That sewing of your garden to the fields
Which rise then stitched with hedges in a mild gradient
   To Ludgvan Church and culminate on ground
Of granite where the brow is wreathed with defences
   And the threadbare back pockmarked with tumuli.

3

One year the marvel was a bush vermilion
   With lucent fruit, one bush, glowing like Mars,
Kept at its brilliant prime for us to see. There followed
   By our hands the abundant bleeding of the tree,
The million berries mounded in a basket. Your
   Own skill is that of transferring the garden
Into the recesses of the house, of cupping
   The summer in a household hoard with no
Diminishing of warmth or light. In jars on shelves
   In cupboards stood the store of amber, garnet,
Jade and when the year closed down the house glowed at its core
   With the essences your working hands put by.

4

Dear ones in Cornwall how golden and leisurely
    The light stays. Nobody can be in haste
Not even to ask for or dispose of stories,
    But a shyness which is perhaps the sun
Slanting so low causes companions to hide their eyes
    And soonest to fall silent, admiring
The growth of a tree set at a birth ten years ago.
    Then to seek anything would seem discourteous
In the fullness we can almost hold to be lasting.
    Again we shall leave and you will write to us
How in October the sky blackened with starlings
    And fell on that mock cornfield like a pall.

5

But now the children are handing you down apples
    That will sweeten the dark under the roof
Another winter. Then the reeds, under a cold sky,
    Are warm-coloured like corn and fire by fire
Towards another spring you burn the logs of cypress
    And apple wood. How much is into us
Of all your gifts and through the long attenuation
    Shall we be able to keep hold? Think the hands
We see on tombs are clasped not only in farewell
    But to impart and thereby are we bound.
By touch the generations glow. If not reunion
    Those held hands are at least continuance.

'Suddenly she is radiant again'

Suddenly she is radiant again.
She sees rainbows through her wet lashes;
In the brilliant light her wet cheeks glisten;
Her talk resumes like a brook, as fast and careless.

She has to suffer the interruption
Of sobs still, that have the bad manners
To arrive after the thunder has already gone
Over the hill, insisting they are hers.

We were a black sky only a minute ago,
Now I'm the one cloud in her clear heaven.
I haven't even begun yet to undo
The hideous knot of anger she tied me in.

I'm like a black old lump of winter snow
Bitterly facing the spring sun. Fair
Is always fair and the ugly, be they ever so
Much in the right, are not welcome anywhere.

I'm not a stone, I'm dirty snow that in
Her sunlight melts. It has no choice but to.
Soon I begin to feel I've been forgiven:
I go down on my knees and fasten her shoe.

'For years now'

For years now through your face the skull has shown
Nearer than through their living surface
The hills' bulk of dead stone;

And for years, watching you sleeping in that chair,
I have wished you might die with your face and hands composed,
Quietly sleeping there,

And trusted death to be so easy on you
That now one moment you would be sleeping and now
Have ceased without seeming to.

But today, watching you dead, I cannot think that there
Is any such slow passing into death from life
That the one might seem the other.

Finally the gap is absolute. Living
At all you were never nearly dead
And dead there is nothing

Vital of you in the abandoned face.
But the lack, the difference, has such nearness
We could almost embrace.

Waiting

We have gathered together
The things you will need immediately
And set them on a table
By the bed you will be born in.
You have three drawers to your name
Of clothes for the first months.

I go from room to room. The house
Is waiting. Our hands are ready.
Even not yet knowing you
We love you; grateful
For how you have increased us; glad
We have it in us to put out new love.

Hands

Round my finger, like a bird perching...
In my hollow palm, like a pebble, a cool bud...
Idling with his hands.

O hands...

The interslotting of our fingers and beckoning in
Your palm and tonguing of
The skin that tautens between thumb and index...
Your hand gives him the breast and the ring shines.

How cold her hands were latterly, and visible
The painful jointings of the long bones.
The firelight shone almost through and the blood's
Network with its many nodes and bruises
Was shown like that of a leaf.
She lagged her ring with cotton but
The days loosened it again.

His sharp nails are like
The fragments of rosy shell lying in pools.

O sands, o future rocks...

In Memoriam 8571 Private J.W. Gleave

who was at Montauban, Trônes Wood and Guillemont

'*So many without memento…*'

1 *Prologue: The Children*

I bade them climb: they must have come to the very crest
And it was beautiful to see them shine
Not steadily but charged at a sudden moment
And for only such duration as the light allowed
The light they caught upon their faces from the face
Already we should have thought sunk out of sight.

There are some dead we see and even see by;
They glimmer for a generation, our looking
Lends them more luminance. I saw the father,
Whom no one can rekindle, appear to shine
Over the earth in the eyes of the gazing children.
They cast his face upon my white paper.

2 *After how many Novembers…*

How soon, I wonder, after how many Novembers
    Did the years begin to seem not paces
Interminably around a pit nor steps deserting
    A place, but slow degrees by which she came
Over the curve of the world into that hemisphere
    His face rose in? Again we have given ground,
The dark advances an hour into the afternoon,
    In the interlude between cloud and horizon
A mild sun scythes the field – so by the last winter
    After an illness and before her death
We saw a similar light dawn on the woman
    Who had been a widow more than fifty years.

She lingered in the doorway of the living-room
    Impelled as people leaving are to say
Some word more than goodnight. I have seen her eyes shining
    Bright as a young girl's on that threshold
Bright with tears. She found nothing to say. But having
    Her purse in hand – the purse she had kept house from
For generations since the Queen died – she took out
    The new, neat, folded notes of her pension

And to the children and their children and their child
  Disposed of these. We do not like to watch
A person look for words nor by whatever gestures
  Taking her leave of table, hearth and chair.

She went to her own room where everything was ready
  To leave, the furniture of her married life
Though in another house, one he had never seen.
  But in that mirror he had seen his face,
They will have stood side by side and looked at themselves
  She will have stood by herself and remembered.
And always she held the two or three photographs
  Which light had fallen on man and wife to make
In an envelope with the notice of his death
  As if to cross over with these in hand
That she should know him again who had been effaced
  And he should know her who had lived and aged.

3 *Notification*

It was the painful duty of Lieutenant Thomas Dinsdale
On Army Form B 104-82
In an envelope the postwoman shrank from touching
To notify my grandmother of her altered state.
The women stood by, they followed the post like crows:
To whom would such a communication come
That morning, to what woman by the hand of a woman
Whose job it was daily to visit that village of streets
And lay the stigmata on certain doors?

So the news came from Guillemont to Salford 5
After a lapse of weeks during which time
She had known no better than to believe herself a wife.

4 *By word of mouth*

Not having seen him die and when
Upon their notification nothing followed
Neither the body to her hearth
Nor any of the late soldier's effects
A little while
As though the outcome could be put in doubt
She trimmed her mourning with a thread of hope
She kept the Suitor from her husband's chair

Showed Death the door
Nightly, until the evenings were long.
He called then with a companion from France.
The neighbours, who miss nothing, saw
Only the soldier leave.

5 *Récit*

No messenger in the tragedies
So mean but coming to the wife, the mother
Or any beloved woman waiting
Recounts fittingly the dead man's death
In alexandrines or iambics
And honours him in the telling.
But who the pal was is not remembered
Nor what he said, nor what the questions were
She had the heart to put nor whether
She lamented there and then, praising the qualities
Of the man lost and hiding her face as queens do
In her apron. Not a word, not the place itself
Reached me in his pronunciation
But as to how and where
She only shrugged her shoulders
And perhaps she had that from the messenger
Who did not tell her that the night was very short
And began in a barrage of phosgene gas
And ended in a thick fog
And a barrage of high explosive
As they moved around the southern edge of Trônes Wood
Across seven hundred yards of open ground
Gently sloping to the village of Guillemont
In an attack understood to be hopeless
But serving the French on their right
Whose attack was also hopeless
And that somewhere before the wire
He was obliterated
In gas and night and fog.

6

But by November the congregation of widows
    Being told it was a reasonable sacrifice
Their men had made saw mutilated trees bedecked
    With bloody tatters and being nonetheless

Promised a resurrection of the body
    They saw God making their men anew out of
The very clay. These women having heard from soldiers
    However little from the battlefield
Towards All Saints gathered black gouts from the elder
    Among their children stared at the holy tree
And envied Christ his hurts fit to appear in.
    Some then insisted on a photograph
Taken before the harm was done – which face they caused
    To appear in the hideous crater of their lives
Upon its slimy water. In time while she pursued
    With wrung hands her business as a widow
The water cleared. On the surface of a peaceful pool
    Decently framed the face shone steadily.

7

There being no grave, there being not even one
Ranked among millions somewhere in France,
Her grief went without where to lay its head.
She would have rested sooner had she had
Or had she even learned somewhere there was
A well-kept place where he was lying dead.

She could not even think him out of harm:
He must be hurt somewhere by every shell,
Somewhere his mouth could not get breath for gas.
She would have scavenged all his body home
Into the shelter of if not her house
At least the roofed and hidden well-walled grave.

But of what comfort is the body home
Which here or there cannot embrace or smile?
And of what comfort is the body whole?
Only the rich and saints do not corrupt.
She almost thought there were degrees of death
And he was more dead piecemeal and abroad.

There being nowhere but the family grave
She went and called her grief out of the air
And coaxed it to alight upon the stone
That did not bear his name. Upon that absence
She grieved as though it were the greater one
And death was lured almost within her view.

She set that feature on the featureless
Visibly everlasting plain of death
She trod a path, she made some little inroad
And placing three or four remembrance days
She netted in their few interstices
Glimpses that she could bear out of the deep.

8 *Roll of Honour*

She never saw his name at Thiepval
Nor even in Manchester Cathedral
But on Liverpool Street outside the Mission Hall
There was a Roll of Honour on the wall

Affixed in nineteen-seventeen
And this she will have seen
Daily (until the Blitz
Blew all the names to bits).

The enlisted men – there were no officers –
Were columned street by street and hers
Was one of those already crossed. By rights
The Vicar should have come at nights

And crossed the others one by one
Until the toll was done.

9 *Like shrapnel*

Like shrapnel in the lucky ones
She carried fragments in her speech
Remarkable to grandchildren
But to herself accustomed
Like rise and shine and left
Left...he had a good home and he left
And a long, long trail a-winding...

Coltsfoot

Coming before my birthday they are for ever your flowers
Who are dead and at whose hand
I picked them on the allotments and blitzed land.

Coltsfoot and Larches

I love coltsfoot that they
Make their appearance into life among dead grass:
Larches, that they
Die colourfully among sombre immortals.

Hyacinth

Overnight the hyacinth opened
In the room left to itself among
Our books and pictures, behind
The closed door and the drawn curtains
Where the chairs had sat the fire out.

By morning the door opened strangely.
The scent glowed through the flower's long fingers
The hand turned for my praise, and as between
Mirrors I saw your face in that dark room
Receding down the years of familiar rooms.

Though windows gleamed and the sky rose
And the ground was already prickly with shoots
Still the unthinking birds whom we can think
Undying, the jackdaw, the white gull,
Called from our roof: 'Remember! Remember!'

Everything reminds. Though into such rose dawns
The roads take up their travellers
And run with a straight intent
Or climb purposefully to ridges
Having such skies behind

Still throughout today and for
Its time consuming in our element
The rose hyacinth has burned
And I have watched faces returning
Down a flight of rooms for want of light.

Johnny

Faces, faces, says Johnny,
The perceptions lingering, lingering, in general
And in the home, for what
Does a man see on the dead wall of his life,
A jakes wall, but among the writing
Faces, faces, beating the brow against?

Jimmy

The belly: a big craw
Come out of the shirt like a goitre;
An angry cross of scars.

Jimmy, your face has the texture of fungus.
Your tears drop like fat
In rapid beads, from under the hair
The head is weeping,

They hit the table between your bloody knuckles.

Billy

The lines, Billy, I am thinking
I should like to run a finger down, they rive
Your face to the bone chin.

Your daughter, you are saying, said
The aborted one, Norma, 15, fuck off
Back to the asylum Dad, your own dad,
You are saying, home
From prison strung you to the mangle naked
And beat you to a jelly. I

Am thinking Billy when he weeps
It is the rent, the creases fill but
What about the rent? And more
Than ever I should like to put a finger in
The runnels of your face
That wants some beating for cadaverousness.

Stuart

Stuart, I would not begin at once
With the obvious. It seems
Too many have and she
Is none the warmer. Her beak
Would gnaw through bone.

The mouth, I grant you, is
A whiskerless rat's; raw
Her hands and one of those trees on the estate
The kids have stripped
Would be as abundant to embrace.

Under hers, as motherly as hail,
The child has lost his tongue. Where then
Should you begin? The eyes
Look for the worst. Could you only
Show them some goodwill.

'But with a history of ECT'

But with a history of ECT
And separation Milburn Margaret Mrs
Did not attain the obliterating sea
She got no further than the DHSS
And on a Friday in the public view
Lodged on the weir as logs do.

During the rush-hour she was attended to
And all the terraces of Gallowgate
Watched the recovery of this female who
Went in the river at the age of thirty-eight.
She did not pass unnoticed but instead
Got seen to being dead.

And at the inquest the Acting Coroner
Inquiring as to how and why she died
Exculpated both the hospital and her
Emeritus husband who identified
That frozen woman in the mortuary
He had four children by.

'Dennis Jubb is dead'

Dennis Jubb is dead. But considering
He certainly never went short of smokes
Nor a dreg of something in the morning
Not to mention the lovely picture books

He often sat behind his barrow in doorways
Grinning at the innocent passers-by over
And when you take into account that all these
Were extras to a living wage we do aver

That Mr Dennis Jubb did not do too bad
Bearing in mind as well all the other things he had
As for example he had a loving mate
And a revitalized house on the Fairhope Road Estate

And that he lived to be forty, a good age,
And got his death by burning on the front page.

'I suppose you know this isn't a merry-go-round'

I suppose you know this isn't a merry-go-round.
The man won't stop it when you think you've had your money's worth.
To get off at all you'll have to jump
And risk breaking your neck
And where you fall will appear strange
And not where you got on.

These have not been flat revolutions
On the enduring earth
But spirals down.
You are lower now.

That being so
I would almost advise you to stay put.
You are in the company of your friends
And for a change
You can always stagger from a horse to a white elephant.
Nobody seems to mind.

FROM

WATCHING FOR DOLPHINS

(1983)

Mary Magdalene and the Sun

Hugging her breasts, waiting in a hard garden
For Sun, the climber, to come over the hill,
Disconsolate, the whore Mary Magdalene,
She of the long hair. But Sun meanwhile,

Scaling inch by inch the steep other side,
At last got a grip with his fingers on the rim
And hoisted himself up. She saw the spikes of his head,
His brow, then his brazen face. So after his swim

Leander's fingers appeared on Hero's sill
And he hauled himself inside, naked and salt
And grinning. She closed her eyes and let him feel
Her open face, uncrossed her arms and felt

Him warm her breasts and throat. Thereupon a cock
Crowed once, very red. And something came and stood
Between her and the Sun, something cold, and 'Look,'
It moaned. And there, casting a shadow, naked

And bled white was the nailed man, he whose
Blessing arms they fixed on a beam, and he crouched
There gibbering of love and clutching his
Thin shoulders and begging to be touched.

He was encrusted above the eyes with black,
And maculed in the hands and feet and in his side,
And through clacking teeth he begged her to touch him, and 'Look,'
He moaned, 'at this and this that they did,'

Showing the holes. Sun, the joker, though,
Had leapfrogged him, and more cocks crowed,
And down the green hillside and through
The waking garden the waters of irrigation flowed

And plenteous happy birdsong from the air,
As Sun diminished the ghosts of fruit trees on the grass
And over the nailed man's shoulder stroked the harlot's hair
And fingered open the purple sheaths of crocuses.

Lazarus to Christ

You are forgetting, I was indeed dead
Not comatose, not sleeping, and could no more
Wish for resurrection than what we are before
Can wish for birth. I had already slid

Four days down when you hauled me back into the air.
Now they come to watch me break bread
And drink the wine, even the tactful plead
With dumb faces to be told something, and, dear,

Even you, who wept for me and of whom it is said
You know all things, what I mutter in nightmare
I believe you lie awake to overhear.
You too are curious, you too make me afraid

Of my own cold heart. However I wash
I cannot get the foist out of my flesh.

Christ to Lazarus

They faltered when we came there and I knew very well
They were already leaving me. Not one
Among your mourners had any stomach to go on,
And when they moved the stone and we could smell

Death in his lair they slid off me like cloud
And left me shining cold on the open grave
Crying for you and heaving until Death gave
And you were troubled in your mottled shroud.

They hid their eyes, they begged me let you stay,
But I was adamant, my friend. For soon
By a loving father fiercer than any moon
It will be done to me too, on the third day.

I hauled you out because I wanted to.
I never wept for anyone but you.

Minos, Daedalos and Pasiphaë

Minos himself, like any supplicant,
Came clumsily asking how it might be done.
Daedalos smiled: nothing the heart might want
Surprised him, who had Ikaros for a son.

None knew, so perfect was the counterfeit,
None among those who ran to take the bull,
Dropping bewildered from coition, in a net;
Only the King, who watched. The woman, full,

Penned what she bore in the Labyrinth to die.
It grew. They heard it roaring for the light of day,
They heard it blunder through the passages and try –
Sobbing with a human hope – another way.

They wished a slayer would come. Their normal child
Looked monstrous to the Queen. Daedalos smiled.

Priapics

1

Godling, your mother, the smiling Aphrodite, though she loved
    Nothing so much as cock, when she had born you to
Bacchus, hid her face, and neither would own you, seeing
    What had lain covert in the divine heart of each.
Associate of Pan, impossible to clothe, they hid you in greenery,
    In gardens to threaten thieves, or you stood where roads met,
Ambushing wayfarers with their desires, and, as Priapus of Harbours,
    To you poor sailors prayed, leaving their girls.

2

He threatened with his club impartially
    Thieves of either sex; served them alike
When, by the bed of leeks or the bed of thyme
    Caught trespassing, boy or girl turned tail.

3

Caught fig-stealing girls departed that garden
    Only on payment of an equitable fine.
'Figs for figs,' he demanded, and the luscious part
    Of girls, the cleft and honeyed, the conducive,
The petalled-back, must cap his club. Then he arranged
    Their stolen figs coolly in a nest of vine-leaves,
And showed them out of the garden by a secret door
    Where trespassers might enter when they liked.

4

Who are under the orbs and sceptre of King
    Prick when he says jump they jump for his
Slightest wish is their command throughout the hours of
    Daylight and darkness. Nowhere by that
Soft nose may you not lead them and to their hearts
    The way comes thence. Dead they will all
Push up the earth in molehills, the humblest
    Among them emerging as *phalli*
Impudici, while the best some flowery
    Hill will brandish as an Attis pine.

5

How soon evasive girls walking alone and wishing
　　Always to bear thus deep under their surfaces
The shadows, the quiet clouds, the shaken moon; being
　　No further in than glances, than the casting,
Like dew on webs, of first love on the common courtesies,
　　Have halted at him set in his covert place,
Grinning, upreared, always too soon, a hamfist,
　　Botching their dreams with sense so blunt and tearing.
'Leave oil,' he says, 'leave honey, you would be wise
　　To smooth me. For I am at the root and how
You grow and flower in the light and how you fume in scent
　　And pass from substance to vapour, crying for love,
Crying for the happiness of your rendered soul, derives
　　From me.' Some women by the way they smile, some wives,
One knows they wear the root-god for an amulet and mirror
　　Skies still and every fineness of sun and stars.

'Misshapen women'

Misshapen women on the Fairhope Road Estate when the wind
　　Presses upon you hurrying to the meat factory
Your breasts are not discovered through a thin chiton, nor down
　　The inguinal triangle do the lovely folds ripple;
And when the sun, winking behind the scrap heap, ends your days
　　You cannot face it smiling like caryatids,
Whom only marble burdened, for you are not fit to be
　　Regarded from any angle. Only from above,
To Infinite Mercy, are your unbuttonable forms and your
　　Poor mouths not an eyesore, and in an interlude
When no sun plays and no sarcastic wind He may drizzle
　　Some charity upon you from a grey heaven.

The Door

Yes, that is the door and behind it they live,
But not grossly as we do. Through a fine sieve
Their people pass the incoming air. They are said
To circulate thoughtfully in walled gardens, the aged –
And they live long – wheeling in chairs. They exchange
Nothing but traditional courtesies. Most strange
However is their manner of dying, for they know the hour,
When it comes, as old elephants do. They devour
Their usual breakfast of plovers' eggs and rise
Then or are lifted by the janitors and without goodbyes
They step or are borne aloft through that door there –
And thus they end. For of course meeting the air,
The air we breathe, they perish instantly,
They go all into dust, into dead dust, and Stanley,
The Sweeper, comes with his brush and shovel and little cart
And sweeps them up and shovels them not apart
But into one black plastic bag with dimps, dog-shit
And all our common dirt. But this they intend and it
Signals their gracious willingness to reside
In the poor heart of life, once they have died.

'Pity the drunks'

Pity the drunks in this late April snow.
They drank their hats and coats a week ago.
They touched the sun, they tapped the melting ground,
In public parks we saw them sitting round
The merry campfire of a cider jar
Upon a crocus cloth. Alas, some are
Already stiff in mortuaries who were
Seduced by Spring to go from here to there,
Putting their best foot forward on the road
To Walkden, Camberwell or Leeds. It snowed.
It met them waiting at the roundabout.
They had no hats and coats to keep it out.
They did a lap or two, they caught a cough.
They did another lap and shuffled off.

Boy finds tramp dead

But for your comfort, child, who found him curled
With crizzled cheeks, his hands in his own ice,
Among the trapped dead birds and scraps of girls,

His spectacles and broken teeth put by
Along the window with a pile of pence,
Remember this man was the son of nobody,

Father, brother, husband, lover, friend
Of nobody, and so by dying alone
With rats hurt nobody. Perhaps he joined

And mended easily with death between
Newspaper sheets in drink and did not wake
Too soon, at midnight, crying to sleep again,

Alive and hung on cold, beyond the embrace
Of morning, the warm-handed. He was pressed
Together when you found him, child, but names

Had left his lips of wicked men released
Quickly in sunlight and of one who baked
Asleep inside a kiln and many at rest

With cancer in the casual ward or knocked
Under fast wheels. These he conjured with
To Christ as instances of mercy, being racked

Himself on boards beside a prolapsed hearth.
His vermin died. The morning's broken glass
And brightening air could not pick up his breath.

Little by little everything in him froze,
Everything stopped: the blood in the heart's ways,
The spittle in his mouth, his tongue, his voice.

Elegy

We hear you spoken of as a dead man
And where you were there is new growth of obituaries.
Someone has met an eyewitness from Darlington –
A liar, it is true. We had thought this was
Only the interruption of one of your stories

And you were working slowly on a smoke
And, tilting your indoor trilby, would appear
Through clouds soon and would broach
Your silence waiting like an untouched beer
For a man back from the gents. Remember the bloke

So bent with *arthuritis* that for his wake
They tied him to a board and in the small hours
Some joker cut his cords and, with a creak,
He sat up grinning? In a digger's jaws
Rising in a shroud of snow at bitter daybreak

You cleared a building-site; the mortuary men,
Summoned to shift you, dewy, from the road,
Have brought their breakfasts up and dropped their load
When you opened an eye. Time and again
From under newspaper we fetched you in,

A foetal stiff. Around the cup you set
Your fingers like a broken basket
And thawing your nose in tea began to tell
The story of a man from Motherwell
Who swallowed three hundred goldfish for a bet

And lived. You lived the part: the Indian doctor
Offering to amputate; nice Ronnie Kray
Visiting his mam; Lord Londonderry
Addressing your father like the man next door.
You hooked yourself a stooge when necessary.

If the liar from Darlington was right then now
The devil is leaning on his fork and you
Are keeping him waiting while you toast your bum
And roll a smoke for what is still to come
About a man you met in Eccles who...

Swans

Not many see the white swans.
Vagrants at road-ends have
Or, waiting for shift-end,
Machine-minders staring
At dereliction through the blank panes.

Not many hear them. Soiled
Drunks have whom the cold wakes
Early lying curled;
Or, nearly sleeping, the innocent
Lovers. After birdsong

That is the kindest light.
Through silver grey, through rose
Across our malignant city
The heavy birds strain
In this season, about this hour

Little above roof-tops
Rapid, whistling, intent,
Steadily clouting the air.
Pity them should they flag
For where is there a meadow

Or any habitable water
And where, landing or falling,
When the day hardens and we
Come down the roads will they
Avoid our fatal notice?

Watching for Dolphins

In the summer months on every crossing to Piraeus
One noticed that certain passengers soon rose
From seats in the packed saloon and with serious
Looks and no acknowledgement of a common purpose
Passed forward through the small door into the bows
To watch for dolphins. One saw them lose

Every other wish. Even the lovers
Turned their desires on the sea, and a fat man
Hung with equipment to photograph the occasion
Stared like a saint, through sad bi-focals; others,
Hopeless themselves, looked to the children for they
Would see dolphins if anyone would. Day after day

Or on their last opportunity all gazed
Undecided whether a flat calm were favourable
Or a sea the sun and the wind between them raised
To a likeness of dolphins. Were gulls a sign, that fell
Screeching from the sky or over an unremarkable place
Sat in a silent school? Every face

After its character implored the sea.
All, unaccustomed, wanted epiphany,
Praying the sky would clang and the abused Aegean
Reverberate with cymbal, gong and drum.
We could not imagine more prayer, and had they then
On the waves, on the climax of our longing come

Smiling, snub-nosed, domed like satyrs, oh
We should have laughed and lifted the children up
Stranger to stranger, pointing how with a leap
They left their element, three or four times, centred
On grace, and heavily and warm re-entered,
Looping the keel. We should have felt them go

Further and further into the deep parts. But soon
We were among the great tankers, under their chains
In black water. We had not seen the dolphins
But woke, blinking. Eyes cast down
With no admission of disappointment the company
Dispersed and prepared to land in the city.

Islands

1 *Bracken*

There were sheep then, they pastured on the little islands,
We took them there by boat. But the grass has gone
And the fold my father's father built with his bare hands
Here at high water has also gone. One by one
All his fields have gone under the ferns again
And now it is hard for you to see how it was then.

Bitter, unharvested, deeper than children,
The ferns rise from high water over the wall.
The fields drown; the swinging gate is fallen
And ferns break round the posts that stand as tall
As men. But from the spring you climbed this way
After the spilling water-carts on a hot day.

You would not think we had any open ground,
But we did. We called it Plains. There was space
For all the island to be sitting round
Watching the tennis or the cricket. Our playing-place
Has gone the way of the fields and I shouldn't know
Where to look for the pitch and the court now.

Sunk flourishing in depths of bitter green
The little islands are lost to us already.
We watch from boats the rats going hungry between
Waste and waste. Remember for our sakes quickly
Where the sweet water places were and when
And by whom the fields were first rid of their bracken.

Sometimes in summer we made ourselves a bed
Under the ferns, where we should never be found,
And looked up through the lovely green at the sky and said
That we were at the bottom of the sea and drowned.
I believe sometimes we slept, but the afternoon
When we woke again was still no further gone.

We lie on the harbour wall and peering down
Where the wrack heaves and hideous claws feel
After food, we see the clouds that do not drown
In pathless water with all of our things lost but sail
Untouched through the coral and the salt flowers
Through the places of this island that once were ours.

2

At blown cockcrow, hearing the driven sea,
You remember the rattling sash, starlight
Surviving faintly on the looking-glass
And the islands troubled with a ceaseless crying.

Scheria, kind to strangers, wept for her ship
Sunk by God unjustly; for the *Schiller*'s
More than three hundred souls there were many in
Two continents weeping; and everywhere

For the sailors of our wars, numberless
Mothers' sons who have rolled in without faces.
Indifferent Hermes conducted them all.
The sea turns and its creatures hunger. Soon

Everything lies under the mercy of day.
The surface flickers with scared pilchards.
Light, above all the light. And the sea comes,
At sunny tide-flow the plucked, the smitten sea

Comes running. The wind then, high-ridden by
One nonchalant gull, batters the opening
Eyes of the sun with water. Far-reaching,
Iridescent, the white surf comes and comes.

Children are playing under a rainbow
On Pool Green; or behind Innisvouls,
Delighted in a rocking boat, they stand
Outstaring the ancient quizziness of seals.

3

Our child when we came looking and calling after her,
And had come through marram and sea-holly to the dunes' crest
When we stood crushing in our fingers plucked samphire
Looking still further and calling and saw her at last

She was remote and small on an almost island
And turned away, at tide-flow, but our fear was less
Of the sea already parting the cord of sand
Than that she was so small and averted from us.

We ran heavily, the white sand sank us in,
But through the neck of the place stole then like bird-stalkers
Over the flat wrack that popped and stank in the sun
Towards her kneeling before big granite chairs

Gently stroking for shells. When she turned and looked up
And showed us wordless in her palm the fissured cowrie
The spiralling white horn of wentletrap
And scallops smaller than her smallest nail then we

With our looks put upon her the fear of death
And the ownership of love. Between our tall shadows
She walked to the safe beach down the snake path
Already sunk over ankles in warm shallows.

Gratefully then the weed rose in the sunny water
And swirled as it liked and flowed and the bright shell
Hoards sparkled before the thrones without her
Who stood between us watching, waiting for tide-fall.

4 *The Drowned*

Flat calm. The ships have gone.
By moonlight and by daylight one by one
Into a different world the drowned men rise
But cannot claw the sleep out of their eyes.
None such can know the bigger light from the less
Nor taste even the salt. Their heaviness
By no means may be leavened. Now they live
As timbers do where shipworms thrive
Only in what they feed. Strange things engross
The little galleries of thought after the loss
Of breath. The white clouds pass, but still
The drowned increase upon the senses till
The moon delivers them. On islands then
Seeing the lovely daylight watchful men
Come down and haul these burdens from the waves
And slowly cart them home and dig them graves.

5

The trees here, though the wind leave off, never unbend.
Likewise when he sat the stick retained
The shape of the sixty years he had limped and leaned.
He would haul from under the bed with the crook-end

His bundle of photographs and the soldier's pay-book,
The usual service medals and a card or two in silk.
The marriage bed was draped to the floor like a catafalque
And he hauled the War from under it. And when he spoke

Of the craters at Ypres he used the pool on Pool Green
As measure, and the island's entanglement of brambles when
He spoke of the wire. He rose, drinking gin,
Massive, straighter than his stick, and boys were shown

At the hoisting of his trouser up the sunless calf
A place that shrank like Lazarus from being raised,
A flesh the iron seemed only lately to have bruised.
And if one, being bidden and not in disbelief,

Put in the hand to prove him right who bet
That he was past hurt there – probing appalled
In that still weeping place the fingers rolled
Wondering between them an angle of iron grit.

For year by year his flesh, till he was dead,
Evicted its shrapnel, as the living ground
Puts out for the Parson or the Schoolmaster to find,
Scouring at leisure, another arrow head.

6 *Spring Tide*

The summer moon was terrible. It beamed
Like Christ on Lazarus. Nobody now,
In daylight, can distinguish what he dreamed
And what he saw, in night-clothes at the window.

It was like All Souls when everything lost
And the smothered dead struggle to rise. Around
Midnight the moon hauled hand over fist
And sheet by sheet the waters were unwound.

But nothing was recovered. Still the sand,
That we saw white and phosphorescent, levels
The slopes and pleasant laps of land
And stops the doorways and the fires and wells.

The curlews cried like springs starting to run.
Then sleep began to fill us and we felt
A weeping rise and flow. Now in the sun
The sea is brimful and our cheeks are wet and salt.

7

Sheer nowhere: the land
Ends, the rocks pile dumbly where they fell,
And hold for any life nearer to ours than lichen
There is none; the useful
Wood of wrecks whitens beyond our reach.

Rain passes, rain on the sea, and sweetens
With all its copious fall
By not one measurable jot the expanse of salt.
Clinging to islands we
Camping with our dead around a sunken plain

Such as we are, late on,
Want above all things passage to one another,
Aid and the sharing of wells
And not to swell our bitterness beyond
The normal allocation of tears.

Journey

1

Someone at least reading about beauty in a room
Above the city has turned from the lamp once having heard
Her step behind him on the creaking board and until
Morning then and until, close in the eaves, birds woke
He was allowed to lie on the narrow bed with her
Under the maps that papered the sloped ceiling
Embracing her freely and planning with her journeys.

2 *Locus Amoenus*

One read of the place where the covert mound rose
    Flanked by slopes, and clear water
Issued below for thirst and the excited mind
    And the senses equally were delighted.
One read of that pleasant place in the writers of pastoral
    And imagined its charms scattered over an earth
Less than so beautiful, and thinking never to come there
    Did: and found it surpassed their praises.

3 *Musée du Louvre*

These courtiers in a wood have come upon her
Rising before them moonlike in a clearing.
She strikes their eyes, their hands are all upraised
At the light she sheds upon them from her scallop.
Far inland henceforth, deep in the heart's covert,
Closing their eyes they will always hear the sea.

4 *Musée Rodin*

They saw the figures of Fugitive Love and supposed them
    Wrought to the condition of subtility
By one another's hands: she streams away
    And the soul may be seen, playing upon her limbs.
The hotel bed was bordered with a mirror
    Where they reviewed those figures, curious
What novel disposition of themselves
    Would lend their evanescence form.

5 *Chartres and Avignon*

One could not look through it nor did the light
   From outside enter as light of day
But passed inward in the form of a persuasion
   That love hungers and can't be filled by
Mere dexterity. That was the window of Mary,
   Of post coitum tristis. Waking
In Avignon he saw her beside him sleeping with
   The sheet thrown off, arms and throat
Already burned from travelling. The dirty pane
   Showed a blueness under which the town
With sprinkled gutters foretasted the dust
   And thin shade under walls at noon.

6 *Gothic or Classical*

Reading that in the depiction of the female body
North and south of the Alps there were two traditions
By stages night after night in disreputable hotels
North and south of the Alps he examined whether
She approached more nearly the Gothic or the Classical
Bearing in mind from Paris a certain Venus
As far as Florence where a lascivious Eve
Displayed her teeth-marks in the bitten apple.

7

The mind then seems to become the burning point
   Of the other senses, when by day
Arches are seen and one's delight converges
   At their tips and down the aisles, and when
In darkness are corresponded all parts having stiffness
   Actual or potential, likewise
All declivities and entrances and more are devised
   And the mind then is the glass, burning.

Bluebells

But then her name, coming to her averted
And more than waist-deep in the ground's embrace,
How queer it sounded, like screaming swifts,
Like bats hurting her ears. Still, she turned

And lifted her face to the rim of beech-light
And the leaf-sieved sky. And again her name
Came down the slopes to her, tugging like grief
With little cries. So she was drawn. The blue ground

Let go of her in a white furrow and where
She had entered at the horseshoe's opening
Now she began in earnest her long haul
Against the streams, ascending slowly by

Degrees of blue under the cavernous light,
A floppy corpse of flowers on her left arm
With midnight hair, with blue dark thoughts, with white
Uprooted feet. Standing in the shallows,

Black to the waist, cradling the lolling doll,
She had no sight nor sound of her lost name.
Her bluebell lips, smiling at nobody,
Clouded the cold air with a breath of roots.

Autumn Lady's Tresses

In late summer the Lady's Tresses
Spiral to light leafless and stand
Almost as bare rods. But flowers
Proceed upwards by an unbraiding or as
When the wind frays
The scything edge of a wave. Thyrsus,
Snake of ivy. Flowers
Without energy of colour, at the least remove
From the stem's green. Torch-flower,
Faintlight, but prized by finders
As much as wentletraps
The white unicorn
The winding stairway shell.

Autumn Crocuses

The naked boys, entering the light,
Their root-whiteness suffuses upwards with a colour. Then,
So long as they hold the sun's eye,
Light through and through and barely tethered,
They stand hovering. They die
When they empty of sun, sleeves
Of their life lie on the soil crumpling.

Sunflowers

Stems wrist-thick,
A pulse of plant-blood;
Faces puffing like the four winds,
A hot light. Sunflowers in the days
When they wear the aureole of power,
The licks of flame,
They lap furiously at the sun
With rasping lion-tongue leaves. But they die
As big men do whose bodies the life finds heavy, they loll
And blacken like the crucified. At evening
You will hear them in the garden flapping their rags
Groaning to fall from the fences
Flat over the grass.

Tree in the Sun

This morning the tree shed
Leaves. There wasn't a breath of wind, not
A leaf stirred on the stem
But fell for an hour or more
After the frost last night the tree stood in the sun
And the leaves fell, there wasn't a moment
When any less than hundreds were falling and neither torn
From where they held nor in their fall
By the least wind deflected as when a day falls still

And the sky silently snows so they
Were shed but it was in the sun
They fell after what cold
In the body of the tree after the withdrawal of
The lifeblood to the heart no longer held
Themselves no longer adhering when the frost relaxed
The dead leaves fell for an hour or more.
Weakened by the sun after that night
The tree shed leaves.

Song of a Woman at the Year's Turning

My children were conceived in February.
I fall in love under the hesitant light
At the year's first singing. Snowfalls
Come like reprieve, like more and quieter sleep;
Lie everywhere in a kind prevention.

Snow on my hair. It must have seemed like grey,
Like ash for a moment. But come the shining sun
Winter collapses off the necks of daffodils;
The crocuses melt, they glow like spar. My hair
I feel jet-black and jewelled with water.

What will not open, what will not rise again
The year leaves for dead. Under that law
The helpless birds sing. What will not turn
And flow now singing will be hung
Like cadavers when the flood falls. I sing.

The purple crocuses open on an iron ground.
They have a frail centre. Birds whistle
Among their frozen dead. Trembling at heart
I shall be bold as purple, unbow like daffodils
And show my wintered face to the new sun.

Atlantis
(for Lotte and Hugh Shankland)

It dies hard, the notion of a just people;
   The wish that there should have been once mutual aid
Dies very hard. Through fire, through ghastly ash and any
   Smothering weight of water still we imagine
A life courteous and joyful; see them lightly clad
   Loving the sun, the vine and the grey olive.
Over the water, from trading, they come home winged
   With sails, their guide and harbinger the white dove.

I

The sea suddenly stood up vertical, sky-high,
Bristling with the planks of their peaceful ships.
The earth roared like a bull. They said Poseidon,
Breaker of lintels, was shaking them. There was fire too
Glaring like a red eye. But the unkindest
Was of all the four elements the purest
And to breathing man his being: the air
Clagged and precipitated in cankers of pumice
And thereafter for weeks in a fine dust.
Wherever the living air was welcome now
Ash entered and the hearts of houses ceased;
Their eyes, hurt by blows, were quite extinguished;
Their mouths, agape, were stopped. Ash filled
And softly embedded household pots, shrouded
Frescoes of air-breathing dolphins. Who survived
When the sun had wept and blinked its eyesight clear
Lame in the lungs saw only dust
Lying now quiet as snow. One inch of such –
That is from nail-end to the knuckle of the thumb –
Will render infertile the fruitful, the man-nurturing earth
For perhaps ten years. To them now kneeling on rock
Who had salted no fields, burned no olive groves
And poisoned nobody's wells, there remained no rod
To sound the ells, the fathoms, the generations of ash.

II

How deep below? None of the warring nations
Had length of chain to fathom at what depth
Atlantis lay. Nobody anchored there. But then –
In the days of death by impalement or the ganch

When Christian citizens of Candia ate
The besieging Turk – with a roar, witnesses say,
Like innumerable bulls, the sea, or the earth
Under the waters, rendered up to the surface
A new island, called nowadays *Kaimeni*,
The cinder. On Santorini the common people,
Scratching a living in the old ash and pumice,
Remembered Kalliste and watched and prayed. But a scholar,
A believer in Atlantis, when the steam had thinned
Pulled out alone in a small boat. How great
Must have been his disappointment if he thought
Some glimmer of Atlantis might be vouchsafed him
(Who had done no especial wrong in wicked times)
If he hoped for some however dim intimation
Of their lost lovingkindness and wisdom: he saw
Only black smoking slag and ash, and smelled
An intimation of Christian Hell. Also
The hot sea soon uncaulked his punt and rowing
Desperately heavily for home he sank
In depths well known to be unfathomable.

Chronicle

Scabby with salt the shipwreck wondering
Upon what shore, among what manner of savages
He was tossed up, found himself received
With a courtesy near to veneration. Lies
Were ready on his tongue but he found
His rescuers, his hosts, discreet or indifferent
And asking nothing. Only once he was bathed
And dressed in clothes held by for the occasion
There was a pause, a silence, and his fear returned
Imagining sacrifice. Solemnly, deferring,
They led him into the church. The congregation
Was the island's marriageable girls. He must choose,
They said, one for his bride. Any stranger
Showing himself indignant or lascivious
Heard behind him the whetting of knives. The wise man
Walked modestly two or three times
The length of the aisle and among the girls after
The heart's true inclination made his choice.
A priest of the church married them there and then.

Next morning early with a harder courtesy
He was fetched aboard a manned ship and so
Passed back into the sea-lanes. Some thus restored
Put off the escapade, some boasted and some
Wandered thereafter for the one bride. She
According to the custom of the island was courted by the best
And if she were seen to have taken the stranger's seed
Then by the very best, and married in her third month.

The second husbands shone like full moons
In reflected sun, their stepchildren
Were called 'the strangers' and enjoyed
Love and privileges above the rest. The boys
Grew proficient with boats, eyed the horizons
And one morning departed, courting shipwreck. The girls
Excited a restlessness but themselves
Waited, knowing they were most likely to be chosen
When out of the sea one morning a salt man crawled.

Sunium

Dawns may be rose and dove-grey
Evenings blue-black like Persephone
Lovely. But the culmination at noon
At sheer midsummer
That is incomparable.

Remember the bay, the water clear
As nectar in a calyx. There the sun
Brought our perception of carnal life
To the burning point.

Then the horizons had no attraction
There was no drowsiness, we watched
And bathed and sweetened the mouth with fruit.

Where promontories embrace an arena of sea
At noon the bivalve opened
The mollusc wings
The lips.

Lasithi

Lasithi: notable for windmills. Summits are
    The petals of Lasithi and their snow
Streams underground. Ten thousand mills, sailing like toys,
    Crank it to surface into troughs. At dawn
The families come down to a lake of mist. Women
    In black unmoor and swivel the bare crosses
To feel the wind. The rods blossom and in its throat
    A well reaches for water like a man
Strangling. It mounts like birdsong then – oh lovely work
    Of slowly scooping sails – it fills the reed,
The wells respire, the cisterns wait like mares and when
    In leaps, crashing like laughter, water comes,
A full wellbeing ascends and wets the walls and brims and
    Down the runnels like amusement overflows
Under the leaves, along the root-courses, and men
    Go about with hoes gently conducting it.

After the evaporation of the mist, under
    The sheer sun, under descending eagles,
Rimmed with snow, veined silvery with water and laced
    With childish flowers, the plateau works. The mills
Labour like lilies of the field, they toil and spin
    Like quivering cherry trees in one white orchard.

The Diktaean Cave

Children, attend. The myths are bloody. In this wet crack
For Mother Rhea, weary of fruitless birth, the Kouretes
Hid God the Usurper, little Zeus, from the cunning,
The child-swallowing Kronos – himself a son who for his mother,
Gaia, the Earth, weary of copulation, reaped from his father,
Vast Ouranos, the parts necessary with a jagged sickle.

The cry a hurt sky makes echoes for ever.
His fading semen splashed Heaven. Seaborn
Of the rosy froth where the unspeakable fell, our fierce
And gentle need grew. Blow out the candle. Darker
Than this and unimaginably deeper is Tartarus where grown
Zeus confined outwitted wily Kronos, having exhumed

Vigorous brothers and sisters from his guts. Zeus lived
The life of Riley then in the upper air, with clouts
Of thunder and strokes of the rod of lightning lording it;
And pressed divinity small into the bull, the swan, the eagle,
The golden dancing gnats, when tugged by Love, the immortal,
For one of the black earth's mortal sons and daughters.

A Relief of Pan

Standing behind you in the looking-glass
I saw my foolish admiration cross
Your own dispassionate appraisal of your dress.
I met your eyes, I saw you wished me gone,
I thought of that man by the Zappeion
Who likewise could not let you be in peace.

I had gone looking for a sanctuary of Pan
Along the dry Ilissos, you by the drinking-fountain
Sat eating cherries. I had gone
Looking unsuccessfully for a relief of Pan and he
Meanwhile, your gentleman of the Zappeion,
Was proffering you his member round an ilex tree.

Brother of mine, the Nymphs will not come down
To dead Ilissos, nor can you watch at home
A girl before her glass from nakedness become
Clothed like a stranger at the drinking-fountain
Nor watch her put off every ornament again
Saving a jewellery of cherries. I can,

I do. Yet I imagine being found
One day in shrubs below her window or by stairs
She might descend or shuffling after her in queues,
Eyes down, with cunning mirrors on my shoes.
I think it will amaze the officers
To learn what lady I have importuned.

Perdita

The brusqued sun returned, but milder, as
Through leaves over water, and silence too,
After the sprung lock, a clamour of birds
On the lake in the heart's forest settling.

Then nothing was between them but her bed
And that narrow. Come near to either bank
And staring neither saw when they began
At the throat the undressing very much of

The other's appearing nakedness since the eyes
Across the pause held them to their purpose
By force of looking face to face. Only
When she reached for the counterpane he saw

How bare her hand was and how thin her wrist
When she took off the covers and they stood
Shivering and unable to get breath
Beside a girl's sheets who with solemn dolls

Behind thin flowery curtains lessening
The strongest light had owned, until he backed
With pressing hands the blank door to, a room
As still as the heart pool of a forest.

Talitha Cumi

1

Lazarus was heavy but she, little sister,
When he spoke to her softly in the common speech
She sat up beckoned by his little finger
Puzzled to be present at so important a levee.

They gave her milk to drink in her usual bowl.
Her lip took a white moustache. She made
Crumbs on the counterpane thoughtfully breaking bread.

2

Sweet breath. She amused herself
Clouding her mother's mirror and with finger-tips
Then causing her re-appearance. Light
In a black grape held between finger and thumb
This pleased her too, and squinting at the sun
To discern its heart of darkness, and on her tongue sometimes
Curiously she felt for bitterness in honey.

3

In dreams she was trailed again through the clear void
And caused the unborn to appear
Twinned with the dead. They seemed
A poppy-head bursting slowly or
The milky river of stars. They hung
Upon her when she returned
Like rime. She sat up thoughtfully
Against a hemisphere of Persephone blue
In which the comets and the little moons were vanishing.

4 *Glossolalia*

She sank or swam. Her father's pier of knowledge
Reached nowhere in that sea. He watched. She drowned
And surfaced, crying out and babbling in a language
High in rapid vowels, a tongue attuned

To pleading, like none he knew. The lamp held
Towards her eyes showed him himself unseen;
And pressing her cold hands he was only chilled
And could not wake her. She had lost her own

True intonation and having passed below
A surface spoke refracted. He feared that there
She had been loved at once and was missed now
And Death came pestering and questioning her,

A mistress of his tongue, and swore she lied
When she denied all knowledge of his seed.

5

Within a month then came
Her first issue of blood. She feared
Another leaching of her strength but this
Was only the moon's small opportunity for life
Spent by her woman's body. Still
She lamented the going of her blood as though it were children.
Her heart was anxious like a linnet in a mine.

6

O Kore with the little hurting breasts
Your elders' eyes are on you worse than mirrors.
Men waver in their looks when you put down
Your childhood one day like a doll and take
It up again the next with lavish love.
The women soon, too soon in their own lives,
All winter long lament Persephone,
Calling on God to send us a saviour,
A radiant child, they coax you out of the dark

Like pale narcissi. Returning girl
Our love of beauty and our fear of death
Oppress you worse than clouds. Look for a clearing
Ankle-deep in red anemones and pool
Your innocence with some ardent fumbling boy.

7 *Chanticleer*

The child's familiar whose stabbing beak
Tickled her palm for crumbs, the strutting lord
And master of a few hens in the little yard
Had never so woken her. The cock's head broke

Like bedlam through the tympanum of sleep,
Suffused, red-lappeted, with a wicked eye.
She saw him swell upon the eastern sky,
Showing the rose, the red and gold, and step

From the sea like God, crowing, splashing salt,
Turning the globe with claws. Her Chanticleer,
Her little favourite, she felt him sear
The dew away and savagely exult.

He had become a lord of thorns and a lord of spurs,
Of thorns flowering, of spurs raking his rivals
Until they streamed. There were no other pools
On the dry ground. The dew had gone and hers,

She thought, was the only charity left to the hard
Flamboyant earth and the brilliant salt sea.
Chanticleer stamped and rioted in the sun and she
Hid from him like the lidded well in the yard.

8

Reluctant child. The family have gone
Calling for her to follow, climbing the fernhill.
Everyone has gone. But she still kneels
And strokes the shingle with her finger-tips for one
More augur, wentletrap or cowrie shell.

Mist. The familiar fernhill enters the sky.
The levels flood. The herd of tumuli,
The graveyard and the little islands
Lift from a drifting ground. The smothered sea
Creeps from oblivion in long winding bands.

Emerges. Breathes. All things become their ghosts.
The sun dissolves. But there are gaps of lightness against
A shoulder or between disappearing mounds
And dunes of the cliff-hill. Like a finger-post
High on the borders of daylight somebody stands

Singular on this island without trees
Calling a version of her name. But she is on hands and knees
Over a pool of shells and if she hears or sees
She pays him no attention. She may be sure
That more than once he will turn back for her.

The drowned are lowing in the fog. Come along,
She remembers them calling. She blinks the wet from her lashes
And sees a white sun shrinking and distending
And someone, stark as a post, more urgently beckoning.
Clutching her shells she begins the trudging paths.

Love of the Dark

We loved the rain, it bathed our minds to think of
The replenishing rain. On a morning then
The cloud had lifted and we saw the whiter
Splash of the stream at the cwm mouth and the wall

Through which the bracken trickled. Behind that dyke
Ownerless herds of fire cropped, unhousing
Little birds but leaving springs in hoofmarks and
On a craterous level above two valleys

The lake where once in a cotton grass summer
White gulls lifted quietly from the surface
And we undressed to bathe. I showed you afterwards
Blood on a stone, feathers and a bridge of bone.

Love of the dark, love of the falling silent
Of everything but the stream...We left the road
At nights, we trespassed over the properties
By the white clue of the climbing stream, by red

Lanterns of rowan. Above the stepping falls
Under the lintel of the lion-gate fold
And through a hogg-hole in the cyclopean wall
We entered our sleep like children. Hand in hand we

Ran some distance to the last skyline. The lake
Still lay in a sun- and moonlight at a time
Of the soft drifting of cotton grass or when
Ice clouded over our full crater of rain.

Moon

Under compulsion when the moon turned murderous
Coldly we walked out during the white hours
Who should have kept ourselves indoors for warmth
Asking of one another only mercy.

Sweetheart, I pleaded, under this hag moon
We must say nothing and look upon nothing.
Come in and sleep now or we shall convert
Our universe to ash and ice and stone.

Her hung and bitter face setting against me,
Look everywhere, she said, once and for all
And speak of everything and show me if you can
Some love still living under my truthful moon.

Turning to look I gave our fields to ash,
I creased the brows of hills with lines of stone,
I struck the wincing surface of our lake,
I wrinkled every stream. In silence then

Standing triumphant by the sobbing ice
I cupped my hands in trickling dust for her
Whom fever shook. Moon love, she said,
This being done how will you warm me now?

Red Figure Vase

Black where he is now who drew them, lightless
    My love, and where they are and all those
Like them, the youth and the girl, and where we
    Shall be, over the curve no sun,
No star ever rising. Black. See how they shine,
    Their fired bodies. Smiling she curves
Ascendant daylight over him to quench
    With her cone his standing torch. That done
Were they living they would sleep as we do
    Sightless, enfolded warm, on black.

FROM
MADDER
(1987)

I mean the Dyer's Madder, *Rubia tinctorum*, that used to be culti-vated extensively in Europe, especially in southern France, where it was called *garance*. The dye they got from it was a deep red, but the plant itself, a straggling, hairy and sharp-leaved plant, is dark green in colour. The flowers are small and yellow, the berries as they form pass from green through red to black, and when ripe they are juicy. The roots are the thing, that is where the redness is, in the thick, proliferating, energetic roots. Madder was planted in July and harvested in November of the following year. It was cleansed of its earth, then hung for months to dry; then ground to a service-able powder in mills. This powder needed to be used within a year, before its virtue diminished.

Garance occurs as a measure of redness in troubadour poetry. 'His face went redder than madder,' they might say – for shame, perhaps, or love or anger. The powder was used against poisons and to heal a wound. And in 1737 an English surgeon by the name of Belcher fed madder to a pig and turned its skeleton red. He fed some to his chickens and turkeys too, and on the third day they were thoroughly red, in bone and tooth and claw. This Belcher fellow made me think of Orpheus.

Adam confesses an infidelity to Eve

I dreamed you were stolen from my left side
And woke hugging the pain. There in our room
Lit by the street lamp she appeared to me
Like something pulled from the earth. She is bulb-white;

Her shadowy place as black as wet moss
Or the widow spider. Believe me
She flattened my raised hands. She gripped
The cage of my heart between her knees,

Gluttonous for mandrake, and fed then,
Crammed her nether mouth, so rooting at
My evasive tongue I feared she would swallow it.
Curtained together under her hair

Only when she rose from drinking
And rolled and bucked as though I were reined
Did I see her face, like a slant moon,
Her eyes smudged and cavernous, her mouth bruised.

She cried like a seal. When she bowed down
Her brow on mine as savages pray
Enshrining my head between her forearms
Then, I confess, feeling her cold tears

I lapped them from her cheeks and let her rest.
My seed ran out of her, cold. On the street
Hissing with rain the lamps were extinguished.
You, when I woke, lay hooped on my left arm.

Orpheus

Styx is only a stone's throw from here,
From anywhere, but listen: here
You can catch Eurydice's scream
And count how long before she hits

That water. Afterwards
He mooched through such a landscape:
The sun was low in the wrong hemisphere
And hurt his eyes, the birds

Were plump and garish and their chorus,
Mornings, a lascivious rattle;
His familiar trees – the willow,
The poplar – were all yellow

But as blanched as what he had seen of the damned
Were the unfamiliar. Through a willow fringe
He watched the people who looked accustomed
Taking their walks and seemed

To himself only as she had seen him last:
A silhouette. Dearest
I think it was such a flight of poplars
He entered finally and turned

At the dazzled end, calico-thin,
And saw his red grief coming for him. Listen:
The whisper of Styx, her scream
On which his slung head, singing softly, homes.

Siesta

On edge again, over nothing
Near to tears, when the curtain rattles
And only the warm wind enters
And not the scent of rain, he sees

Garance (it is the name of a flower)
Leaving the water as he approaches
And putting on her clothes.
She ages rapidly around the eyes.

Any more songs, he cries, any more stories,
Any more entering as sisters arm in arm
And leading me to believe you in the shuttered room
Barefoot on the marble

And you can look for me in spots of blood
Across the ponds of cotton grass.

Yseut

The white company of the lepers
Whom we pitied a little and left food for
Whose myxy eyes skenned down the misery slit
At our virgins receiving the Saviour

They have a new white queen
And we go out less, nobody picnics, theirs
Are all the pastorals of this season.
What have we done, what have we let happen?

The King's glee was shortlived.
When the gate banged and he heard their jubilation
He turned the colour of the underside of fungus
He was of a weeping texture, feverous.

One of us shot into the pack today
When they were feasting with their blunt hands
At the cressy well. Now their bells
And clappers are louder and we are nervy.

The King stands looking at the lonely post.
He wants her back again in the opened cloak
Of faggots: to see her soul like a water-baby
Scat heavenwards through the smoke.

He will put a bounty on his Queen
And send us hunting the scuttling herds.
He sweats at the thought that she will give birth.
Her progeny, his doing, will people the earth.

Ignis

This land was crazy with the loves of Christ:
Straight running of the lame, a dance,
The multitude picnicking.

Ones he unfastened the mouths of
And got their tongues going
They ran about charged with the word 'ignis',

They babbled to right and left of an interdiction,
Their mouths overflowed
With tongues, with lucifers, and ones

He took out the darkness under the lids from
And told them not to tell
They saw the light of the eyes into everything.

He said to follow his trespasses
And convert the charnel lands
Where our brothers and sisters still go cutting themselves.

Martyr

This man, if we can call him that, this foetus,
This white larva, he was there at the Dry Tree
As a merry child, a pig-minder, when Christ,
So we believe, (the dates do tally) did that
Trick with spittle and two dead eyes and the sight
Or was it the ensuing loud hallelujah
Or being spotted in the stinking mayweed

Tugging away at himself no doubt among
Our burned-out necklaces and the handy stones
And Jesus telling him to cross his heart and
Hope to die if he told a soul about it
(Everyone did) and him telling his mam? It
Blew the wits of that doughty little witness
Of many occurrences on that bloody spot.
His mam never saw the stars of his eyes again.
She watched him curl and eavesdropped on his nightmares.
She even petitioned the travelling Master
To please come and wipe her little man's vision
Clean of the miracle. We reckon in his fist
(Observe how over the years he has eaten at it)
We'll find the crooked sixpence Jesus flicked him
When our blind brother saw the heavenly blue.

Oh, Jemima…

I was there, I was the man in black in case
His ticker burst, but I watched Jemima
Whom they were yelling at to look and the sweet thing
In boots sucked on her barley sugar and throughout
The uproar of the ducks and when our man was in
Rotavating the water with his white arms
And his legs were fighting one another she
Only did as she was bid and looked and of course
Never screamed nor covered her eyes nor wet herself.

She saw him crawl up the bank with muddy eyes
And weed on his tonsure and his busy-bee stripes
At half-mast, Flo handing him his glasses
And a cup of tea and Arthur a handkerchief and me
Going in with my little silver ponce to sound him out.

And I was there coming down from Ethel's bed
And the same little nod our Jemima gave
When they wrapped Uncle away I saw her give
That morning over her bowl when Flo's card came
Saying that Jim, the learner, the brave tryer,
Was took on the West Coast doing his few strokes
Up the Acheron, against its tide, into its freezing mouth.

Don't jump off the roof, Dad...

I see the amplified mouths of my little ones
And dear old Betty beseeching me with a trowel.
I am the breadwinner, they want me down of course.
I expect they have telephoned the fire brigade.

They have misinterpreted my whizzing arms:
I am not losing my balance nor fighting wasps
Nor waving hello nor signalling for help.
These are my props and I am revving up.

From here I have pity on the whole estate.
The homegoing lollipop lady regards me with amazement.
I shall be on the news. Lovely Mrs Pemberton
Will clutch Mr Pemberton and cry: It's him!

Ladies, I am not bandy, it is the footing I must keep.
My run-up along the ridge-tiles will be inelegant.
But after lift-off, breasting the balmy wind
And when I bear westwards and have the wind in my tail

Then what a shot I shall make, going for the big sun,
Over the flowering cherries and the weeping willows,
Beating along Acacia Avenue with a purpose
Towards the park and the ornamental lake.

The Meeting of God and Michael Finnegan in South Park

Sunday, early; foul with dreams
Entering the empty park between two bent railings
I found his crutches towards the bottom of the hill
Lying on the long undulations of grass
Like spars of wreck. So, I thought,
Michael has met God as he always said he would.

He will have dropped from them last night
Having swung this far out of the soiled city.
Here is his jagged bottle. This morning then,
Waking with scabby lips, he saw God walking in the park,
Dewy-grey, delighted by blackbirds and songthrushes
And the scent of the mown grass. Look, God said

To Michael Finnegan, how beautiful the city is,
The white spires, delicate as a moonshell,
Reaching from sleep into the soft blue daylight.
And see the well-spaced leafing trees: that copse
Through which is passing even now a frisson of joy,
That single poplar in a brave plume – and there

A damp place which is a beginning stream
To water the pale city. Begin again, said God,
Leave your crutches lying and no excuses. Don't,
For example, be telling me you must wait for the keeper
To let you out. My fence is vandalised
Where you came in and above, higher,

Passing that single and admonishing poplar,
That convocation of oaks, that company
Of beeches downed like youths in Homer,
Leaving behind and further and further below you
The city sparkling like a hoard of shells
You will find a gap I made for the convenience of the children.

So Michael Finnegan spewed up some green bile
And wiped his lips and saw blood on the back of his hand
And found his feet and climbed the long slope unaided
And far below him in the moonlike city
From towers, faintly, fell the notes
Of an hour that was still unearthly.

Don Giovanni: Six Sonnets

1 *Act 2 Scene 18*

When he had gone, burning in hell fire,
And the valet in black had drawn the cloth and they
Had sung the restoration of order in a choir
In separate silences they turned loosely away:
Facing a nunnery, marriage to a fool, marriage
To a woman in love and service more tedious.
He was their sun, his fist had held them, each
Released now travelled down a different radius.

Turning on a widening wheel, come spring
After a winter they will rake his fires to life
Under the heart's ash and his singing will begin again
Coursing through them like sap. Thirsting then, burning,
Servant, nun, husband, unloving wife
Will scan the linen for his last wine's stain.

2 *'How can men want wearisomely to philander?'*
LEPORELLO TO DONN' ELVIRA

Burgos is full of women and Burgos is only one
Of the cities of Spain full of women and Spain
Etc. They are a drop in the ocean
The thousand and three. And it's all labour in vain.
He's ladling at women with a sieve
And like the proverbial good shepherd he'll leave
The one to chase the missing ninety-nine
Up hill down dale in the wind and the rain
And lose the one. Lady, he never lets up.
The poor man hasn't had a holiday in years.
He sees himself as one of life's almoners
And bringers of sunshine, handing his loving cup
To rich and poor, fair and ugly, and the shriven
Kneeling with sinners for his French stick of heaven.

3 *Zerlina*

Waking this morning I was someone else:
A wife who knows she has conceived, but the shock
I felt under my heart was remembering how he struck
The strings with the backs of his fingers and my new pulse
Was the starting again of his singing in my veins
Sotto voce. I have gone about the house
And to and fro in the garden hearing his damned voice
All day under my clothes carrying his tunes.

He swung my soul, he showed me how they move
In very presence, those whom an innocent love
Flings to the dance. And I believed his tongue,
I swallowed him, we married there and then.
I am his lawful widow big with song.
I have danced all day, believing him again.

4 *Zerlina*

He had a house, if I would follow him in
He promised we should debate the old question
How many angels might dance on the head of a pin
He guessed in my case more than a million.
There was music for what we felt, he said,
But as yet no dance. I was to imagine
Things overlapping, things deeply interlaid,
Crown-knots of fire. His hand on mine,
Our fingers so interslotted that we could not tell
Left from right, his from mine. I was to dwell
As dance on the interleafing of warm waves
Over a sand bar, their passing through themselves,
Their continuing rippling on the tide that weaves
A depth of them in which the island dissolves.

5 *Leporello*

Forked in her moorish arches, standing sentry,
I watched the summer heavens teeming down;
I dozed under her generous balcony,
Dopey with orange blossom and moonshine,
Hearing their silly laughter above my head,
His rapier clattering to the marble floor,
Rustle and sigh of things of hers discarded,
A rose thrown over into my lamplight square.
When he came down I kissed his ungloved hands
And we escaped then through the skirting gardens.
Once, in the wolf's clothing, using his voice,
I drew his starved wife down. Inhaled the perfume
Of an amorous woman, saw the abandoned face
That hurt my eyes even through my borrowed plume.

6 *Donn' Elvira*

I see my face in the black window glass;
I touch my throat, feeling for Christ's chain;
I think of charitable casual women
Who at the throat begin to undo their dress.

Christ knows my visions and may forgive me them.
They are of women and my spouse in Hell.
They stand among their fallen clothes and smile
And show him their white places without shame.

I should have smiled, I should have had their ease.
My love was like the terror of the lamb
Under his knife. Don Juan never saw
Amusement at his passion in my eyes.
I am the widow of a man at whom
I never smiled as though I were his whore.

Confessional

Where, in a French church, stuck through
And dreaming of haymaking in Liebenau,
Should he go to die? Not in the lee of the altar
Nor spreadeagled under the tower.
He hid in the confessional and died seated
Leaning forward as though to the priest's ear.

Americans were brought in dead
And laid down the hollow nave to the altar steps
And from north to south on the transept
And peasants with faces like the Conqueror's
Embarking in their church windows made
A white cross over them with armfuls of June flowers.

The dead man from Liebenau sat still
Behind the curtain in the confessional
Pressing his open mouth to the grille.

Thoughts of the Commandant of the Fortress
of St Vaast-la-Hougue

My boy keeps up appearances.
He props the dead soldiers in their embrasures
And fires their muskets from time to time.

By candle light in the nucleus
With a bitten finger I patrol our miles of walls
Hearing at every turn the claws of a grapnel
Or the moat bleeding away through a wound.

And what is worse: low tide when we
Padlock our throat and cordon the slit with salt
And the birds stalk over the foetid mud
Bayoneting the overturned soft crustaceans?

Or full: when we are brimming with fear
That our besiegers thus will fall quietly upon us
With the soft wings and the demon faces of moths?

They have surrendered oceans of freedom to beat these walls.
How furious will be their disappointment
After the falling silent of my ragged bird-scarer.

Pillbox

Dome of the sun. So we shall burn
Immured in a head, peering through hyphens.
Though we are prickly with angles of vision
An intelligence may calculate our blindspots
A hand rise out of the earth
To post us flames. Somebody squats
On the skull with a trepan
Where our flailing glances cannot dislodge him.
The surf is placid at nights
And soothing the scent of camomile.
We have nailed this coast. Buried to the eyeballs
We shall burn like lampions.
The quenching Atlantic will back away from us.

Nestor encourages the troops
(after Iliad *ii. 336ff.)*

My dears, you sound like little boys
Still pimply before they redden out
With bloodlust. Who promised then? Did not
We all with drink and a handshake
Cross our hearts and hope to die
For Agamemnon? Yapping, though we yap
Till kingdom come, will get us nowhere. Sir,
Lead them cheerfully back on to
The killing-ground and let
The one or two malingerers, the schemers
For early home-time, the impiously
Unwaiting to hear God's final word, let them
Drop dead. I personally
Believe we were given the nod and the wink
That day by Zeus. It lightened, did it not,
Righthandedly when we were boarding
Our snouted ships for Troy. Well then
For Helen's misdemeanours and your wasted years
Anticipate a just desert
Of married Trojan cunt. When we are in
And the pretty fires are burning and only toddlers
And snivelling old men encumber your knees
Remember then you thought of going home. However
If luxury to come (shitting on silks)
Will not embolden you try running and we,
Your lords, will stick you to the ships.

Garden with red-hot pokers and agapanthus

The link flowers that stood in a loose sheaf
Cock-red and yellow-wattled
A clear honey dabbling their waxy spikes

When you pushed open the gate in the garden wall
They dubbed your bare shoulder
When you went down the granite steps

Pushing open the gate that was always half-open
You agitated the flames and the embers
When you went down into the cool agapanthus.

The green iron gate was always half-open,
There were three steps down. The agapanthus
Is shock-headed and slim. Love, through a caul,

Through slung cells dotted with life,
Through sunrises and rose
Windows of webs I watched for you climbing

Out of the place of quenched fires
Dew on your hair, your flinching shoulders
Touched with yellow pollen.

'Looking for nothing'

Looking for nothing but a place in the sun
We found the cricket-pitch that nobody
Finds by looking: an outfield head-high,
A plateau of curious topiary
And twenty-two paces of asphalt battened on
By gorse like sea-slugs. Over the boundary

The wind streamed downhill in a bright sunlight
Through choppy bracken with a watery din
And entered the sea. Wading in
We found the drinking trough of lichened concrete
Still holding water that had fallen sweet
Nowhere arable, nowhere beasts might feed.

We lay in the sun's cupped hands
By the undrunk water mouth on mouth
Below the cricketers' flat earth, beyond
Their lost sixes. We opened
Rapidly from diminutive springs, like breath
Surfacing butterflies wafted down the wind.

Sunset Shells

Sunset shells, of which there were millions
Banked at our bare feet, like a flint scraper
They fit exactly into an idle
Skimming grip between finger and thumb.

That day whilst the sun blew and the long-
Sleeved tide harped louder over the sandbar
Until the island was awash for the last
Half hour we were launching sunset shells.

Oh, we threw thousands, they saucered up and
Cut from under by the sunny wind
Each at its curve's high-point paused spinning
And was returned overhead into

The sea's incoming arms with a sound
Like kissing and floated briefly, we had
Behind us a flotilla of little
Sinking coracles and in the sky

Always any number climbing to
Their points of stall and boomeranging down
The windslopes. The sun laughed and the tide
Like clapping drew the last white curtains.

Oranges

I

Mother has linen from the *Minnehaha*,
I bought the ship's bell for half a sovereign
From Stanley, our dumb man.
Everyone has something, a chair, a bit of brass

And nobody wakes hearing a wind blow
Who does not hope there'll be things come in
Worth having, but today
Was a quiet morning after a quiet night.

II

The bay was coloured in
With bobbing oranges. What silence
Till we pitched into it
Knee-deep the women holding out their skirts

And the men thrashing in boats
We made an easy killing
We took off multitudes
And mounded them in the cold sun.

When Matty halved one with his jack-knife
It was good right through, as red
As garnet, he gave the halves
His girls who sucked them out.

III

The beams we owe the sea
Are restless tonight but every home
Is lit with oranges. They were close,
She says, or else the salt

Would have eaten them. Whose popping eyes,
I wonder, saw them leave
Roaring like meteors
When the ship in a quiet night

Bled them and they climbed
Faster than rats in furious shining shoals
In firm bubbles and what
Will tumble in our broken bay tomorrow?

Sols

*(for Alice Thomas, in memory of her son,
my cousin, who died in 1943, aged three weeks)*

1

Planting is hard, so much stooping uphill,
But leisurely and we can lob
Some conversation over the high hedges,
Share forenoon in a strip of shade.

Picking is desperate though, the wind
Reaches in like a bear fishing.
We get them out earlier and earlier
Hurrying under frightful red skies.

The market demands it, however green
They are and tighter than shut beaks.
Packing them is a stiff business,
So many rods, box after box. Some die,

That's certain, die at sea, and what
Could we deal worse into the roofed homes
There to be broached behind drawn curtains
Than a Christmas box of sols

With wrinkled eyes that no one's hands
Taking them up or water will freshen?
The house had already imagined
The scent of gratefulness in every room

Which is the breathing again of sols
When a woman lifts them like a love child
Out of the ark that crossed the wolfish sea
From the world's end at the time of miracles.

2

The harvests were golden once and every room
Of that formal maze had a fire of flowers
Whatever the weather constantly fuelled
With cradled armfuls. The little paths

Going through our roofless windy city
Like cracks in brickwork by two or three steps
At slits in the tall euonymus
Trickled with gold. The trundling carts

Climbed to the packing-house, the long shed,
Like royal hearses. From a broken rim
The harboured steamer received into her hold
The burden of busy gigs and launches.

3

They worked all the hours God gave
They could never pick fast enough
The fingers of the women were raw with tying
They were minting gold
Hand over fist, the currency of grief,
And bloating the steamer with condolences.

4

Christmas, and not a candle showing;
The steamer kept coming, the markets of London
Were lit with flowers, by grief's
Osmosis they were drawn

Through every capillary:
Down highways in a slow march
Sinuously through lanes and cricked
At stepping angles through the slums.

5

Put off alone in a white ark
He scents the room like bread
Fresh on a board, like sols
In sparkling vases. But silence is natural
To the breathing of bread and sols and nobody
Pushing open the door ajar
On darkness would listen thus and crane
And tiptoe in and lean with an ear downwards
To be certain they still lived.

Curiosity, since by daylight
He could never revisit the unroofed slums
To peer inside or glance at a slice of living-room –
Its tatters of floral wallpaper and dog's

Hind-leg of a flue – he never saw
In a winter daylight the exact layout
Of our cemetery fixed among the lines
Of railway, box-like factories and canal,

Never swooped low in the sparkling frostlight
To observe the neat little casts of the newest graves
And their cut flowers and perhaps a cortège
Pushing, as though congealing, through a back street.

So curiosity brought him low over the bulbfields,
Gentle township of evergreen walls,
Corrals of sunshine open to the sky
Whose goods nothing worse than a south-easter swipes.

And there were little people busy at the source of flowers
Who ran at his roar, dropping their burdens,
And hid where we look for shade.
He came in low, he saw their white faces.

7

Since it is sleep that makes possible
The coming of the sackman, cherry-red,
Who can pass through soot with his white beard immaculate,
Sleep and the darkness, a black heaven,

A sheeted firmament, darkness in the attic,
Darkness in all the sleeping rooms,
The children are desperate to sleep and clench their eyes
Fearful they keep the red man listening at the door

Unable to enter, fearful he will turn on his heel
And shoulder the sack, but worse, almost,
Should he mistakenly believe their breathing
And enter the knowing darkness with effulgent whiskers.

8

Concave over the magic box
My father holds his breath and a small soul
Has appeared in the Brownie eye. Then light
Admitted is severed with a click.

Soon I am entered in the quilted album
On the first black page. All babies look alike
But here is my name in small white capitals.
Ergo sum! My resting place

Is the Morrison built not to give
At the knees or cave in under
A rubbled house. It easily took
Your leaden grief in a box till he

Was sided away to a third-class plot
In the big necropolis
In perpetuity. Lid the cradle
And that is how it looked, with flowers,

In a blacked-out house when he had flitted through
The lit rooms, your cock sparrow.
But you had pictured him for ever.
As we go forward now

Print after print and you are saying what
He would have been, I blur with light
Like streetlamps when our eyes are wet
As if his ghost got in.

9

Had he come down from the dark
Even three or four of the fifteen stairs
He could have looked into the living-room
And seen the fire and the lord of the fire:

Father in a long dressing-gown,
A shield on his arm, the black blower;
A sword in his hand, the silver poker;
Ushering the flames up. When Father kneeled

And tinkered with the damper
The flames became a quiet curtain
This side of which there was a smell of hot soot
And a trail of Woolworth's glitter.

Hugging the cornucopia,
The lumpy stocking from the bed-end,
Had he come in the table was laid for him
Its leaves extended as though for company.

Crusaders in a fort; a farm:
The lovable animals, the health of the green fields;
Houses, a lighted church, the whole world
Looped by a tremendous locomotive.

[St Martin's, Isles of Scilly / Salford 5]

Cold Night

We saw the pent fish redden the ice
In a Grecian park where the Cnidian
And Pan accustomed to nightingales
Stayed out all night with the owls.

The trees are brittle, the streams wrung dry;
The ice yelps at the least thing
Like a railway line; along
The scoured road there are drifts in a drove.

Drifts: they are water thrown
Under the undulating air, they are
The manifest line breath took
When the clouding water set. And we

Where are we? Listening to the owls
Or the ice or the rim of the moon:
Something that cries with little cries
Under the lake moon, under the ice

Where the drifts move in their shapes
Like seals or whales and sound
For one another down the bloodstreams
With a strange phoning, like owls.

'As though on a mountain'

As though on a mountain, on the sunny side,
The view over seven counties suddenly palled
And the stream we had bathed in, our loveliest,
We fell to damming so that not the least
Of relief could leak through, no not a mouthful;

As though downstream somewhere, still naked,
We seated ourselves on the two facing rocks
And made some conversation until the air tasted,
The shallows got tepid and our mouths dried up
And we listened to the waters piling behind our backs;

As though we joined hands then, still bleeding from the labour;
As though the waters broke; as though together
With rubble and furious fish and trees the chute
Of waters shovelled us off the mountain
Eating each other's heart in the mouth out.

To be honest, I'm losing my nerve. One day
We'll finish in town like that, on show,
A phenomenon come out of the sky, beastly,
My beautiful, ingrown, rooted through.

At Dinas

The sea runs, the long-haired breakers
Come on and on with a constant thunder;
They wear the pelts and manes of animals,
They show their throats.

At the sea's edge you look run to death,
You turn your face towards us shining with tears,
You seem to hang from your surrendering wrists;
But the sea lifts

As though you raised it. For if grief tears
The head back so will happiness, the throat
Intones and maybe your mouth's drowned
O is singing.

We three look monstrous, our heads so close
The blood beats through and across our open mouths
The wind howling. But thus we accompany you
With drum and flute.

Local Story

I

When a tree falls
The rooty place
Is beloved of children.
We opened loaves
And fruit for one another;
At the tap-root
Drank a white drink.
All we asked was to flower
In one another's features
And be apportioned
Fairly below.

II

To the black cwm
Through the sunny forest
By way of the stream.
Though I often turned
You continued following
Bare to the waist
You three were following.

A grey snow
Hurts in the cracks of the face
Long beyond spring;
Scree, wreckage,
A circling echo.
Where have I led you
Shivering?

III

Reading the excreta
Of crows and foxes
We fell on whortleberries.
We had inky fingers
And the mouths of the drowned.

On a high headland
In a form of heather
We entertained the lord of the place
Old Proteus
With our curious love-knots.

The light changed
The hill stood up and brushed our picnic off.
God watched us out of sight with other clouds.
We were never hived
We were less than crumbs of pollen.

   IV

We lit a last fire with our swag of seed.
Under the coals
Among the kindling of splintered driftwood
It sang and cried.
We swallowed souls of firelight in our wine.

Mynydd Mawr

All night sopping up rain
At daybreak the wells of the hill opened;
The animal in my crystal valley
Doled itself downstream more rapidly.

Everything flows, it must, the skull
That lodges in the stream exults
At the eyes and at the widened mouth. On Mynydd Mawr
A high wind bearing the law upon me

I let this house go, turning it
Into the rivers from the rainbow's end
Let go our beds and fires
The bowl of berries and the driftwood in arms

The holly, the harebells and the only rowan
And the long icicles brought home
I dealt them down the wind
I conjured everything out of me

Owls and curlews and a peck of jackdaws
And the tunes of dreams. Turning then
There was a steady scintillation
The wet was shining off every surface stone

As I came into the quick of the rainbow
Into the roar with widening eyes
And over my thin skin Mynydd Mawr
Flowed out of the sky, cold silver.

Swimmer

(in memoriam Frances Horovitz, 1938-83)

In summer the fires come and feed here
Like starlings. If the earth knew
She would feel a shiver of memory.
Ash on that crumpled ground.

The lake in a luminous silence, sunlight
Shed generally through the air,
A light of dreams; no lapping, shingle and
Water in a still seam.

Swimmer, the hills say, having come through ash
And snagging stumps and now
Idling on a warm surface to the midpoint
Naked, alone, try standing,

Swimmer, the sky says, tread water and feel
How thin the warmth is, thinner
Than the earth's burned hide, as thin as the Holocene
On Time's shaft and below

What a pull of cold, what colder than stone depths
Your feet are rooting in
And the cold rising as though cold were the sap
And blood of a new flower:

Death. Try calling a name, swimmer at the hub
Of a lake in a wheel
Of hills, your voice will flutter on the black slopes.
Kick, then, enjoy the surface.

Butterfly

A year and a day. Then too
There were daddy-long-legs wrecked on the flagstones
And ladybirds heading nowhere.

He offered me something in his closed hands
So suddenly my breath came with a scream.
He said was I frightened even of butterfly kisses?
Did I think he would feed me a spider?

He looked bound at the wrists
Until the flower of his hands opened
And he showed her spread and gave her up to the sky
With whole days still to live.

Fly away home: the poor shell creatures cannot
Nor can the crippled dancers lift
Off these immense piazzas.

'Then comes this fool'

Then comes this fool, muttering about freedom
And stands watching my hands and makes me nervous
And says there's a better game he knows with hands
And undoes everything, and what *he* does

Looks complicated, like a cat's-cradle,
And frail as a web and more and more like a rainbow
When he makes that wicked sign with his thumbs and fingers
And purses his lips and softly begins to blow.

And I'll set sail, he says, there's a nice breeze,
I'll probably be in paradise by tea-time.
I ask what the life expectancy of bubbles is.
They go far, he says. He says in the first dream

When I had hidden he was only passing
And kissed my whitened knuckles on the window bars.
I wonder how I undo what it was he did.
He will push off soon, muttering about the stars.

Mistress

Women whose hands know the feel of a baby's head
Push them confidently in among the melons
And their strong brown thumbs side by side,
Beautifully cuticled, feel for give on the crown.

That summer of the hot winds and the fires
The melons were sold split. He held me one
Before we had paid for it, before all the people,
To smell the inside of at its small
Opening fleur-de-lys and we went down
In a river of laughter between the banked stalls
Among all the people swinging our fruit in a net.

He made the cuts but I opened it
And for a moment my hands were a bowl of flames.
I served him cradles and the moons of nursery rhymes
And a family of rocking boats. We ate
And our mouths ran over with luscious smiles.

Then he closed my hands into a fist and held them shut.

'Wet lilac, drifts of hail'

Wet lilac, drifts of hail; everything shines
After the white rain, the gutters stream with seed;
Glistening in a fierce sun the road pitches
Downhill into an entrance of chestnut trees.

Tonight shall we cross the same meadow
And steal in the long gardens? I wore
Blossom in my hair, I wore a white dress,
I gave him my shoes to carry and ran away barefoot.

In love's month, after the first winter,
Apple trees revive in the memory of the dead
And they remember pink and white apple blossom
Flung down on the grass like a girl's clothes.

After a year the entrance is lit again
With high candles and the dead wait in the dark
For somebody coming, their flowers of hope
Plucking to nothing in fretting fingers.

My empty-handed love, someone will come
Soon bringing me armfuls of stolen lilac,
Sparkles of rain in his hair, and the black earth
Tonight when I run barefoot will quake with sobs.

Poplar

He slept at once as though
Escaping, he slid from my mouth
With a smile of thankfulness
And at the temple then his blood
Quietened upon my heartbeat, as though
The sea had pitched him far enough
And now withdrew, but I
Came to and heard
What I thought was a river
Passing overhead through our crown
Of leaves, I seemed
To be lying in a downpour, one
That drenched and blessed
My sleepy sub-self, the ground
Of me, and I wondered at
His fear of sadness
And of new desire like that
For snowy mountains rising again
Always too far distant,
I could conceive of none –
No thirst, no sadness, no distance –
My downpour could not answer.

Apples

(for my father-in-law on his 80th birthday)

The daughter has a taste for sharp apples
And lolls in a fork, munching; little brother,
Blonder than corn, can dangle one-handed
Far out. Elsewhere, so I believe,

These things are forbidden, there is a scarecrow
And it is not you who strolls by
To see what the children are up to
But old Mr McGregor or God the Father.

On the lawn all you are judging
Is the likely parabola of apples when the tree
With a shout next fires one off;
You resemble a Green Man

Fielding eagerly at silly-point,
Your nettle-proof hands seem to be praying
Apples will fall. Those we miss
Bruise with a white spittle

And some my ring nicks, we lay them down
For immediate pies. In the apple light
Among the globes and leaves
The lucky children have ascended again

To the era of pure monkey tricks
Where lichen roughened us
And we were barked and greened. Our little Lob
Has stuffed his tee shirt full

So that I wonder, and perhaps you do too,
Who are four yards and forty years away,
Whether apples in a shirt
Have the feel girls have. Catching apples

And once my daughter's core
All afternoon I have been praising Eve,
The starred girl, the apple-halver,
Who has redeemed us from Mary-without-spot.

Pictures

Whether to take down the Kissing Swallows
And the Modigliani nude
And blu-tack something else there: a child,
Say, on fire and running towards us

Down a long road; or this little dot
Whose belly looks almost bigger than
Her mother's did; or any
One of those solemn witnesses we stand

In our photographs of a new mass grave
Like gentlemen in an old print
Modestly indicating by their smallness
Something phenomenal. The children

In this photograph from El Salvador
Are that international pair, a boy
And a little girl on a roadsign
Running, and below them, his head

In the gutter and his black blood
Being lapped by a row of dogs, on a road
Empty but for the photographer
A man has fallen among worse than thieves.

Amber Seahorse
(for Mary-Ann)

Europe is ripped through, my darling,
The resinous trees have little spastic arms,
The golden routes are leaden and the lap
He came from can't imbibe much more. I read

That the hippocamp is a sovereigne remedie
Against the byting of a madde dogge. Hold on
To him, it may soon come to that as
Every day they open up more badlands,

Burnish him, love, for some fluorescence
A while longer and note his canny eye,
His long shrewd nose and the springy tail
He rode the flood out on.

Traveller, bright thinker,
Remember the wreckage of the woman of Sindhos
Lying under glass like Snow White
And the finds where they were found:

Amber where the throat was, given her,
I think, and worn for love; a bowl
Lying in her vanished lap, her dusty
Hands had grasped it, proffering.

Eldon Hole

They fastened a poor man here on a rope's end
And through the turbulence of the jackdaws let him down
To where everything lost collects, all the earth's cold,
And the crying of fallen things goes round and round
And where, if anywhere, the worm is coiled.

When he had filled with cold they hauled him up.
The horrors were swarming in his beard and hair.
His teeth had broken chattering and could not stop
Mincing his tongue. He lay in the rope and stared,
Stared at the sky and feared he would live for ever.

Like one of those dreadful fish that are all head
They saw him at his little window beaming out
Bald and whiskerless and squiddy-eyed
He hung in the branches of their nightmares like a swede.
They listened at his door for in his throat

Poor Isaac when the wounds in his mouth had healed
Talked to himself deep down. It was a sound
Like the never-ending yelps of a small stone
Falling to where the worm lives and the cold
And everything hurt goes round and round and round.

Sunken Cities

(for Lynne Williamson)

Some wrecks the fish steer clear of and no
Life at all will inhabit them; others
Are cheerful tenements. Since you told me
Of dolphins living in sunken cities

On any blue clear day I imagine them
Arriving here and circling the spires
Slowly like eagles and down the standing
Canyons going faster than bicycles.

For rubble will not do. We must sink entire
Like Ladybower under the reservoir
Or under the two oceans that collide
Around the Wolf and under our ships'

Black shadows Lyonesse. After snow
When the white dome and Saint Mary the Virgin
Look frail on the sky and the gardens
Are blank and silent and sometimes

At evening when the great libraries
Light up like lanterns we are fittest perhaps
For the seabed and to open our doors
And windows to the incoming dolphins.

Landscape with friends

It was like hands when they extend
To greet us or offer fruit in a bowl
Or release a dove. The sun unclasped
And we admired the mountain in a new light.

It was the hour of the very long shadows
Pointing nowhere across the big fields
When the cypresses tap the darkness under the earth.
The fleece of forest on the mountain bloomed.

The gesture of the sun was almost sorrowful
Over the heads of our joy, as though
We missed the point. I praise the light,
I praise the mountain too that had

A self to show, but mostly I praise you
Little enough in the empty field against
That sea-green hill who stood your ground
Embracing and showing me your lighted faces.

At Kirtlington Quarry
(for Simon)

Catch, cricketer. Another year or so
Before you love the fit of a lampshell
Its promontory and pedicle hole
Quite the way I do

Or a section of the honey golden bed
Where the molluscs are lying as thick as leaves
Puts you in mind of Jews in chamber graves
Horribly impacted.

On the old floor, innocent and loveless,
Shapes were shapes, the lampshells swayed
Like nothing but themselves. We made
All the analogies.

Two hundred million years above us
The shape comes, ahead of its roar;
Seems too heavy to float on the surface air;
Has amazing slowness.

Lampshells shining in the oolitic snow;
Stars above all. The guards took bars to prise
The families apart. Here comes the noise
And shadow over you.

Tea-time

Tea-time. Instead of the tea-lady
Enter Aquarius. Fish, she says,
Marry me quickly. Backs the door to.
He sits like Piffy on the window-sill

Knowing she can see behind him, head-high,
Her river with its chunks of ice, stiff sheep
And the homes of fussy coots
Turned upside down. Do it, she says.

Handling the tiller of the tall window
He lets in the din and smell of the black melt.
In her bright eyes he is riding high in the stern
Of a ship of fools. Then the books lift,

The strict papers and the tight-arsed files
They flutter, they butterfly,
They snow up the room like doves, beating it to
The slitted window. Yes, she says, oh yes.

He has an ear for discipline. He hears
The lift land Mrs W.   Girl, he says,
Hold that door handle tighter than Katy did.
Oh come, she says, we shall be gone, she says.

NOTES

Piffy: a creature of indeterminate character and sex.
Mrs W.: the tea-lady.
Katy: the brave Scots girl, Kate Barlass, who bolted
the door with her arm to save her king.

Burning

I

Brick tholos, heat
Humming about it in a strong sun.

She served in the dough
By a long handle. Bread
On the air, we lay
Idly in the camomile.

II

Thatch, it burned;
The doors puffed open, the panes
Shattered like that woman's spectacles
On the Odessa Steps.
Bread had gone into the oven.
It burned.

Tashes of ferns for the pigs' bedding,
Hay for the cattle
Burned. The gorse in flames,
The broom ravelled to nothing;
The heather crackled.

What a squeaking of shrews.

III

At low tide we entered a sea-cave.
There it was cold, fireless.
On the sea, as in an old perspective,
We saw charred little boats.

When the sea came home
We backed into the gullet,
Admired the vehemence of past tides
That had so rammed things in.
We remembered a picnic above:

How the sea thumped the air
And the ground blew cheerfully.

He felt for us.
Above the boulder choke
There was a small breathing space.

IV

Our land is bumpy with tumuli.
The fire uncovered them.
Looters came
With bars and rooted at a blocked entrance
Or stove in the crown.
They will have found
Poor skeletons
No gold
A little earthenware.

V

The fire blew into the sea.
The black earth raised innumerable foxgloves
Where in living memory there had been none.

We used to think the willowherb came in with the bombs
There followed such a flowering on the sites.

VI

Into the dunce's cap
Inserting your little finger
Which is the little-bird-told-me
The listening finger
Inserting Baby Small
Under that snuffer
Wish, child,
Wish hard.

'We visit the house'

We visit the house: two blackened gable-ends
Their bedroom fallen in. They had perfected
The gift of lying still and sharing breath
Under one roof their tongues necking in silence,

He in her, fled to a small bud, inside,
Under her thatch, her lintel-bone, her capstone,
Shut-eyed, hibernated, and neither knowing
Exactly where it was, in whom, in what,

A new springwater was divined and roots
Struck quietly. Had they lain apart
They would have heard the low clouds tearing and
The fleeing constellations crying out.

Mother and Daughter

Mother and daughter were found standing
Unharmed in the bloody arena
On stage in the stepped hoofprint
Packed in mud. They had survived

A long bombardment of hot stones
And days of ash. They were found by feelers
Put out choking from a new well-shaft
Sunk for a villa riding high

Among sweet fields. Gently, gently
Resurrected they were thought to be vestals
But no, for certain, they are the mother and
Persephone still dumb from kissing Death.

Nobody loved the earth better than Demeter did
Who trailed it miserably
Calling after her child and nobody's gifts
Withheld were more pined after.

Mother and daughter passed north
From prince to prince and latterly
Survived the fire in Dresden. How Pompeii
Seen from the air resembles sites of ours:

Roofless, crusty. Look where Persephone
Wound in rags
Leads blinded Demeter by the hand
Seeking an entrance to preferable Hades.

The quick and the dead at Pompeii

I cannot stop thinking about the dead at Pompeii.
It was in the Nagasaki and Hiroshima month.
They did not know they were living under a volcano.
Their augurers watched a desperate flight of birds
And wondered about it in the ensuing silence.

There was sixty feet of ash over Pompeii.
It was seventeen centuries before they found the place.
Nobody woke when the sun began again,
Nobody danced. The dead had left their shapes.
The mud was honeycombed with the deserted forms of people.

Fiorelli recovered them by a method the ancients
Invented for statuary. When he cast their bodies
And cracked the crust of mud they were born again
Exactly as they had died. Many were struck
Recumbent, tripped, wincing away, the clothing

Rolled up their backs. They were interrupted:
A visiting woman was compromised for ever,
A beggar hugs his sack, two prisoners are in chains.
Everyone died as they were. A leprous man and wife
Are lying quietly with their children between them.

The works of art at Pompeii were a different matter.
Their statues rose out of mephitic holes bright-eyed.
The fresco people had continued courting and feasting
And playing mythological parts: they had the hues
Of Hermione when Leontes is forgiven.

Fogou

We are watching the sky in a certain quarter
For the look of iron. The house we leave
May be hospitable with the smell of baking bread
When we enter the ground again at the ferny hole.

What pity we shall extend into the sunlight
For our molested rooms, and what rank fear
That men will come prospecting with crowbars
Or slip in dogs at the mouth of our shorn hill.

The cold or fire; or to be sat out
By hunger; or as at Trehowlek
Where there were grave finds: a doll,
A photograph, the family loving cup.

At Pendeen something unspeakable
Must have happened to the woman of the house.
She appears in winter in a white dress
Biting a red rose.

Christmas

If his snowy manoeuvres
His chimneyings
Always seemed feasible
Why should not the big ship

After the seven seas
Sail our curdled river
Our stunk canal
And the unlit alley alley-o?

When the sky shrieked
And shapes were nosing through the water
And our big hospital
That could have blazed like a liner

Tried to hide, the galleon
Flew in like an owl
All sails breathing
Hoarsely like a baby

Behind the blackout
Hove to in our front room
And put off towards you
A coracle of oranges.

Hyacinths

The tortoise earth seems to have stopped dead.
Certainly the trees are dead, their limbs
Are broken, we can hear them clattering.
It must be about the midpoint. Last year
At this time you knelt for the hyacinths.

You brought them in like bread, in fired bowls,
From secret ovens of darkness. Three or four rooms
Soon had a column and a birth. Pictures show
The crib shining similarly
When Christ flowered from Mary the bulb.

The Kings stand warming their hands on the light.
Their gifts are nothing by comparison.
I suppose they feared that without some miracle,
Without the light and the bread of hyacinths,
The earth would never nudge forward out of the dark.

Mappa Mundi

1

This was a pleasant place.
This was a green hill outside the city.
Who would believe it now? Unthink
The blood if you can, the pocks and scabs,
The tendrils of wire. Imagine an apple tree
Where that thing stands embedded.

2

There is nowhere on earth now but
Some spoke will find us out
Some feeler from the impaled hill. On sunny days
That broken thing at the dead centre
Its freezing shadow comes round. At nights
Turning and turning like
The poor shepherd Cyclops for his bearings
It colours moonlight with a hurt eye.

3

Blood then, in a downpour.
For weather continued, the sun
Still drank what sea was available.
The indifferent wind herded his sagging clouds
That wept when they could not bear any more.

4

Our nearest sea lies at the mercy of certain rivers.
The rivers themselves cannot avert themselves.
They begin blindly where, so we believe,
There is clean ice, snow and rare blue flowers.
They come on headlong and before they know it
We have them in our cities.

If they could die that would be better.
If they were lambs and we their abattoirs.
But they emerge like many of our children
Suddenly old, big-eyed,
Inclining to apathy. What was before
What they saw in our cities
They cannot at all remember. Day after day
They sink their trauma in the helpless sea.

5

The flat earth is felloed with death.
At every world's end, in some visited city,
Diminished steps go down into the river of death.
The salt river fills the throats of severed bridges.
Mors, the serpent, encircles the world.
His tail is in his mouth. He lives for ever.

6

Paradise lay in the river of death.
Before we slept we listened to the lapping water.
Our sands went steeply down, we bathed,
Rolling for joy like dolphins. Smiling,
We felt the dry salt on our faces;
Salt on our lips. She could halve
The mouth-watering apples exactly with her fingers.

We had four cardinal springs, they rose at the centre.
They rose from a love-knot continually undoing.

One day Charon arrived in a black boat,
One morning early, we were still sleeping.
Naked we were taken away from home.

7

The rivers of Paradise swam under the sea,
Unmixed with salt, death had no hold on them.
They surfaced miles apart, like fugitives
They calmed their breathing, they assumed
A local pace and appearance. Inland somewhere
Ordinary people
Receive driftwood from their broadcasting arms.

8

All rivers, even this, remain persuasive.
We have a house whose open windows listen.
At nights, my hand on your cold hand that rests
Upon your belly where our child curls,
We listen anxiously. Suppose we left,
Suppose we left this place and leaving below us
City, town, village and the interference
Of fence and throttling wire, suppose we found

121

The crack in the ice where one of the four emerges
Thrown, gasping, lying in the thin air
Like lambs that wait for strength from the sun to stand,
What could we do, holding that dangling thread?
Where could we go, knowing our need for breath?

Frightened at nights, hearing our city river,
We feel through our divining hands the pulse
Of the first four springs, we feel the kick
Of their departure diving, sweet through salt,
Their shouldering like smooth seals,
Their wriggling through the earth's rock like white hot quartz
Passing the creatures pressed
With starting eyes in carapaces
Whom fire and weight put out from the shape they had.

9

We shall not harm them now, they seem to pity us.
They have come out of a few last hiding-places.
They are solemn and curious, they have formed a ring.
Little by little they are coming forward, shy as birds.
We might have fed them. Or perhaps they are drawn
Against good manners, thinking it rude to stare, but as
Our children used to be drawn to pavement corpses
When deaths were singular. They are all true, all those
That we imagined; but many we never imagined.
They stare particularly at our little ones
Who cannot be frightened by anything we imagine,
Who are not alarmed by Blemyae and Sciapods,
By Dogheads, Cyclops, Elephant Men,
By some mouthless, feeding through a reed, others in a caul,
Some with the stumps of wings, some webbed, some joined, some swagged
With dewlaps, some diaphanous, some thin, with eyes.
Our children smile at them all. They are glad perhaps,
Our children, not to be unprecedented.

FROM

SELECTED POEMS

(1991)

Local Historian

Come in for a reference he lay down,
The book on his chest, his finger trapped in its pages.
Slept, and the sea did what it always does
When we sleep and listen, the sea drew nearer
And the neighbourly black cypresses
Almost leaned over the house. Starlings
Drove like hail to the collection in the marshes.

Slept, out of hours, late winter in the afternoon,
His finger marking a reference, and with a whisper,
A shush, an exhalation, his library
Dissolved and a thousand saints and the local worthies,
Every carn and cross and cove, as fine as flour,
Sucked from the room like dust, like spores,
Name after name after name, the parishes,

All of Cornwall, slipped from his lease
Towards home. When he wakes, in the darkness
For a while he will not know where he is,
The sea making a din, the cypresses overwhelming.
But I know that man. His finger marking the place
He will go back to the lighted room where his writing is,
He will recall the truant parishes, once more.

A two-seater privy over a stream

All work, hitting at the buckled hills,
Stopped long ago. Trees have exploded
The dwelling house, but where they went and sat
Side by side for the resumption of innocence
Like pharaohs on two full moons
Their feet on a slate rest placidly
Their hands on their knees in the dry and out of the wind
(Except that the water shot through
Under their feet and moons and on the cold water
A colder draught was riding)
That place still stands. Well-built,
Homer would have called it, well-roofed.

124

The smooth wood is wormy but will support you.
I went in to eat an apple out of the rain.
Their bony hands. So high above Trawsfynydd
They had nobody upstream after the Romans left,
Always new water (after a rain
Like boiling quartz) and downstream not their worry.

The Pitman's Garden
(for Bill and Diane Williamson)

Man called Teddy had a garden in
The ruins of Mary Magdalen
By Baxter's Scrap. Grew leeks. What leeks need is
Plenty of shite and sunshine. Sunshine's His
Who gave His only begotten Son to give
Or not but shite is up to us who live
On bread and meat and veg and every day
While Baxter fished along the motorway
For write-offs Teddy arrived with bags of it
From home, which knackered him, the pit
Having blacked his lungs. But Baxter towed in wrecks
On their hind-legs with dolls and busted specs
And things down backs of seats still in and pressed
Them into oxo cubes and Teddy addressed
His ranks of strapping lads and begged them grow
Bonnier and bonnier. Before the show
For fear of slashers he made his bed up there
Above the pubs, coughing on the night air,
Like the Good Shepherd Teddy lay
Under the stars, hearing the motorway,
Hearing perhaps the concentrated lives
Of family cars in Baxter's iron hives.
Heard Baxter's dog howl like a coyote
And sang to his leeks 'Nearer my God to Thee'.
He lays his bearded beauties out. Nothing
On him is so firm and white, but he can bring
These for a common broth and eat his portion.

Leaving town, heading for the Ml,
Watch out for the pitman's little garden in
The ruined fold of Mary Magdalen.

The Vicar's Firework Show

Because he wanted St Paul's, full,
And a singing of praises to raise the roof
And got Duxford with Penton Mewsey
And a bare quorum to observe his puffs of breath

He thanks God for gunpowder. All Souls,
The tongues of his flock of dead ignite again
And whisper visibly. He climbs the hill outside
To pull a multitude, like Wesley

Packed to the mouth with speech, he draws a town
Of people roaring into the dark
And does what it is his call of work to do:
He gets them to look up: at the lifted word

Spilled on the sky. When that night
He offers the finished work of his hands
His year of peaceably fiddling with saltpetre
And all his secret inventions go up from the ground

With a thump and arriving rapidly
Out of a pinpoint open and hold
Wide open falling their pent-up souls
And the people respond with numerous similes

They call to one another what it is like
And repeat the brilliant insights of their children
So multiplying his illuminations
And a congregation of innocents is looking up

Earth seems an enviable place, a small
Warmth in the universe, and God's
Face feels for it like a blind man's. I name
That vicar the hope of those who join

And their hearts still hunger. I wish him
Snow for Christmas, deep snow, a hush
Over everything, a cessation, whiteness,
The town dumbfounded, and one sprig of flame.

A calvary on the Somme

It stays: a thicket of clenched fists,
A pack still menacing him with hands like maces or mines;
And beggars even as love fails
And a black hole is sucking him away

Still showing him what was done to them by diseases
Or by the law. It lasts on his retina
And here, inflicted: trees like guitarists
After the Civil Guard had wrecked their hands.

A skylark opens. One dead poet writes
Of shells that they sprinkled out of the sky like mimosa.
He wished his girl's breasts might be reddened at the nipples
Beautifully by the blood of him raining.

Every year the ground breaks out in an eczema of iron,
Lead and the bones of men and the poor horses
And somebody comes here with his instruments,
A gardener. The field raises its colours

On slag and larksong falls in generous handfuls.
Inborn in hands is the love of opening,
They love to race into leaf. A fresh forest
Soon assuages the head of Christ the medusa.

'He arrived, towing a crowd'

He arrived, towing a crowd, and slept
That night at the house of Simon
The leper, in Bethany, three miles out.
We know the rest. But Simon adds
A leper is good company for
A christ, each in his skin
So lonely and viewing the ordinary loves and trades
From a star through frozen lashes
(Simon whose face
Shines in a certain light like mother-of-pearl
Or a silverfish). And when he blew
On lepers and pushed them gently
Back into the camp this only whitened him
The more. He was the cold
Blood-brother of Lazarus anointed by
A whore out of alabaster. His feet
Felt heavy in her net of hair
Like twins
Like bastards drowned.

The Saint observed at his Vigil

It was a strange sight.
He entered the North Sea like a candle
Long and upright, a pale man,
He entered and made two pauses:
Waist-deep, to suspend the animation of his parts
Chest-deep, to stun his heart.
I was afraid he would go under utterly
But at the chin he halted
And I saw his head alone on the sharp sea
And heard him yodelling across to God
His head under the whistling mobiles of the stars
His shining head
And the incandescence
I believe this was the soul of the saint
Climbed higher and higher in her drowning house.

Man on his holidays

A man my age at Morecambe when the tide
Went out he went out after it with a little spade
And built a nude in the sand, her feet
Towards the sea. He did her open-eyed

Flat on her back or sleeping with her arms
Her pillow. He would be hours out there
Patting her with the spade and then with his hands
To get her curves right and the difficult hair.

Nobody came. At a distance, it is true,
There were some others with their trousers hoisted up
And hankies on their domes looking for scallop shells
And one playing noughts and crosses and one poor chap

In tears at a prospect of the Lake District
Across the bay. But when my friend had done
He sat back in his folding chair and waited for the sea
Which always came: it seemed the horizon

Unrolled, it came in rapidly, little low
Nibbling waves, and he watched his work: her feet,
Her thighs, her breasts, the careful likeness of her face
Blur and collapse under the sea's cool sheet.

Returning then he says he always felt
An old terror: of being so far out,
The sea teasing his ankles, the shore beyond his strength
And nobody adult who would hear him shout.

Came hurrying in with his little spade and chair,
Pressing his hand on a sharp stitch in his ribs,
And asked what he'd been doing out there that long
When he could speak he told the usual fibs.

Mandeville remembered

In spring I wheeled him through the garden
Crushing the cockle shells, the paths
Enraged me, their perpetual
Digressions and dead ends, I couldn't think
My thoughts, letting him coast,
But must manoeuvre and shove hard and turn about
Seeing his dappled hands
Addressing an audience, and worse
His crown in its blather of white hair
Like the world egg
Lumped in chaos, the monologue
I swear was in the old coot's head
Like beaks, tapping for egress, he was cracked
And a swarm of dickybirds
In there was ready for the off.

Mandeville

He saw the agave flower and knew
A woman who had watched the phoenix burning
But for the once in a blue moon flooding of the Labyrinth
He found no witnesses and yet
It was the story he told best: how when
It happened the creatures congregated
To play in the turbulence as though this were
The bursting well that lies at the heart of Paradise
And swimmers passed, dreaming hand in hand,
Over the corridors of the Labyrinth
And viewed them from a height
Like Icarus. He evoked
The coming up of water
Out of the deep ear: the sob,
The chuckle, water's cleverness,
Her delight in rapidly solving intricacies,
He remembered this. I asked
Where was the Minotaurus when the waters rose?
He answered: the Minotaurus slept
The heavy head succumbed on his folded arms
Like a beaten boy, he wept, wept,
He dreamed himself a bubbling source of joy.

The Scaffolders

I

These are my days of lead. I stare across
At Mandeville's great library where he beached
With all his souvenirs. Last week I watched
The scaffolders against the aqueous glass

Labouring upwards on the other side
In silence like the things without a shape
In depths of sea, in terrible depths of sleep,
Arrested things, aborted, efforts at flight

Sunk and encumbered, and although I pitied them
(Still beating) how could I wish them air
At last and the light knowing that what they were
Would always flounder and be burdensome?

II

The gales lifted the leads. Raising my eyes
For once (a screaming of swifts) to the library's
Long and spacious roof I saw a man
Ascended there and strolling with a younger man

Against the sky, so shapely, so exact
Their living lines, and leading him to inspect
The drop on either side, and into every wind
He stood him, pointing. We are so far inland

But on high windows, after a southerly,
Like frost, I've heard it said, there'll often be
A lick of salt. The pointing man embraced
The boy around the shoulders, bare to the waist.

III

They have come this side. I raise the heavy window
And watch them spit on their hands and begin the escalade
With a racket of iron and singing. I see now
That rising to where they will bask and promenade

Is nothing to them, thin cheerful men
Stripped for the sun, a bone charm at the throat
And a shining spanner on the thigh. When they have given
The uprights a sure footing they repeat

A pattern of bracing slants, they plank the walkways,
Lash in ladders sharp and rig at the head
For the roofers a handy crane so that with ease
Against gravity the parcels of new lead

May be called up and the traveller's fruitful ark
Be weatherproofed. Every last bolt
Is tight through its clasp. The scaffolders embark
On a quick and patient work, and leave it built.

Clare leaves High Beach

(for Steve and Sheila)

Others also were muttering and went
Each alone on the designated ways
Tipping their headgear. Said Doctor Allen,
His kind keeper, for such men
The best company in the world is trees.

Turmoil in the head, tempest: a beech
With its arms ripped off, the yellow bone
Showing, rags everywhere, the shriek
Of roots in air, and the mind reached
Into the crippling. He bolted then, for home.

Lay down, beat, his head the needle
North for the morning, he lay between
His two wives quietly and the love was equalled.
Woke. They were gone. The sadness welled
Out of the ground and through his eyes again.

A face came over him, it had a crown
That bulged from a wreath of hair, a face
As large and a dome as bald as the moon
Beamed down at him. It was his own:
Good-natured, cheerful, and quite crazed.

He lay for the north. Out of him travelled,
As though he bled, the love of certain trees
In place, a spire, a stile, a golden field,
Lapwing in thousands. How much he held
And must crawl after now on hands and knees!

'Under that bag of soot'

Under that bag of soot, when I moved it,
Something had been trying to grow. The light,
They think, as soon as the earth warms. Eyelessly
Start pushing. Then to be flattened and on the belly
Have to go feeling for help... Sunlight,

The gift of singing comes back to the birds,
And the things that had been doing their best to grow
Get up, they are white, they are a damaged yellow.
Nobody will ask such things to flower, only
To turn a decent green. A man like that

Released into the community with a shaved head
And the marks of fangs on his temples stands
Every day at the lights and when the green man shows
And everybody hurries he stands still, through red
And the next green he stands there like

Caspar on the asphalt with his wounded feet
And one little scrap of speech: that what
He wanted was to be a rider, but
He could smell the dead still growing in the soil
And the green he needed made him vomit.

The gardener of all this raises a merciful spade.

'There used to be forests'

There used to be forests beyond the peripherals.
We knew whenever one burned: it quietened our wheels
With skins and beheaded beasts would appear
Upended on the market and into the centre

There was a fall-out of the bipeds it evicted,
You saw them in the queues; or in the precinct, stupid;
Or getting the shittiest deals under the bridges;
And I used to think of Pan, naked, uprooted,

Limping on his goat-feet, come into town
After Daphnis died, and I tried hard to imagine
This town on a grief like that. Midsummer again.
Last night I woke from a dream crying my heart out.

Lovers forget the news. They will ask for places
Heard of near the perimeter and put
A pretty shock through the network but
Where will they run to when you catch their faces

Like souls in your blaring lamps, their clothes
Already fallen away and root and stem
Already they are being translated and from their mouths
The need for a forest babbles, bewildering them

Like antlers, the need for glades and pools, and as
Beasts they arrive where a whistling forest was
And clothing again is impossible and the moon beams
Back at the ash its last programme of screams?

The Forest

Pity about the forest gone up in smoke
And what comes out of it will surely die.
Not just the meat, also the funny folk:
The sow, the goat with faces haunted by
Humanity, the cross-betweens we give
A quid to goggle at, they never live.

Was on the tube once years ago in June
Late, on the wrong line, sleeping, very tight.
Opened an eye at let's say Bethnal Green
And slept again, thinking this can't be right,
And somewhere later, let's say Leytonstone,
Opened the other and a man got on

Naked as Adam, with a donkey's head,
And sat twiddling his ticket. Woke again
Somewhere, I don't know where, the place was dead,
I heard that wind come down the tunnels, then
Girl's steps running and the girl who ran
Got in and sat beside the donkey-man.

They filled my eyes, and when I heard the din
Of our wheels enlarge and we hit fresh air
And were into fields, outside, and blossom blew in
And touched his limbs, her dress, their heads of hair,
I felt we were a well of happiness
Struck luckily and coming up to bless

Mankind. They stood to leave, he steadied her
Against the fall, I saw how bare he was
Below the nape and how the head he bore
Flowered from a spine like mine, how courteous
And solemn his attentions were and what
A pride he showed, handing her down. I sat

Like some forgotten dosser in a pew,
The doors wide open, scents, a hubbub or
Music, a river noise – I knew
It was the forest they were heading for.
My ticket was wrong. I let the damned train start
Back for the city, back to its knotted heart.

Miranda on the Tube

An empty carriage – or nearly, there was a girl –
We all piled in, bigger than usual,
And sprawled or hung and the first strange thing
Was how we had kept our distance and left her space,
And then it stopped. I ask you: nowadays
Who stares like that? No man who wants his face
Leaving alone and certainly never a girl

Who's normal, but we flick our eyes at a face
And off again before the owner comes
Or stare a girl to the floor, but there between
Stations halted, a nightmare for a girl,
She stared at us, at every one of us
In turn and all together and the strangest thing
Was this: she thought us beautiful, it showed

Like an open flower, it shone, it seemed her eyes
Were hands already learning over us
The human, the phenomenal, incredulous.
O faces soft as roses! We reviewed
Our boots, the worst came up in everyone
Like puke, out of the heart, our mouths were full
Of reason upon reason why we should not be

Looked at as though we were beautiful by her
A total stranger halted nowhere near
Help and wanting none. A carriage comes
Empty almost never and a girl alone
Never who looks like that. I sometimes see
A face a bit like hers: it hangs between
The smashed-up stations, sad as a bag-lady's.

A blind elephant man in the underground

He is still under the park where I saw the girl
Sunning her face. Her eyes were closed and such
A blessing she gave mine, smiling to herself,
I wished it down through the roots to cure London.

Travellers nearer the surface may send up
A tremor into our feet but where he is
Is where the nearly sheer escalators end
And haul themselves out of it. People gave him

The wall and a thoroughfare along
Their cold shoulders and he came through untouched
Like Moses, sweeping with his stick, and his
Right hand was open to avert us. But if

No girl like the one in the upper air
Has let his fingers model another face
On hers and practise smiling on her smile
Then he has no comparison in his head

During his lifetime in the multiplying
Corridors under London when he rides
The worm and alights in the small hours somewhere
Deserted and draws his head into shelter.

Jailed for Life

In where I put her she had always said
There was a frightening thing but I put her there
And slept on it, to teach her. Morning after
I went down with my candle. First our steps
Then it was different: a weapon in my hand
And I was knocking against wet walls and louder
And louder there was a roaring noise, it stank
Like in a cage and I was going down on paths
Calling her littlest name in like a shell
Or lug, hearing a roaring, seeing the stumps
Of legless men and smelling an animal.

Then out. There was a beach and she, my kid,
Was leading the thing she had been frightened of
By the hand and it was blind and its great head
Was hurting it in the light, an arm like Samson's
Thrust out, and ballock-naked, the poor thing
With its bull's head, and she was leading him
With daisies in her hair to a little boat,
Some men of the island bowing.
                                                Stood there
With my daft candle in the sunshine, gripping
Our coal hammer and watched her sail away.
The men put on their caps and looked right through me.

Quay

The launch is late, we wait on the hot quay.
Our farewell conversations are giving out.
That little shark from yesterday
How white it looks, how sad its mouth;

A team of crabs is operating on it.
Crabs are the stupidest among the living down there.
Netted with shrimps they never mind the net
But crunch like fun. You can haul them anywhere

On anything edible. Stag's littlest daughter
Is gouging a limpet out. End of the season,
They will be gone home soon. With his father,
The Drowner, mothers used to shush their children

And some still do, with him: his one eye,
His black appearance. Hunched in his tractor
He is thinking he will kiss that holiday woman goodbye
If she looks his way once more.

His girls have landed a crab on the hot concrete.
It sidles and fences, bubbles at a vent;
Black in the sun. They squeal for their bare feet.
Its scratchy legs pick at our nerve-ends.

The launch rounds the point like sudden death.
Clatter of starters, the tractors edge down.
We shall leave, we shall be over and done with.
Stag's girls are screaming, that crab has gone to ground

The last place it should: under his wheels
And he is on hands and knees searching the shadows
With his head's one eye and his hand crawls
Under the racket of the engine after the claws.

His shirt rucks up, we see his white backbone
And are glad when he surfaces, though the black lid
Over his eye has slipped. His hand has won.
He fits the crab snugly under the tractor's tread.

Oh, we have time enough to interfere
And look a fool. The crab merely waits
Folded between the concrete quay and the tyre
And nobody moves. We wait. I see its

Eye. Then Stag backs over the carapace.
His girls giggle. The woman, in tears,
Comes through the mêlée from her rightful place
And bruises his mouth with hers.

The Island of Curieuse

I wake. She wakes. I weep.
She knows I am weeping for the Island of Curieuse
So clear to me: the rain
Like nothing we witness here
Coming with the lightning
In sheets the blue of Hell
And the storm-wind when I wake
Continues for several minutes in broad daylight
The surf rakes everything to itself
The sea wins
The killing sea takes all.

Lilith

I think of her more when it is cold.
Snow-light: waking very early
I saw nothing in the garden that was alive
But puffy birds. Last night my son,
At the telescope, called me into his freezing room.
Threads of the light of his eyes, minuscule darts,
Had traversed an infinite cold distance
And struck into a moon.
He was bent over the slide, making a commentary,
But I was looking down the white garden
To the fence and the one lombardy poplar
And could see nothing that was alive.

'I should not be dreaming of you like this'

I should not be dreaming of you like this.
There was a staircase, we were not surprised
After the fountains and the tumbled statues
To begin a marble stairs. You ran ahead
Lifting your sodden dress, and I should have known
By your laughter which was not like the laughter

Of a real girl out of breath but like
The merriment of water it was a race
And I was trailing. Where the stairs gave out
Where they were broken off you waited for me.
I saw you backed against finality
Quite still, your open hands were by your sides
And you were showing me your pointed breasts
And smudge of hair and smiling at my grief.
We were so high above the ruined garden
I was afraid and you were not afraid.
You took my fingertips, I felt they were cold,
And blew on them and weighed them in your hands.
I knew that you were turning me to stone
And all the buoyant blood was in your veins.
Then cracks ran through the marble from my feet.
You stood me on the lip. Now fly, you said.

'In the ocean room'

In the ocean room, in the history of voyaging,
The best he showed me was the giant nautilus.
We were cheek by cheek, pressing against the glass,
When one or other of us began imagining
Sleep underwater and the old way of breathing.

He was the pearly nautilus and I
Allowed my body to the way he rocked.
So we tolled forward and with my fingertips
I read the scrimshaw: poems, fables, the log
Of landfalls, idle beautiful lines

As long as thong but flowering queerly
And becoming another creation. Couched on him
I read and silvery tickling bubbles
Hurried from my mouth. In the next case
There was a photograph of a savage man

All mapped out, he wore the fabulous
Whole world, not an inch of him was free,
And he wore it under the skin that rubs away.
His wife (I read) with the point of her tongue
And nails at night had inked and coloured him in.

Swimmer and Plum Tree

The clod was between his legs, the thin trunk prone
Across his thigh. I came and went,
I could only watch so long, but all afternoon

He sat on the dug ground in the sun, content
With his knife in the roots. He said it was ditched
And they had brought it home. The roots were pent

In a net, impacted, desperately stitched
In and out of the mesh through every single square
As fine as centipedes, embedded, clutched.

Not looking up, he said he remembered my hair
When I was swimming, water through all the strands,
Such a fine combing, and did I not wish I were

Unravelled out of him? I watched his hands
Feel gently with the knife, his fingers tease,
Loosen, release. The swimmer's hair extends

Her down the river, as though the sea's
Moon-ridden body sucked on her she slips
Easily into water. I sometimes raise

The swimmer I was – the river parting from her lips,
She holds steady with strokes, her head
Wearing the river like a bride – and then she dips

And drowns. The bole was upright in his fist. He said:
Now it can breathe again. He showed it me,
Its shock of gladdened roots. I am afraid

Soon he will write that the frail arms of their tree
Have blossomed while I am clenched and the small cone
Of the soul under my hair is weighing like mercury.

'I am inconsolable'

I am inconsolable because of her laughter.
You must have put something into her mouth
That flowered and overflowed like the living water
Between her lips she had flowers coming out

And dribbling down her neck and throat and all
The length of her like Madalena's hair
When she sat up it was a waterfall
Of laughter and nothing else that covered her.

You must have put something under her tongue.
I heard it entering her blood like power
And I lay dumbly where I don't belong
Like somebody else outside your open door

Thirsting to death and given nothing but laughter –
Hers – to drink and wishing I could swap
My tongue for hers and clog her mouth up where
The laughter was coming from and make it stop.

Emblem

Here is a woman holding an orange tree.
She must be waiting to change houses
And by the way she holds it in her lap
She will not part with the little orange tree.

I suppose the time of year to be winter
But the orange tree holds the three living seasons
(Leaf, flower and fruit) in the woman's hands
In earth, in an earthen pot, in her lap.

Bare boards, windows bereft of curtains,
Gaps on the walls where there were pictures:
But she is sitting quietly on a broken chair
In her warm coat, holding the orange tree.

CASPAR HAUSER

A poem in nine cantos

(1994)

'Where the devil should he learn our language?'
THE TEMPEST, II.ii.

NOTE

The facts of Caspar Hauser's story which matter for my poem are as follows. Incarcerated for most of his childhood and adolescence he appeared in Nuremberg at Whitsuntide 1828, able to write his name and say, without understanding it, one sentence: *I want to be a rider like my father was.* The city fathers put him into the charge of a retired schoolteacher called Georg Friedrich Daumer, and it was in Daumer's house, in October 1829, that an unknown assailant struck him across the forehead with a heavy razor. Daumer, an invalid, soon afterwards asked to be relieved of the responsibility of looking after him, and Caspar moved in with Clara and Johann Christian Biberbach – but only for a few months. Clara conceived a passion for him, which he did not reciprocate, and he was moved into the safer keeping of Gottlieb von Tucher, still in Nuremberg. Then the eccentric Lord Stanhope appeared on the scene and made Caspar his ward, removing him to the town of Ansbach in December 1831 and lodging him with another schoolmaster, one less humane than Daumer, a man by the name of Johann Georg Meyer. Stanhope himself, having shown great fondness for the boy, went travelling, and after January 1832 never saw him again. Caspar was murdered just before Christmas 1833. He went to meet a stranger at a monument in the the public park in Ansbach. He seems to have hoped that at this meeting the truth about his life would be revealed. But the stranger stabbed him. Why he was confined, let out, assaulted, murdered, has never been quite explained. Probably as the jurist Anselm von Feuerbach believed, he had a claim to the throne of Baden; but because of his innocence and the extraordinary reactions of his untried nervous system to a life in the daylight, people at once invested more than a dynastic political, worldly interest in him. He was an enigma, and excited all kinds of hopes and longings.

In Germany there is a vast literature on Caspar Hauser. I have read a good deal of it, but experts will soon see that I have taken many liberties in the pursuit of my own conception of the subject.

In six of the nine cantos I imagine Daumer, Clara Biberbach and Lord Stanhope, each near death, reflecting on their dealings with Caspar.

First Canto

I

Whit Monday 1828 he stood
In Nuremberg in the biggest empty square
Bang in the middle of it where

They burned people and broke them on the wheel
And showed their hearts and bowels to other people.
He stood there swaying on his sticky feet,

His head was bowed, the light had hurt his eyes,
The pigeons ran between his feet like toys
And he was mithered by the scissoring swifts,

Their screams and shadows, then the hour
Rolled off an iron tongue in an iron tower
And clouted him, like ferrets sound

Screwed the discovered burrows of his ears
And through the cobblestones
Another massive novelty of pains

Entered his fork. Even an embryo
Raises its little paws against the din
But Caspar stood there sucking it all in,

Dowsing for more of it on the square's navel,
Arms stiff like compasses, at the end of one
He held his letter of introduction

'To whom it may concern' and at the end
Of the other a wide-awake hat,
Both very tightly. There he remained

Just as the man behind him had set him up
On a morning of primary colours in the time
Between the moonlit and the sunlit crimes

In the town's arena, wept and wetted himself
And felt the blood in his boots, until the windows
Folded their wooden lids back and in rows

147

Diminishing to points under the eaves
From all the openings of their ordinary lives
The people stared at their accustomed space

Larger, as it seemed, and quieter and emptier
And all their beams were gathered at the centre
As by a heavy ore, or by a vacuum.

Caspar was tugging them. Down the stairways
And down the alleys of their daily bread
Blind as a mole he drew them by the eyes

Singly, hand in hand, in families,
Lifting the children up and shoving gently like
The beasts towards Adam, towards this stake,

This tree, this thing blown in by Pentecost,
They inched, already aghast
At all the questions he would make them ask.

II

Perhaps in a pitch black he would have been spared it
But there were eyes on him, the outside
Dimly through the nailed lids peered in

Down the length of him from beyond
Where his particular self came to an end
And in a darkness riddled with motes of light

He sprouted, whitish, his faint soles
Slowly, slowly, pushing towards a daylight
Only a shade more white than midnight

And even at noon never cruel. In time
The timbre of his grunts deepened
And curly dark hairs came up around

The ignorant staff of his sex. His pulses ticked,
But time for Caspar was as Luther guessed
It might be for God: all in a heap, at rest.

His repeated wakings did not seem to advance him
Only brought water, every time he woke
There was the water he loved in a clay beaker

And a clod of bread speckled with carraway seed.
He believed he slept these necessaries to his right side
Handy by, he ate, he drank, he fed

And watered the little horses, he dressed them,
So that it was a pleasure on his eyes,
With blue and red ribbons, and how they raced then

To and fro on their wheels at the end of his arm,
Their colours fluttering, an electricity went
All through him from the happiness of the movement.

The exhausted bread pushed through his coils meanwhile
At a certain pace, nosing like a mole
For its own moment of exit. Then he slid

Left over a hole and let it go through breeches
Cut out behind. Suddenly his sleepiness
Reaching a certain level tilted him backwards.

Everyone said there must be more to him, more time
Than the small space he recalled
When left and right he could touch the two cold walls,

More below that, at least the usual
Pit of years. I know a well
On an island where the clear fresh water rests

On the salt and lifts with it. Like that lay
Under Caspar's thin memory
An ocean in which most of him had sunk.

III

Right, the precipitates of sleep:
The bread and the water. Left, his sunken pot.
And left and right when he laid himself out flat

And sent his fingertips as far as they would go,
Two walls. A daylight faced him
Dimmer than the shell of the full moon on blue.

That was his room. If there was a ceiling
It never bothered him nor he it.
He slept between his little horses like a king.

149

Events came from behind. Waking, he rose
By a force, there was a hot wind on his nape
And like a stocks a wood lay across his knees.

He saw his hand, the playmate of his horses,
Under another of its kind, not his,
That clambered on it like a crab and fitted

A hard stick in and made queer jabs
And slides and slippy loops and when it stopped
Writing had come over the desk top.

It did it more, again and again and again,
Until the knowledge had taken
And Caspar's fist could move without a rider.

Those were his first steps on a white sheet,
Clutches of wriggling letters in black lead
Like tracks of worms on the Precambrian mud.

Sleeps came and went. Along with the bread and water
They flew in sharpened pencils and white paper.
He practised hard. Then he was overshadowed

Again by the hand. Riding his own
It pressed one of the little horses down
Hard on his writing and a pair of lips

In at the hairy opening of his ear
Down the quaint passageway
Again and again on pulses of warm air

Spat the one syllable, the hand
Working the plaything under Caspar's hand
To and fro, to and fro,

Until the name had come up through its wheels
And down the flex of Caspar's arm and muscles
And speech and writing touched their fingertips

In the horse's wooden body. Later he had
Sounds for himself like that, force-fed,
Trodden like a goose. The ghost hand

Busily applied them to him everywhere,
Belly and heart, mouth, eyes and hair,
It set the letters on his sunless clay,

150

Even drew up the cold balls of his feet,
Even went out to the limits of his reach,
To show how far his name was meant to stretch,

IV

Why then? With hindsight
We see the lessons were to equip him for life.
'Horse', he could say, and 'Caspar Hauser' and write

All three. But why, why start him ever,
Ever shunt him out of his silent shed
Into the traffic, who decided?

And then, what is this 'then'?
Suddenly the dust, the living grains of him
Are dumped in a hopper and begin to run

And the quiet heap of time is undermined,
Gravity riddles it, it begins to slide.
Then is when our clocks start, the hurrying kind.

Somebody shoves him off, he drifts, he sets,
He goes away faster and faster towards the falls.
Somebody connected him. Why then? Why at all?

When I dressed my son from behind, leaning over
Like a cosy sky, like a safe house easing on
His cheerful leggings, socks, and smallest size in

Soft boots, I remembered gratefully
That I was warmed like this and had my back covered
And things done for me with a sweet silly commentary

Close in my ear. But Caspar woke on the dirt,
Stark, the hands were yanking breeches up him
With a bum for once, and boots that hurt.

He flopped like a mongol being dressed,
He was as slack as a collapsed marionette,
A giant one that has lain in its box and grown,

And against his delivery into the lives we lead
He offered the passive resistance of a corpse
Dragged out by a muffled man towards a cartload,

Or of a protester at a sit-in against the War
Gone heavy in the arms of the Law,
The hands making a buckle on his chest.

His underworld had steps and reaching these,
Arranging him on the third like a man of sorrows,
His keeper came at him on hands and knees

As if in obeisance or like
A fireman getting in under the smoke
And folded him over his shoulder upside down,

His nose on the itchy jacket,
And humped him up, up, a long climb,
Frequently resting, against the pull of home,

Against the needful love of the little horses.
He was a heavy earth. Dug out, he groaned
For his abandoned shape under the ground.

Divers need time, they need to come up slowly
And Caspar needed months on every step
To harden. He was hurried. Only

The night-time was a mercy, on his eyes,
The colours sleeping, light at its quietest,
A bearable visibility. The rest,

All the waiting world, all the backed-up years,
As though he bled, as though through all his pores
He called for torture, when what little film

He wore was blown away, this all
Assembled like piranhas. He was the hole
Nature has a horror of, the greed, the thirst

Dug in her body, so the universe
Fell to filling him in. The winded man
Wheezing behind him like a buggered engine

Held him vertical on spaced feet
And the first rip-tides of nausea travelled him
Over the brew and fumes of a sweet May night

And terror when his flinching soles divined
The nervousness and hunger underground,
And he felt the moths on the dipped lamp of his face

And when he heard the winds of the stratosphere
In the hurtling planet's bright delighted hair.
Hung over chaos by the scruff he made

His three shaped sounds. 'Caspar', he said,
And 'Horse' and 'Hauser', but it did no good.
He felt like ants in a stabbed and burgled hill.

Then the march began. It began like this:
The man behind him pressed his thigh on his
And strode, the right, the left, the right, the left,

Holding him slumped. Anyone who ever
Rode on his father's shoes and took giant steps
Worked by his greater legs will have an idea,

A kind one. But the knack of it or the need
Lapsed out of Caspar after every stride
Until the man behind him kicked his heel

And the leg remembered. So towards Nuremberg
Little by little Caspar's feet were booted
And all the way the man behind him repeated

His third lesson, in at his heels it went
To the rhythm of their stiff trudging
In at his ear, a long statement:

I want to be a rider like my father was.
I want – kick – to be – kick – a rider – kick
Like my father was – kick, kick,

Caspar weeping. Thirty yards or so
In inches was as far as he could go.
Then the man behind him let him down to sleep.

So many sleeps he had on the way to Nuremberg
Face down on the heaving black-green earth,
So many hangovers, his poor head stupid

From the fragrances. Waking the first time
He met with the brutality of plain daylight:
Blinked, the world watered, everything went white.

Days in a white-out; even the night-time
Though it eased his eyes it put on perfume
Like a woman coming to bed; rain fell

153

Out of a sky he did not know existed
And water came to his mouth at the end of an arm
And fists of carraway bread.

Pairs before them have stumbled through the spring.
There was Antigone and the blind king,
Also the little girl and her blind minotaur

But Caspar never had a hand in his
Only on his neck and when the darkness
Would have allowed it he never saw a face

And when he sagged he kissed another patch of grass
And when he rose all his encouragement,
Spat in his ear, kicked in his heels, was

The difficult long sentence which he spoke
In pieces in a muddle with his name
And the sound for a horse and always meant the same:

Lay me down, make the pain less,
Sheath me in the dark again with the ribboned horses,
Only let me be. Instead

Head down against the birdsong and the scents
He barged his boots through flowers and the dried
Blood of the last stage in them liquefied.

One daybreak then, dewy themselves, they bowed
Their faces over the city of Nuremberg,
The light still kind, the squares, the houses showed

Gently through a veil. Hung by the neck, his lessons
Rattling faster and faster off his tongue,
He tumbled down to meet the citizens.

Second Canto

GEORG FRIEDRICH DAUMER
1 January 1875

I

Born in the spring of the century's first year
Lately the big questions have seemed to him answerable.
Where were we going after all? Answer:

Head down into the Age of Iron.
And thereafter? Nowhere. Iron is the last.
Or maybe lead. Some days it has that taste.

Iron or lead. Lead in the souls (the souls?)
Of such as us, the poets and the scholars,
Iron in the fists of those who govern us.

I should have been born in 1770
With Beethoven, Wordsworth, Hegel, Hölderlin,
I might have gone to Paris at the age of nineteen.

I should have moved to the centre.
Goethe would have welcomed me, I might have read
My Hafiz to him, but by then he was dead.

I am as old as the century.
I might have gone to Paris at the age of thirty
(Heine did) and in '48

I could have been in the *Paulskirche*.
There was never any shortage of barricades
I might have been on. Deeds,

However, were not his forte and look where
What was has got him, the reading and writing – here:
Loneliness, penury, a sad end

Among the poor who were always poor,
Poorer than they, they address him
As what he has been for fifty years: Professor,

Courteously, and leave him a cabbage on the step
Or a couple of billets of split wood or best of all
Half a bucket of slack brown coal.

Truth is, he has begun burning his library
Tome by tome in a strict order
Of greatest to less inefficacy.

The Bible first, a large one, he began with Revelations
Then back to Genesis. In twists with little cakes
Of wetted coal dust and the week's

Dried rinds it warmed some of the air and the side of him
Next the stove. The vellum Rosicrucians
He fed in like brickettes, transmuting them

Into heat and smuts.
The smuts continued falling on his head and hands.
Snow likewise on the streets.

Last to burn – he is as vain as the rest of us –
Will be the four dozen volumes of his published works
And first of them his *Cry of a Convert* which was

Of his innumerable wrong roads
The wrongest. He is saving
His three books on Caspar and the twelve boxes of notes

Till last, and prays (prays!)
He will die in a warmish interlude before next winter
And spare that fuel. For what? Who knows!

He saw Caspar again the other night
In the pitch black, white
And pointing at the wound in his side

So that the teacher come to the last dead end
Muddles his own and Caspar's peace of mind
Feels neither teacher nor pupil will ever rest

And burning books in the worst street in Nuremberg
Under their fall-out as the stove gives up
Its ghost of a warmth and his dewdrops drop

From a little height on to the old words
And on to the new ones written big on flattened shop-paper
He ponders for the last time over Caspar

Over his being, his origins, his innocence,
That above all – his innocence – but the truth
Seems to have lain a million years beneath

The dripping accretions which are
The writing of doctors, prelates and legal men
And of Professor Daumer again and again and again

Who to the bitter end cannot desist
But tortures the experience he indisputably had
After the meaning he feels he may have missed.

II

My good and learned friend
The jurist Anselm Feuerbach whom they poisoned
At Whitsun in the year

They stabbed poor Caspar during Advent
Laid on the grounds of his peculiar wrongs
The definition of a new capital offence:

The murder of a childhood, but the victim
Only felt pity for the man who had done that to him,
And wept to imagine the anxiety

Of a man jailing a child of his own kind
Twelve years in the dark, he said
He would not like to inhabit that man's mind

For it must be a dark place with nothing in it
Except the wrong that was growing by the minute
Bigger and bigger in a place that could not grow

Because its walls were the walls of a grown man's skull.
Later – and I can tell you precisely when –
It was the night of 1st August, we were in my garden

On the riverside, near my white statue
Which has gone now and with it the garden and my house
And what has been done to the river I will not tell you

But we were in my garden, Caspar and I,
More than two months after his appearance above ground
When I lifted up his face and he saw the starry sky.

There were showers of gold that night and the usual stars
Seemed nearer and many we had never seen
Were pressing down at us between

The black interstices and even I
Given the vision of his eyes
Felt the nearing of beauty like a booming noise

And shook at it, his heavy head
Lay back in the hollow of my hand and starlight filled
The vast pools of his face until they overspilled.

He lay collapsed across my lap
And such a weeping came up in him as though
He were a fountain for the whole earth's sorrow

And bitterness, and yet he could not bear
To wish on the man who had cut his starry nights
By thousands the forfeit of more

Than one. Later he grew
More into our way of looking at these things
But I will remember him when he was new

During the time when I had him in my house
And before I induced him to eat meat
For then his compassion was infinite.

I had him from our gaol where they had taught him
Fire is hot with a candle flame
And where he had set his fleas at liberty

One by one through the window bars
And the inrush of everything had almost killed him.
At twenty-eight I was already an invalid

With a few private pupils, living on the island.
My mother and sister kept house.
There in the river's arms we had some peace

And Caspar mended, a little, it was never enough,
For where can you walk in an average town like ours?
Nowhere, the public squares

Reek, every domicile
Does its own butchery, a hare hangs
Bleeding brilliantly at the nostril

From the fist of a woman gossiping in the sun.
Cooped, trussed, flayed, Creation
Emits only a little of its rightful scream.

Caspar heard the rest. Worse still
Even a wooden depiction pierced him like the real thing,
All those Christs, for example, hanging

From nails, in silence, with open mouths,
He asked why they must be perpetually tormented
And never cradled in our arms and tended.

I had begun to view the world as he did
And remembered watching my playfellows
Pin back a thrush's wings on the door of the shed

And spit her pimpled babes, to roast them.
I had begun to flinch as though there were blood
On every hand I shook and wherever I trod.

III

If the cold endures or the charity of the neighbours fails
And Professor Daumer begins to feed his stove
His own children, his titles,

Though he will preserve his Hauseriana to the bitter end
Last before them will be his efforts in rhyme,
His effusions to Zoroastra, to Womankind,

Nature, the Nine Virtues, the Four Last Things,
The East, the West, the Orphic Mysteries,
And his versions of Hafiz

And the English Lake Poets. He was noticed
Favourably more than once and Brahms released
A handful from prison in the century

By lending them music. Yesterday he addressed
Caspar's slandered shade
In seventeen quatrains no worse than all the rest,

Was Caspar Orpheus? On 4th April 1829
He greeted the beginnings of a new life
In forty-seven lines that rhymed

In nice writing and he might pen
Something on Duty, Friendship, Virtue, Fate
For a lady's album now and then.

But no, it never looked likely he would grow to be
As good as Professor Daumer at poetry.
Nor could he sing. And yet... One morning

In the first summer of his six above the surface
Caroline Daumer was playing Schubert in the garden room
When Caspar appeared, like a ghost, she said, his face

Was shining like a hill with streams,
His fists were clenched, his forearms crossed
Like cross-bones hard against his breast

And he said: 'It feels him strongly here'
And that sadness in him was enough already
Without the music making it any more.

He felt he was saying goodbye to the shape he had.
The music unravelled him and he was sad
To be coming loose so soon

Never having set into anything definite
Never having made himself at home under his name
Always unsure where he and the outside met

Where his own writ ran. His ears, for example,
He was only led to discover by our gaoler's son
Who took his finger and thumb and pinced the lobe of one,

The nose likewise and conned
Over the bumpy braille of a face with its own hand.
But shown the lot in a glass still nothing clicked.

Pain, in his feet, say, caused him to realise
He owned extremities, but not who this 'he' was
Nor where it lived. When our phrenologist

Took Caspar's head in his long cold hands
Poor Caspar begged him not to unfasten it.
Everything threatened to quit,

The heart pulled like a learner and receiving music
Almost shut down. It troubled Daumer
That Caspar never made the first person stick.

However often corrected he would edge
Out again and again into the third
Like a man on a window ledge

Outside himself. That summer
Once he was on the mend Professor Daumer
And Dr Osterhausen put him to the minerals

At the index finger of his right hand
And measured the shock. Lead hit the elbow,
Iron the shoulder, diamond

Via the eyes (they spouted) drove
As far as the pit below the heart. Degrees
Of cold, distances travelled, intensities

Felt of cold, out of the infinite
Waiting cold of the earth through the little ambassadors
Gathered in Professor Daumer's cabinet,

Gold, silver, platinum, mercury, and malachite,
Amber and amethyst, copper and zinc were let
Into Caspar's side, the right,

For the left conducted without the least resistance
And shock after shock of cold to the heart's pit
They dared not risk it.

A crystal glass released
From the corners of his mouth and the centre of his lower lip
Three icy lines that fused

In the throat, and sank. And this
That he was chased through and through with veins,
Courses and capillaries

That sucked like vampires at all the holes and tits
Of the earth's cold matrix fits
Caspar for the fraternity of Orpheus who are

Much too open and fray like spume
And dance in the warm sun – or the cold moon-beam
Equally gaily, like dead dust or genes.

He was too long in the ground, no wonder
He could smell the dead who are there for longer
Like a seam of coal. He said the mouths

Even of the lustiest were draughty. His spine
Felt like a column of mercury
If Professor Daumer fifty yards behind

161

Wagged a finger at it. Horses too
He said blew cold at him. He sat as though
A magnet in the earth had found him through

The shoes, the stirrups, the iron in the saddle frame,
So that the one sentence dinned into his ear
That what he wanted was to be a rider

Must pull him back again to the little horses
He had been buried with. Though horses stand
Plumb in the sun, four square, and lend

A shape of the air more bodily warmth than we do
They tap the cold of the earth as Caspar did,
It springs up where they tread

So cold it hurts the throat. And this was true
Even of Pegasus who kicked off and flew.
Caspar had a large red roan. She shone

Like those under the Pyrenees that shine
In a sort of upper room
Above the pit, only when the torches come.

IV

To the pure water he loved
At the end of August I added a first drop
Of beef tea. Since he had caught us up

In many things by then: could do
Long multiplication and long division,
Wrote a fair hand, drew

Heads, fruit and flowers nicely
And played a piece of Schubert tolerably well
I thought him ready for meat. He could smell

The cling of it on a white bone
At ten paces and my one drop in his full stein
Caused him to sweat, shake, weep and vomit

But I hardened him drop by drop and then
With fibres as fine as the stigmas of saffron
Until his appetite was redder then mine.

He wore a top hat when he rode out.
I began him on Latin and the preachers
Were sidling as near as they dared, like vultures.

His stools which had been as regular as clockwork
And as sweet as a horse's shifted uneasily
And stank. Sad to say

Our savage cat who would come to nobody but him
And sought him in the garden with a length of coloured ribbon
And they played for hours, it was a joy to watch them,

She smelled the change, and left him. In spring
We put him to the metals again.
None mounted him as it had done:

Lead to the wrist, iron to the elbow,
Diamond to the shoulder. Even his left side now
Took them up bearably. But that same day

He composed his first verses: on the new life
Opening before him, as it seemed, and mine too,
My life, my verses, at last came true,

I thought, as I busied myself
With the marvellous boy while the light still
Lasted around his head, before night fell.

Caspar the fading coal, the Way that led
Or would have led down Daumer's cellar steps
To the Mothers perhaps

Into the zone of the EN KAI PAN
Where everything moves and flows and man
Enters the round of the angels and the animals.

There was more of this. For even as Caspar's soles
And palms hardened and he put on weight
And the light went off him as off a landed rainbow trout

Daumer consulting his faeces
Monitoring the performance of his six senses
Logging his speech, his thoughts, his dreams

As he showed him in various circles
There occurred, he said, a leaching of virtue,
A transmission of zest into himself, the minder, who

163

Until then had only moped in life. He wrote:
I stopped shielding my eyes. I saw the radiance
Of a life everlasting in the near distance.

He meant it figuratively, of course. The eyes
In his head watered as usual and he shielded them
And perhaps the lasting life he saw was only fame

As the curator of a freak,
His archivist. Or – Daumer again – more like
His disciple, his priest. He would have been

My psychopomp and let me into the first circle
At the strait gate from where the circles slant
And spiral one below the other in a long descent.

Even on the threshold I began to sing
Even going in and down only a little way.
Kairos, the moment, it was my opportunity.

V

Poor Daumer. He was reckoning without
Terror. He knew from literature
That where the tight earth split

At Delphi, say, or Cuma, the truth was cold
And anyone drinking it was riddled with shock for days
And floes of it jostled

Among the corpuscles thereafter
Never quite melting. Did he suppose
It would be warmer in his reasonable house,

Mother there, a sister playing Schubert,
A title before his name, the century
Getting on nicely into modern times? In May

Caspar drew the head of an ambiguous angel
And dreamed in every detail
A palatial home: the flights, the suites,

The mirrors and statues. In Caspar's copperplate
Daumer gave a version to the newspapers
Under the epigraph (translated)

'Clouds of Glory'. Seen again
The angel had a smile about as friendly
As the flayer Apollo's. Daumer s garden,

Allowed a measure of self-expression in the English style,
Let rip with poppies as though an old wound
That night had suddenly opened

In a fit of weeping. Indoors
Caspar drew little arrangements of quieter flowers
For ladies' keepsakes. So far as the sun knew

And the blazing stars he was a year old.
Like everyone else he meant to make a decent score.
Soon he was not much odder than foreigners always are.

Everyone liked him: his courtesy, the way
He pieced together what he had to say
Before he delivered it, making a ring meanwhile

Of his thumb and index finger and splaying
The others out hard. He had an honest face,
A striver's, a washed and brushed-up ploughboy's,

And shone goodnaturedly in his Sunday clothes.
Everyone said he was doing very well,
Better than Bishop Fricke's negro, for example,

Or Lady Amalia's Huron Indian. Neither lived.
He fainted less and ate
Even sweetbreads. Swifts and swallows arrived

And nightingales sang in Daumer's garden
On the lovely continuo of the parted river.
Soft days, a mild sky, lessons in the open air

Near the Cnidian and against the darkness
Over our quiet suppers or a game of chess
We shone like tableaux. Then one morning

Mother went in to him: nothing belonged, the room
Looked to have lost what ever made it home
And he had backed into a far corner

Behind the ramparts of his knees and arms
Very small except his eyes
Which begged her. We were days

Reasoning with him: his colossal strides,
His vaster hopes, our greater and greater love and last,
Gently as we could, his duty. He complied

And bowed himself once more to the timetable
But always as though he were cold across the shoulders,
He looked in mirrors often, he seemed unable

To leave the back of his skull alone. It meant
He had lost the dispute with his visitant
And the heart in him was swapped for a source of dread.

So I suppose. He must have suffered
Proof such as music is
Or falling in love but to the contrary and stared

Life in the face until her eyes,
So beautiful that summer, opened
Like old shafts and joined

The nose and mouth. We were gentle with him,
Nobody called but friends and when, as always,
We let the children in to climb the cherry trees

He was the one they honoured with the bowl,
The cherry bowl that has that name all year
In waiting for the renewal

Of its wood by fruit, and when the pirates set
Their head of cherries on the table where he sat
Like an orphaned king, I saw his hands,

Opening round the appearance in quick belief,
Suddenly disciplined as though to say
This may be real but why show it me?

His present, the little bridgehead
He had made on life, by now
Had entered the shadow of a lifted

Weapon so that he shivered on the warmest day
And through our company
Peered like a marked man through his bodyguard

And this, being looked through, being looked behind,
Serving as taster on the gifts of summer,
Having to weight the words of life with more and more

166

Conviction, wore the Professor down.
Mother laid the orphan in her widowed lap
And sang the old spells in an undertone

All the while working with her fingers at his haunted skull,
But Daumer monitoring the more or less of sadness,
The more or less of anxiety dressed

Every morning with an effort, spoke with care
As though his voice would crack, and seeing the core
Of the cherry tree abruptly evacuate

A pack of crows and the unscared
Rats retreat with an insolent slowness
Down the cellar steps he felt his life had queered.

Autumn was beautiful. The conkers shone like cherries
And the leaves amazed us by their size
Like hands descended from a pediment

And with the willow leaves they yellowed over
The pitch-black water in the backs.
Blue days, never any hurry, the smoulder

And flare of fires, a whiff of mist.
He followed me everywhere like my living shadow,
My shade, I had almost said, my chilly ghost,

And I braced him less than a teacher should,
The encouragements went rotten in my mouth.
The fear had become so strong, a mould

Of it followed us wherever we went
Like faith, that in the air
Once made a space for the white unicorn to appear.

Thanksgiving. Even now I love the festivals.
Gratitude is as much our mark as grief.
I love God's house, the barn of our collected souls,

When it fills with thanks, I sidle in
For the birth, the resurrection and the harvest,
I think I love the festival of autumn best:

The crammed ark on the brink of another winter,
Every space and ledge is heaped with stores,
The windows lighted bravely with asters,

We know the perils, we sink or swim together,
We pool the innocent produce of our hands,
And cast ourselves upon the mercy of the weather.

We minded Caspar in the family pew
Behind four walls in a singing congregation
But it did no good. He could not sing. He knew

The fearful vacancy was filled,
I felt him trembling against me when we kneeled,
Heard him plead. No good. The angel came,

And chivved him. The Saturday
Waking he sweated, froze, clutched at a pain in the abdomen
And accompanied Caroline to market. When

She stood he tugged at her skirt like a two-year old
For the travelling atoms of his fear reassembled
Behind him while she gossiped.

Because of his sweats and frosts
I excused him a mathematics lesson with Dr Wenders
And carried another book of mine to the printers.

Mother was in, and Caroline, also the servant girl.
I consult his own account. At eleven he answered a call
Of nature in the privy in the hall.

Finished, he was considering how to describe it
For my records, when the house-bell sounded very lightly.
He rose, buttoning himself in the friendly darkness

And opened the privy door. His fear stood
Made visible with gloves and bandages like the invisible man
And played a measured backhand across his forehead

With a heavy razor. That was that.
Over the eaves of his eyebrows a downpour of blood.
He whimpered, crumpled, lay in the wet.

Waking, he seemed to wish to slobber everything:
The flags, the stairs, the banisters, the landing,
All my house and home. He sullied books

Lent him for learning in his room on the first floor,
He blundered like an escapee from an abattoir,
His prints were everywhere, his drops exploded on the boards.

168

He wanted Mother. She was on the second floor.
Blinded, dumb with the blood, in such a bewilderment
When I remember that he went

Down, not up, down all the slippery stairs
And raised the cellar trap, making for the dark, and I remember
The rats in there and how the water from the river

Seeped in and the big rats splashed in it,
This cold room where I sit
Thinking suddenly drops another degree or two

In terror, which I note
With satisfaction as an evidence of being,
Or having been, alive. I met

The women where the puzzling blood had brought them
At the open hole, found him
By candle on the far side of the water.

It was hard to uncurl the child again
For of all our pleasant house, of all its sunny rooms
With views of spires, trees, white clouds sailing, none

Suited him now like the cellar for it most
Resembled the pit he grew in and where his fear was least.
He masked his face against my candle with his hands

And through his leaky fingers he seemed to be weeping blood.
He was as red as a savage when he lay revealed,
Drenched, and as loose in all his limbs as a man on the wheel.

VI

We gave him a new room, whitewashed,
And a few late flowers. Sitting up bandaged
And making the sign of the circle with his left hand

He spoke an account of what had happened to him.
I took it down verbatim
Like scripture, like the Word

Sprung, unhusked, shining for the first time in our vernacular.
When his own hand was strong enough he did me a copy out fair,
Illuminating it with asters and candles.

Now all his gifts were upon him again
As in the days before he ate flesh.
Seizing the hour I alerted Dr Osterhausen

And very gently we put him to the ordeal of the metals.
He took them up his blood as though electrified
And we were obliged to spare his left side.

Visitors came, across the two bridges,
The police, the church, our dignitaries,
And the common people queued like the people of Bethany.

I let them in in threes and they stood at a distance
Making a dumbshow of condolence
And everybody felt a mite ashamed.

At the removal of his bandages
A painter should have been present, our visages
Were fit for history when we saw the mark

Of the cutting edge of the angel's wing across his brow.
It was an almost sightly disfigurement, far
Easier to look at than a duelling scar,

More like a line of thought. So for a while still,
Bled and delicate, in a white room and the lower floors
Scrubbed clean, he lived in my house until

My spirit, my nerve, my hold, whatever it is
We need or cannot speak, move,
Go about our business, converse with friends, love

Anyone, do anything
That helps, it left me, suddenly one early morning
Of rain, of black conclusive rain.

Poor man. He had soaped his face like Father Christmas,
Wetted his cut-throat and a voice whispered:
Why not draw a thin red smile with it from ear to ear?

Mother found him sitting in his shirt, still lathered.
He looked as old as her long-dead father.
The blade was folded near the copper bowl.

Questioned, he said he had had enough of everything:
Caspar, angels, the Mothers, blood on his books.
He was a scholar and an invalid, his shakes,

170

Runs, turns, were coming back again. A whining monotone,
Geriatric. He was twenty-nine.
He shut his poorly eyes and Mother shaved him.

Through the study window he could see the two policemen.
They had built a little lean-to and were quite at home
With a charcoal stove. They checked whoever came

At the point of a bayonet and anyone
Leaving with the ghostly Caspar had them tagging on
At just the right distance for a constant mockery.

The salutes they gave were clownish. Now and then
They fired off their muskets at a pigeon by way of a joke,
Frightening Caspar silly. For perhaps a week

Receiving the town in his little bedroom
He had seemed beyond fear, martyred and over it,
Soon we should have brought him the halt and the lame

And expected signs. Now he was animal again
And clung to Daumer as a cowardly Jesus
Might have to a fatherly Judas.

And the Professor peering ahead saw nothing but horrors:
His nice house darkened by Caspar and the jailers
And sapped by rats. He jumped if a door slammed,

Wept if the milk was late. Then bad reviews
Prostrated him behind a migraine for two days
And he listened to Caspar whimpering through the ceiling.

Mother, he said, see where I am with this trouble,
My eyes worse, not a thought in my head.
Will I ever put pen to paper again? He lay in bed

Turning his face to the proverbial wall
And heard a voice whisper
Deliver up Caspar and all will be back to normal,

The onus gone. He wanted to be let off.
Things as light as a drop of rain or a leaf
Weighed on him when they landed

But Caspar squatted on him like a nightmare
All of lead. Enough of the frontier,
Enough of heights and depths and having his dim eyes opened!

Professor Daumer wanted the golden mean again,
The little manageable *train-train*
On half pay, and his bowels in order.

Advent. There was a skull
In every little window Caspar opened. He could smell
Betrayal coming. Daumer had them

Padlock the cellar door. He lay sick.
Whenever Mother entered he was worse and worse.
Whose mother was she then? Of course

She took the hint and begged him to think of himself for once
And put himself first and his important work and put
Caspar on the Parish. He held out

All the while weeping with relief in the inner man
Until it was clear that it was *force majeure*,
Mother, he bowed to, a mother's love, and her

Fault, not his. Mother made me, he said,
To all and sundry in the years to come and yes, she repeated,
Until the day she died, I made him,

I fetched him pen and ink. That was the hardest
Writing he ever did, Professor Daumer used to say
Though every 'i' was dotted, every 't' crossed

Already in his head. With regret
And expressions of gratitude for all he had done to date
The Elders accepted the Professor's resignation on health grounds

From onus for Caspar. The howl
When he was fetched. It clung
Like bats against the walls and ceiling.

Daumer covered his ears with another pillow.
He saw the attraction of a dark cellar,
He conceived a horror of his shaving mirror,

And opened books in dread
For on more pages than he remembered,
On more and more, as it seemed, Caspar had bled.

Third Canto

CLARA BIBERBACH
24 May 1852

I

'Clara' I liked, and for an after-name
I took my mother's when I had gone from where
Behind my back they called me Mrs Potiphar

And Mrs Johann Christian Biberbach to my shameless face.
I ask you: Biberbach! He sealed
His deals with a beaver beavering away

Like him, day in day out, he left at six,
Came home at midnight, sex
He set aside ten minutes for

After evensong until I had a son
To carry on from him when he was gone
And then he stopped it. I was twenty-five.

I joined the Union of Charitable Mothers.
The Father when I said
I was having the bad thoughts in the early mornings said

Count your blessings, mostly wives confessed
All they wanted was eternal rest
From it, and I would keep my figure at least

Only having the two. For what? She tried
To age as little as possible after Caspar died
Since he could not. If she went home to die

At least they would concede she has worn well.
But she will be buried with her mother's people
As Mme Clara Citelle, a widow

Childless and respectable. In Nuremberg at fairs
Over her children's heads she watched the whores
Hooking soldiers, and her heart beat

Like the hooves of scandal getting close.
She lay in the early morning sleepy shallows
Elaborating pictures of herself

Masked and naked in a *maison de passe*
For a couple of captains.
She said: If it happens it happens

And put herself daily nearer to where
It might. Marry
And burn is the worst of both worlds. Standing there

One evening she was looked at like the girls
Straight in, and that was itself the fall
For after that she was sure every man could tell.

Her face allowed it. Sooner or later
Somebody calling would be bound to twig her.
It was a youngish gentleman from the comptoir

During the lassitude after lunch. Her hurry scared him,
He left dispirited but put the word about
She was a pushover. A lie. I made a note

Whenever it happened in my private diary
And but for that first week
When I was catching up as you might say

Once a month was the most and only then
If I couldn't help it. Johann Christian
Some Sunday evenings said I was looking well.

The hour reminded him but I made excuses
Nicely. He gave me money for dresses
Instead, and nodded off. So it continued

And I could live with it. I was never in love much
Before Caspar and generally what I saw
When the waves of it came on me were more and more

Lifting on the rim of infinity
And I wanted those too, I wanted them breaking in me
Down where some chap was rooting the best he could

And I stared over his shoulder
For a sight of heaven through our fancy ceiling.
Any woman would. It was my idea

To offer sanctuary to the Child of Europe.
I saw him in his little bedroom sitting up
Like Lazarus. The Professor was cool with me

And his mother sniffed. To be honest
I liked the idea of a police escort.
By that time – I was at my scarletest –

They were already saying he was a king's son
And God would justify him. Holding court
In a spotless shirt he looked like someone

Not like us. There was quite a crowd
Followed them dragging him off the island in the snow
And a man with his belongings in a wheelbarrow.

Upstairs, looking for them coming,
Clara suddenly opened the flimsy curtains on herself.
Gentlemen doffed their toppers, but for the moon-calf

Within a week she forsook them all.
Their cards collected on a platter in the hall
Like season tickets after expiry.

   II

I felt like royalty myself when we walked out
Him on my arm and the six-foot
Fusiliers marching behind us.

We did the shops and took a stroll in the Nuns' Garden.
He wore a black fur hat, the first
Gift I gave him, so that he should look more foreign

As I desired it. My sable swept the snow.
Or we drove on the ramparts and had a view
Of tracks, villages, woodlands come out black

On the utter white. We rode there too.
He had a mare of a peculiar burning red
And fitted her, or she him, as Eve did

The gap in Adam. I ended jealous
That she had secrets with him. But all was
Novel in the early year, the town

I was sick of brightened and tasted savoury
When I dismissed his other teachers and we two
Wandered. Once in the ghetto

We met the Professor. He wore a plaid
Like an old man. He eyed
Our guard. I remember a beam of sunlight coming in,

A canary singing and the spiced air
Whispering Yiddish and I was proud of my adventure
With Caspar and prouder still

When the Professor asked did the blue devils
Plague him any the less and Caspar slid
My arm under his wing, so to speak, and said

The devils of every colour had flown away.
We were all deceived. I checked my gaiety
Enough not to call Professor Daumer Grandad.

He looked like Judas had he lived
To see Christ risen. An early Easter. My heart set
Finally on what it could do best:

Love Caspar. He loved her clothes,
Had Caroline's but Daumer corrected him.
At Biberbach's no fatherly friend protected him

And he fell to the woman. He loved her dresses,
The infinite work in each, the intricacies
Of fastening, the slips and loops, the minute markings

And the amplitude, like chestnut trees
In flower at Whitsun on a sunny breeze,
And scarves and veils and all her underthings

So soft and light and sheer.
He rose early, did some scripture
And simple book-keeping left him by Biberbach

But when the house was quiet, the children
Governed, he felt an attraction
Attack him through the floors, walls and doors

From Clara's clothes as she chose among them.
She chose slowly, expecting him.
He came and sat there like a dumb waiter

And she laid the day's things across his arms
In the order for putting on. One colour
Of love was running into the next in her,

176

A red. Ladies who dress
And undress in the expressionless
View of their black attendants

Were on her mind. April 3rd
She and her shivery image in the glass agreed
She had the same permission. Clara heard

The pretty tolling of his usual hour.
She turned to face him with a different look,
Counting ten. But the tenth stroke

Fell together with a pistol shot
A worse noise than the rooms of a house can bear
Or the ear's caves and corridors will ever forget.

Then in the damaged silence she heard a thing
Shouldering towards her through a labyrinth
Always thwarted, so that now it was nearer

And now cold again and she there at the centre
Could only sit, neither call out nor lift a hand
But only sit like the prize in a dream or legend

Somewhere unbearable for what might be delivery or murder
To slither and bawl closer. Her bedroom broke
Open on Caspar. He wore a hood and cloak

All of blood, he smeared and slopped
The day's light pastel pretty colours and stopped
His brute encumbered crown

Against her lap's
Deeper and deeper diaphanous soft shelter
And Clara mired her hands. The guard disburdened her.

It was an accident. He had furrowed
His head near the right eye. Biberbach showed
The ball to visitors, lodged in a beam,

Like the mark where Luther threw his inkhorn at the devil.
The Elders said he was wrong to leave a pistol
Handy where the unhappy Caspar

Bowed himself every morning to the study of God and Mammon.
Caspar said it was the angel's wing again.
Clara kept the négligée with its vast stain

In the lap and burned the rest.
The house resumed. She filled with haste
Seeing him marked twice across the brows

And ended his convalescence with the slow
Unclothing and slower clothing of her body before him.
He sat immobile like a dead pharaoh.

Morning after morning thus, the sun streaming in,
She stood so that it watered on her skin
And over the blackness of her shock of woman hair

And on her breasts' dark haloes. In silence then
Against her wishes she dressed from the tray
His arms made, and this was the sum of her sin,

Except once when I made him nuzzle me
And once, God forgive me, I felt whether
His thing was stiff, but only his arms ever were

And they held out like iron under my day's
Costume. Truth is
He liked me better dressed and when everything was on

He was as pestering as a puppy dog
And I sobbed inside, in there, in my womb
For him to be like other men and want the same.

It was the time of the first *vita*,
Riddled with errors, and the exaltation of him as Europe's Child
Or the Once and Future King. Daumer appealed

In the name of Virtue and the Sciences
For his removal into more appropriate circumstances.
And Clara beat her sunny nakedness

Day after day against him helplessly,
Against his smile, against his absent stare,
Like a moth that cannot flare

Only beat and beat. The pack meanwhile
Whom Caspar had ousted, wanting to be back in,
Dropped hints into the cuckold's ear his jewel

Of a lady might be in some peril
At home all day with Caliban. One morning,
A morning when everything was going wrong,

They saw him suddenly snap a pen and mess
His thin fastidious
White hands and leave hatless.

It was after ten. Clara sat
Hugging her left knee on the window seat,
Naked, receiving the sun and weeping quietly,

Caspar the clothes-horse distant. Clara says:
I took the lie he offered me, the lie
Everyone knew was one and not for his and not for my

Good name but to spite the clod
Caspar, my heart's sole want and hope, and to end
My hellish mornings. Johann Christian penned

An explanation to the Councillors who roared
With laughter but shifted the boy I could not look in the eye
Away. And then I whored,

I sobbed and howled under one after the other
Till his bed stank of it and he slept
Curled away from me like a cheese rind and crept

Off earlier and earlier. I saw him play
With the pistol but I sent
For a clerk from under his nose as one sends out for tea

And the butcher's boy, calling
With a little bloody package in his soft hands,
Climbed to the master's room and I received him kneeling.

Then stopped, it was over, my life there.
Husband, the necessary son, the unnecessary daughter
Looked at me blankly as from a family portrait

Done two hundred years ago and where I should have stood
I was painted out. Nobody touched me,
I was like a leper. Only Caspar saluted,

Passing to a lesson under guard, he bowed,
He would have come across to touch my glove,
But they hustled him on. He forgave

Or was ignorant of everything. Then came
The devil himself in the shape
Of Philip Stanhope,

An English lord, and of Caspar's blood, some lost
Already on Daumer's books and more running to waste
In Clara's disappointed lap, the rest

Which might have gone with hers
To make a little dynasty of innocence
Ran out at Christmas

Over the snow in the town of Ansbach
In a public park
And down the whited streets.

I broke my heart crying when I heard,
Abroad, incognita, I sat and stared
Like a nun at my brown relic,

Guilty. In my house
All the first week he had barred his frightened face
Against me with his fingers

But I loosened them and ceased
Being jealous of Caroline Daumer's hands
Playing on his for mine too phrased

Life differently, he said himself
That he was lifted up on the new year
As when a wind comes and we see the grey sky tear

And the blue that is always there above it spreads
Like certitude
And the high snows and the washed green fields are made

Visible quickly, all in a smaller time
Than it takes us to open our heavy clothes to it
And breathe again, seeing a road run straight

Somewhere elsewhere, somewhere not like here,
Among a different people, where we might have lived
Only a little oddly, I believed,

As man and wife, and the great houses,
The lawyers, the clergymen, the philosophers
Would have been as distant as another country's wars

And Caspar safe but he
Is dead long since and I soon shall be
And all I have of him is a patch of blood

And depths, depths that in between
His murdered childhood and his barely come of age
He sank in me. For I was shown

The way out of a life gone wrong and told
This is the only true
Way out and it is not for you.

That Whitsun everybody called the best
In living memory when they met
On the streets, especially where a street

Gave into any greenery
Entering the avenues and the parks, say,
And most where the colossal chestnut trees

Gored at the blue sky with their horns of plenty
The phrase 'in living memory'
Came on people's tongues again and again

Because of the scent, I suppose,
The wetted dust, the debris of blossom and the streaming seedpods
Because of the wind that was always tousling us

And lifting the unsettled strata of our years
And quickening the spores
That lie for example in the folds of dresses in a wardrobe

She woke feeling the day already flowing,
The body's atoms shivering,
Tears in the eyes, a desperation in the throat

Craving to melt, and Pentecost
Was borne upon her as the season of living memory,
The past obliged to dance, and the rest

Standing unwanted in the long mirror
Seeking to make her fingers meet around her waist
She saw it panic through the straits

Into the sump where all the grains
Are dead sand. Everything moved and flowed
But Caspar sat so that his shins, thighs, back, arms made

Exact rightangles and I laid out
For Whitsun of all my dresses the favourite,
Too girlish, I suppose, so light that in it

The breeze and I were wedded: that dress lay
Over the bars of Caspar's respectful arms
Like water, air, fire, or the corpse of me.

Fourth Canto

PHILIP HENRY STANHOPE
1 March 1855

I

Stanhope, Philip Henry, the Fourth Earl,
Dying abroad nowhere particular
I wish to be shipped home like an admiral

In brandy, I have a longing
To enter the mouth of the Thames on a flood tide
And settle alongside

Eleanor Mary, my poor wife, the children
Lawfully issued between her narrow hips,
Henry Philip, Mary Eleanor Ann,

There being no bastards, I can swear to it,
And Caspar dead without issue,
Dead and beyond amends, if they will pay my transit

The rest is theirs as they feared it would not be
When I was famous for my fondness for Caspar,
Everything theirs in perpetuity:

A maze, a thousand-year-old yew, a black carp pond,
Forty-four windows opening south
Over the Garden of Eden of England

Unless I dreamed it and the whole estate
Is this tin box I rest on in which are
His letters, his pretty paintings, a lock of his hair

I cut myself the day
I committed him into a tributary of the Acheron
That took him like a magnet and I turned away.

Famous Stanhopes are ten a penny. I
Wish the mark I have made on life were made
On rented sand a little above low tide

But I am shackled to a revenant,
I and that woman and the dim professor,
The chief of police, the parson and the mayor

And Stephanie the Duchess, all
In the yellow livery of betrayal
We tag along whenever Caspar walks.

They called my father Citizen. He swore
By the youthful dead at Valmy and Jemappes,
Wept like a widow over Thermidor

And when what rose at last out of the lake of blood
Was only an emperor's head
Citizen Stanhope returned to private life,

He laboured night and day at merciful inventions
But all his hopes were consigned to future generations,
To a new race, he said, one whom

The true republic would fit
Like the easy clothing of the Greeks. Till then:
Work, work. Us, his children,

Gazing ahead he entirely overlooked.
Nothing could come of us, born when we were
In dead time. We fled the centre.

Two were in Greece. Spencer
Got the topography of the Peloponnese by heart
Walking. He mapped Olympia. I sometimes thought

He would go down and down among the exhalations of the dead
Knee deep, chest deep, by degrees
Vanishing, and map Hades.

Leicester was more with the living at Missolonghi.
He said they would raise the temples again on a real ground
But sailed on the *Florida* from Zante

Home, with Byron's corpse. I was abroad somewhere,
Nowhere particular, when I read in a newspaper
Of my brother committing the poet to the grief of the nation.

If I can get any ship to ferry me
I shall berth quietly and keep
My grave like a man who knows he will not sleep

For Caspar calling. Famous
More or less crazy Stanhopes litter the earth.
Hester swelled in a ruined oasis

East of Palmyra like a queen bee
All day in bed smoking a foul black shag,
Men in her *ruelle*. Each with his swag

Everyone left her when she began to die.
They ran away down separate radii.
She lay at the empty centre, turning.

I made little sorties away from home
On the usual routes. Truth is
No sooner across the Channel I began to dream

I would be happier at my garret window
Staring down the dead straight drive to the Temple of Virtue
Or down the long diagonal across the deer park

To the wood all afternoon or leaned
Against the far wall of the nursery
Watching the door. No sooner abroad I dreamed

I was summoned home for a game of hide and seek
And went from room to room like a jovial father
Always calling so the child would never fear

He hid and no one sought and he might hide for ever
In a dark place and no one seek
And life close over him, but in my dream I spoke

A constant reassurance out loud
And the rooms brightened when I entered them
And I woke hearing the word 'welcome'.

Some evenings in a foreign language
In Baden, say, I hit the sickness for home
And my tongue ran on alone like the wheel of a crashed carriage.

Some nights I was visited by the pure ghost
Of thirst, but not for drink, and hunger, but not for food,
As though the poles pulled equally and the needle was denied

Even the relief of pointing. The trick is then
To spin a new thing as God did
In the space for Adam but Stanhope was a weak man

And soon swung to Chevening
And Lady Stanhope and the two children
And posted home, ignoring

Devils at either ear who whispered he would mate
Like a stupid bull with a counterfeit.
I lost heart the moment we entered the drive

Like blood from a slitted pig. The property
Faced me like the water, the leper
Or the five thousand had I

Impostured Christ. In the summer of 1829
Drifting among the princedoms vaguely south again
He read Caspar's dream of a stately home

As Daumer had made it public in the *Bavarian Courier*
And Feuerbach's note: that no dreamer
(Unless God) creates *ex nihilo*

But the flutes and vistas, the rides, the water-gardens
Must have seeded themselves long since
Through little apertures and feelers of sense

And survived a vanished childhood as seeds do
Ice and fire to flower now
In speech from the boy's mouth.

I was 47, slipping.
All I had in my favour was restlessness.
His dream of a home, only lodging,

Touched me, lodging, whose large estate
Whenever I came to feast on it with the five senses
Shrank and stiffened as though I sickened it.

I had resolved to kill myself at 50
But hoped God knew and would lean down
And stop me on the road with a clear sign

And reading Caspar's dream in an old journal
I thought that if it fitted my own grounds and rooms
At last some blood might vivify my phantoms

And I bore towards Nuremberg post haste,
Breaking an axle. The news there
Was all of his near-murder.

I queued with the common people on the island.
He was bandaged still. He raised his hand
Making a lorgnette of his thumb and finger.

A miniature: sunk eyes, thin lips,
The long Etruscan nose: impossible to tell
If what his Lordship wants inhabits heaven or hell.

II

I open easily. The eye,
Ringed like a burning glass, entered me without resistance.
I would have declared myself at once

And offered him Chevening for his dream
But suddenly blood showed
Through the white bandage and the mother shooed

Us out. We were three. I stood between
A butcher and a witch with a harelip
Who said the blood was a bad sign

And crossed herself. The butcher shrugged. I shook
Like a quaker then and let speak
What was in me, saying God has pointed, the little start of blood

Marks it and I gave my name, saying
Remember this, and the name of my house in Kent,
Saying remember this too and tell your children you were present

At the start. Tongues,
The French, the German, the Italian,
Came easily to Stanhope, he went headlong

Down the rapids of difficult constructions
An ace in the art but helpless so that his family lived in fear
Of what he would give some foreigner

His word on next. Below the nose
His face fell away in a small landslide
Which he raised a hand to hide

So that even speaking the heart's opinion
He seemed to defer and wish to burden
A listener only with a filtered truth.

He backed away. He considered flight to the frozen poles
Or Africa but trailed in spas and the little German capitals,
In the wings, within earshot. Lives appeared

And the first hostile pamphlet: CASPAR HAUSER
NOT IMPROBABLY AN IMPOSTER.
Stanhope paid his valet a bounty on every item.

Tall, uneasy in his clothes
(For years he wore green against all advice
So that they called him Grasshopper or the Praying Mantis)

He sent to Paris for a novelty in morning suits –
A Caspar Hauser – and stood in it
At fairs among the illiterate

Gawping at a Caspar raised high
On a banner in bright colours with his wide-awake hat
And heard the ballad of the wonderful boy

Sung by a hurdy-gurdy man, a dame
Teaching the people the stations of his life
To date, frame by frame

With a stick. He says: No stanzas
Ever went home into my heart like those.
Further, I saw him staged in five cities

As a clown, barefoot, matted,
He swam in the aquarium of my tears.
And yet it was half a year till I admitted

I was no freer than a petty moon.
Nuremberg sucked on me like the hole in a maelstrom
But I pulled away as far as Amsterdam

All the while knowing this: a peer
Of England with ten thousand a year
Being the big fish in Germany's small ponds,

Though nothing much to look at, if he muscles in
Who will resist the star, the garter, the ermine
And drafts on ample funds in his thin hand?

Stanhope expects a decade off his time in purgatory
For every month he held
His person at a distance. Lord Chesterfield

(An uncle) challenged any man
To distinguish a long vain struggle against temptation
From the judicious deferment of a gratification.

Caspar was riding out with Clara Biberbach.
Her black gelding, his red mare,
The silver waistcoat he wore

Which she had sewn for him with ghostly poppies
Were known to everyone who read the newspapers.
The accident of 3rd April

Travelled like starlight to remote salons.
Caspar was rising like a drowned man
In the consciences of person or persons

Unknown, and Anselm Feuerbach
Was nailing him with facts to a family tree
But Stanhope mooching on the periphery

Collected evidence like a lovesick chambermaid:
Gossip and nonsense, playbills,
The first poor lithographs, the booktrade's

Beginning boom in Hauseriana –
He drew it all upon himself as though he were smeared
With honey and so martyred

By bees and ants. In Delft his hostess
Wondering would no one save the Child from wickedness
He felt God's finger on him

And rode at Nuremberg, but lost
Heart or found the strength to resist
And swerved to Teplitz, sending from there

A Present Help, (London 1828),
Being a Pharmacopeia of Prayers for a Soul Beset,
His own work, and a bare card:

A Friend. He waited. News came
Jostling through the news of the July Days
That Caspar, innocent as Joseph, was put out of house and home.

Stanhope thanked God for the efficacy
Of prayer, but dreamed that night he was kneeling with Clara
Before Caspar, and like the Celestial City

Chevening shone behind them. In Carlsbad
Exercising in a formal garden
Shoulder to shoulder, arm in arm, tête-à-tête

With nodding members of Old Europe
He heard it said for certain that Caspar Hauser,
The automatist, the idiot of Nuremberg, was heir

To the throne of the Grand Duchy of Baden
Being the child of Stephanie
Stolen from her still bloody

After a hard birth. And more:
That the righteous were arming themselves with proofs and power
To carry Caspar home in a rush of glory.

Stanhope vanished. His valet tracked him down
To poor lodgings on the German plain.
He lay curled like a hero on his sword

Or a green caterpillar, skewered
On jealousy. The whore Clara was nothing after all.
Mannheim was his rival:

A palace. He saw the illumination
Of every window in the House of Baden
And the veil of his own house rent in twain.

The year turned. He was becoming fifty.
He asked for a sign. None came. The resorts were empty.
He crossed and saw his home again in a bitter starlight.

Ice cave. The Master fled
And wintered in a priory near Dover. There
He thought a good deal about his dead father

The Citizen, and a large idea for the regeneration of Man
From a source in England (Chevening)
Through innocence (Caspar) ran

Wild in his head. He says:
I wrestled against my feeling of election
And lost. He sent his valet to purchase

The best grammar of the English tongue
And quitted his cell. He sniffed the sea and the spring.
A thousand happy devils were rollicking in his heart.

III

Pecca fortiter, says Luther. Do it, if you must,
Hard. Stanhope came on
Full, as an English gentleman,

But behind a handkerchief sidling away,
Drawing his listeners after him in a shuffling orbit
Around Caspar who stood as stiff as a spit

Rotating. They danced thus
In the drawing room of Jakob Friedrich Binder, Nuremberg's mayor.
Gottlieb von Tucher was there

As present custodian of the Child's virtue
After Clara. Stanhope,
Blushing, retreating, offered up

Thanks to God on behalf of the human race
For havens such as Gottlieb von Tucher's house
In a naughty world. Caspar was dumb but turned

His friendly beam on the green lord.
The Mayor, scenting money, encouraged them
Into the walled garden for a private word.

The policemen were at the gate, helmet to helmet,
The common people lined their heads along the coping
And every window craned over the stooping

Foreigner and the boy prised out of the earth
Three years since exactly whose small hands
Were good with horses and whose countenance

Ruddy enough to pass for one of ours
Carried the marks of the razor and the ball
And hoped for kindness like the fleece under the dewfall.

Everyone's breath drew in when Stanhope arrested
The boy's shoulder and read
His lifted face for a while, and when the walk continued

Caspar Hauser was clamped to a new patron
By a fatherly arm. So the town
Where he had landed saw him being taken

Off the books, a saving, off their hands and out of their lives,
A lightening, a grief.
The Earl laid a finger on his lips

And Caspar grinned. Something was on the child
No one quite liked when Stanhope
In the hearing of all of them who had called

Him theirs, said my –
My Caspar, my poor child, my dear boy –
And gave him a grammar and primer of the English tongue,

The speaking made easy. Lodged at the Blackie Boy
Stanhope sent for him out of a scripture lesson
To ride on the ramparts, luncheon

In a greenery, a stroll
With a long following, a farewell all
The polite and vulgar walkers halted to witness.

Five hundred gulden crossed from bank to bank.
We name no names, said the *Courier*,
But raise our hats. The Lord's long finger

Opening the fob slit in the waistcoat sewn
With pale poppies let slide
A gold watch into Caspar's side:

A plain face, time passing
No faster, of course, but with a quaker frankness.
How often we saw Caspar press

His left hand there, puzzled, as though
He were reminded of an old trouble
But could not put a name to it and when he drew

The timepiece out he looked like a conjuror
Who has amazed himself. But the way he wound the thing in public
As pompously as an alderman and listened to it tick

We said this is the corruption working. His first pleases
And thank-yous in the English tongue
Caused us to laugh behind our hands as would indecencies

Taught to a parrot. However
His meeting with Clara Biberbach cheered us somewhat.
She was walking alone, no one would speak to her,

In the Nuns' Garden, and he was arm in arm
With the long-nosed lord saluting the world
And when he saw the scarlet woman who had done him harm

It would be right to say that his face lit up
From within, from out of the core of his generous soul,
And from her face which we admit was beautiful

Light also fell and he smiled
Just so, like a field
When the sun comes suddenly. Taking her hand

And Stanhope's, the way he beamed
Icebergs would have melted
But not them, they repelled

Being like poles bent
Equally on Caspar, they stood off stiffly
Though he joined (we heard him say) present

And past kindness in their hands
Babbling until Milord with English courtesy
Cold as a gorgon gave her good-day

And pulled the harder. It was that afternoon
He paid for privacy at our bathing place,
Setting sentries, and went down

Under the eyes of the valet who held a towel
Naked into the pool
Hand in hand with the unbaptised Caspar.

But for his small hands and his face
Grown used to the sun how white he was
But for the one dark place

His parts inhabited like fledglings in a nest
How white was all the rest
So that I thought and thought of his years in the earth,

His unfired clay, the dough of him
Unready for eating like
The unrisen Lord stretched in the cromlech.

But as for swimming, he was more stone than fish
And I was obliged to buoy him, he lay
Face up on the palms of these same hands, he trusted me,

I whispered him into believing the miracle
He would float like a compass needle
On the water's skin. I spoke of sea-baths

And of dips at Chevening: how we ran, would run or would have run
As man and boy on my estate
Bare foot through the grey dew and the cuckoo-spit

And took the towel from my valet whose eyes were as cold as flint
And sent him to fetch some warmer covering
And I turned myself to Caspar who was shivering.

I towelled him dry as any father would. The wet
Lay on him in the sunshine like a night sweat
As I rose with my hand into the fork of him.

My valet clothed him in a tartan cloak.
Both watched me dress
Suddenly in a hurry over my nakedness

Fumbling and red, I made them turn away
And shook and wept by the quiet pool
For reasons I cannot name even today.

IV

Flights: the second
Was after the occasion at the bathing place
When the sentries opened

A path for the Earl, still dressing,
And Caspar in a tartan cloak
To the cushioned carriage. As though a snake

Were threading his vertebrae
Stanhope had long repercussions of the river's cold
For days, especially

Seeing Caspar, seeing down his stiff arms
Shock after shock of welcome travel
Into the proferred palms

193

And spiked fingers, each day, whenever he,
(His guardian angel, they had begun to say)
The Lord, appeared, it smiled

So without apprehension over Caspar's face
Most of us looked away
As from a thing we had no right to witness.

It was early June. The river's cold
Or some equivalent in the subterranean child
Shaking his Lordship daily like malaria

He announced a necessary absence throughout the summer
To recover vital heat
At spas, lying in sulphur,

And left money for tuition in English
And let it be known it was his wish
The boy should be addressed henceforward as My Lord

Adoption being very likely
Into the bosom of a fortune
And elevation to the rank of firstborn son

Who must embrace an undertaking
As large as Christ's
From his (the Baptist's)

Home. He fled
In wraps and furs on a broiling day
Yellow and ill. The people crossed themselves, they said

There goes the devil posting back to hell
And we assembled at the Blackie Boy
Where Caspar waited to be said goodbye.

I could not. Neither then
Nor when I left him last. I am the man
Who wrote a letter to the boy he loved

Knowing him dead
As though the letter might be forwarded
Knowing the Christmas snow

There in the little town I left him in
Was red for all to see
With scribbles nobody could understand but me.

Fifth Canto

GEORG FRIEDRICH DAUMER
1 January 1875

I saw him last in the summer before he died.
August. He visited me. It was being said
His triumph was near. One of our kings,

De passage in Nuremberg, received him kindly.
The woman had gone by then, to France,
I believe. Good riddance,

Everybody said, seeing her poor children
And poorer man, but I said nothing for I had begun
To pity her. Caspar wept

There on the street below her windows
Seen by all, and hurried to find me on the island
And we had two days

Reprieve in the house and garden. Near my statue
Shutting his eyes he asked could he recite
An English prayer and when we ate

Would we excuse him meat. The river wreathing us,
I congratulated him on his recent confirmation
Exhaustively reported in our newspapers

And I saw him troubled
As he never was or could have been with me
And I wondered who had enabled

His innocence to this.
I said I knew his pastor for a decent man.
Caspar replied: Lord Stanhope wishes

Yourself particularly a long life
In better health and begs that you will think him
The honest friend of Caspar Hauser through thick and thin,

Blushing. He gave me lettters, a fat wad,
And I saw my name like an insect trapped
There in the netting of his Lordship's German script

And felt the cold again, remembering Feuerbach,
My comrade in the struggle for Caspar's good,
Dead at Whitsun, poisoned, leaving his book

Shoulder to shoulder with mine in a world of calumny
And I envied him
His tomb for its quiet and safety.

Caspar slept in the room of his convalescence.
I read the letters as he wished me to,
Hurting my eyes, the Englishman's

Too fluent reproduction of our tongue
And characters was like a skin
That something writhed and shone and postured in,

Something I will not put a name to even now
But say: a man whose mania
Was covering paper here let himself go

Over the white sheets of my Caspar's heart and soul
Scribbling and scribbling till the boy
So written over never would clarify

As a person should, from ferment. I was there,
Though ill, in November 1831
When Stanhope by the main force of his peerage won

Custody of Caspar out of the honest hands
Of Gottfried Christian von Tucher and left this town
More like a kidnapper than a guardian

Caspar waving through the carriage window
To me especially and to the woman who
Unveiled herself and showed a face so full of sorrow

Eyes were lidded. We had said
The fondness, the embraces and the kisses
Stanhope allowed the child exceeded what was right and witnesses,

Myself, though ill, among them, spoke against
His seizing. In vain.
I lay in the dark a week and heard the rain

And felt the river swell and let itself
Into the cellars of my house
And wash the rats on rafts from shelf to shelf

And land them on the steps. But then my book was out
With Anselm Feuerbach's in a brave tandem
Against the lies already taking root

And for a testimony of innocence
And preservation of our century's last chance.
In vain. My Caspar slept

Where we had laid him in the whitewashed room
After his wounding, safely, there
I had him safe still in my house and home

And never slept but wounded my weak eyes
Over the devil's close calligraphy until
Birds sang, light came and I resolved to seize

My life's last chance and his. The sun appeared
Thin and white. I stood in my garden
Like an eloper willing the windows of his room to open

On the sharp air. I sent
Mother in to wake him early. She was present
And Caroline too when I

At the end of the summer of 1833, his last,
Over the last meal he would eat with us,
Spoke with a young man's boldness

Astounding the women
To Caspar, my ward and pupil,
There breaking bread for the last time at our table

And drinking milk. Firm of purpose
I begged him to leave the servitude in Ansbach,
The waiting on an absent lord in a brutal house,

And leave the priests and their unnatural creed
For me, but not to come
Into the shelter of my moated home

There being none, no shelter, no asylum –
Witness the black
Ribbon I wore for Feuerbach –

But leave with me, leave house and home and town
And petty fatherland and walk
South, under other names, as teacher and pupil, down

The almost autumn roads and over the snow,
As pilgrims, going poor
For freedom and the mind's enlightenment and no

More dread. All this
Shielding my vision but in a steady voice,
With a young man's resolve. The women said

Your eyes. I answered:
The unclouded light and the long views will cure them or
Caspar will lead me. Your books, they said.

I answered that my books, except the last,
On Caspar, belonged in the stove, to stoke,
And nothing would come of me in Germany that woke

And lived but in the south it might,
A proper writing, a book fit to read,
About escape, about the soul's right

To life grasped firmly like a bowl of wine and drunk
Into the bloodstream, like bread
Ingested, to give heart and feed

Faith up when it lapses and we settle for less and less,
A book men who profess
To teach should write, or none,

Turning to Caspar. He sat
As though the sun on him were ice
Shivering, white, and little heads of sweat

Stippled his scars like leprosy.
Cannot, he said. And must not. He was bound
To wait in lodgings to be summoned

By messenger or till the guardian angel came
Whose mansion would be Caspar's for the rest of time
In person. He reached

The letters into a hiding place
Next his heart. Then all
My column of spirits fell

Into the cold bulb,
And the screaming began again out loud
Where we had hushed it and the stink of fear and the blood

Returned to the rooms we had aired
With fires and breezes and scoured
Nearly white and Caspar backed away

Past the privy and the trap door
His left hand pressing the lump of letters on his heart
His right warding me off as though I were

Incarnate death. And that was our goodbye:
My Caspar backing to the bridge
Stooping and crumpled under the sort of knowledge

Masks have uttered through their mouth-holes
And seen through empty eyes
In theatres in the crucibles of hills

Where men and women were cradled for the gods
To grind. He ran. I lay for days
Hearing the winds strip the big chestnut trees

And the rain come, sufficient rain
To sluice away a massacre. I rose to watch the snow
Whiten over everything around my house and in the town

And then came news of the red pocks,
The red script, the red desperate prints
Over the snow in Ansbach at the time of gifts and cribs

And the nativity of the innocent
Lamb. And see me now
In Bismarck's day, in Nuremberg, the snow

Descending calmly, knowing its resources,
Knowing the leaden heaven
Can snow for ever if it chooses

And cover everything. What Stanhope wished me
I had half of: the long life, outliving them all,
Sickly, behind the rising courses of my wall

Of books which I will cram the stove with
Faster and faster while the snow falls, and less
For warmth than to be rid of myself, to cease

Leaving nothing, since nothing
Has come of me but words and I am making
Smuts of writing still on another page.

I hope the snow falls, on and on,
After the ash of my own substance has fallen
And there is whiteness over the streets and parks

Only whiteness over the whole town
And on the whiteness, when I am dead,
No smuts of print or ink, no spots of blood.

Sixth Canto

PHILIP HENRY STANHOPE
1 March 1855

I read their books and grasped this:
That he was fading, the light
Off him, the magic in him was less and less

And I must rub him like a used charm,
Massage the heart and suck
Hard for the virtue sunk back

Towards his centre. I blamed God
To His face for not crossing
My line of life and the boy's at the beginning

That first Whit and letting
The Professor have him for a curiosity
And the corrupters touch him while I

Dawdled somewhere in Europe,
Nowhere particular, empty and my
Heart withering up

For want of the flood of grace. Fleeing
Again and again (like a man who
At last gets his hands on the last few

Sybilline pages and leaves those
Somewhere ridiculous where the wind blows
To rest his fitness to own them in the lap of merest chance)

I dreamed of Caspar as a vial of blood
But white, enshrined
At the very heart of my house in poor England

Pulsing, giving forth
Even through the body of the reliquary
Like a vast opal a power to ease the earth

Of every sin and affliction and when that dream came
I whined in terror, told his name
Over and over against the stacking odds,

Swung like a weather cock and thrust
At him again from a lodging on the edge.
Once I had got him in my tutelage

In Ansbach naturally
I reverted his diet to the vegetable.
In vain. Wherever the source lay we

Were far below, he wasted in the ordinary sun
Like the Ice King fetched down
From the glaciers into a dull town on the plain

And I blamed the Professor for not swaddling him
At once in something impermeable
And letting the wicked and the social

Crowd leach him. So he withdrew
As would the face on the Turin shroud
If we hung it merely as a curtain at our window

And the clever jurist drawing a family tree
Of dead branches, rotten fruit
And a trunk as stabbed and scabbed and poxy

As any in Europe was all astray
And only made a beam and a gallows tree
To crucify him on. Fool

Having understood
The offence was the killing of a childhood
And the injured party the soul itself

Then to pursue the poor requital in their gift
And reinstatement into their charnel-house
As though you graft

The mercifully severed one good hope
Back on disease. I would
Have carried him into my desert like Aaron's rod

And rammed him home there
Where it was fittest he should flower
For all our good. My children stopped me in a Baltic port

And wrestled with Satan for my soul, they said.
My flesh, more like. Ten thousand pounds
A year of it. But I had promised God

To rescue Caspar out of the Cities of the Plain
And fetch him into the mountains
And live among simple people, beginning again

The crippled trek away from our damnation. But I slipped
Down from my fastening on his outstretched arms
Down and wept

And swallowed gall and wormwood like the Madalene
And see his face still, flat and blank as the moon,
Not exactly smiling, rather frozen

Into an expression not of his own making,
A sort of smile, but too preoccupied
With its own puzzle, the eyes too wide

And blind to smile on me. So I have lived
Year after year and watched him rise
Nightly over the edge into my cold skies

And hang there puzzling and afraid
And never once incline his face to me
However I begged. He bowed

His head last when I asked him to
When I was leaving, let it fall abruptly
As though my asking him withdrew

His ownership. I cut
A lock of hair off with my nail scissors
And pocketed it.

Seventh Canto

GEORG FRIEDRICH DAUMER
1 January 1875

I read their books and I know this:
He died badly, they were gathered round,
Meyer the brute, the decent pastor, the whole crowd,

Hoping for words such as he spoke
To Mother, Caroline and myself
When the Visitor bled him and it woke

His powers again, but all
That issued from his mouth was babble
Of wrong and horror. The pastor grieved

But it was so. There stood
Taller than any others at his bed
Something he never took his eyes off and called

Monstrous, the monster, that word showed
Like the hand or face of a man drowning
Time and again in his flood

Of tongues. And this:
Too strong, the monster, too big, too many hands it has.
And also this: Let my Lord Stanhope

Guard against evil. And again:
Monster, monstrous. And I have it for certain
What drew the child just come of age

To the monument was Stanhope's name
And the promise of news
Of him, lodged, spider or fly, who knows,

In the outer web. Late afternoon
And barely lit by snow
Already crisping, the families gone down

Into the streets and homes
Only the birds left fretting
When a park becomes

As chilling for a town to contemplate
As the gaps in constellations
Caspar entered, hurrying. No one's

Face ever lifted as his did on a hope of welcome
Nor heart opened and often
I called him only for that reason

To see his face and saw
In the measure of his joy how far below
His heart's deserts I fell and so

Uplifted
Whoever called him away from the lighting lamps
Saw him, and slid

Into the opening between
Rib and fob an icicle
Whose watermark was the hour glass and the skull

And saw his simple expectation of a kindness
Curdle to something more
Suited to the truth of us: terror.

When the snow was gone and with it the blood in the spring rain
And Caspar had a tomb
As safe as houses his Lordship came

In a sweat to Nuremberg, seeking me out.
I would not receive him on the island in my house
But answered at the Blackie Boy. Is it thus

We shall appear for ever under Caspar's eyes:
Yellow, unable to sit still?
The man spoke pell-mell

And always through his handkerchief as though his breath
Stank, which it did if by the breath
We mean how the soul breathes

For Stanhope's soul had died
And against the stench of it rotting he had need
Of more than a hand and a handkerchief.

He said he hoped I lived safely
And nothing worse than voices would be raised against me
And never an arm fitted with a cutting edge

And best to err, for the sake of my womenfolk,
On the side of the new truth
And this (suddenly, with a bare mouth,

And starting eyes as though he shocked himself):
Whatever we say it cannot hurt him now.
There was a diary. We knew

His Lordship had sacked the Meyers' house from cellar to attic
And opened the belly of Caspar's stove to sift and weigh
The delicate leaves of his last auto-da-fé

But could read nothing. He feared
My heart, having beat with Caspar's a last time,
Might be the repository of some gloss on the word

Monstrous, which by then
Was known in every salon as the burden
Caspar dragged with him through his agony.

We faced each other across a common table.
His Lordship looked to be already burning
In ice, which strengthened me. Next morning

Sleepless, my eyes as sore
As cockscombs, I had in mind to stick him to the door
With questions, but found him breakfasting

On meats: on kidneys, livers and a sheep's heart
And rare steaks as fat
As policemen's soles. I stood, he ate,

He fed some hunger in him far down,
Watching me, and never spoke and fed
On meat that dribbled red,

Kidneys that spurted, a flecked liver,
A slop of lights and all the while
He eyed me as though I might contest the spoil

Or like a man caught itching at a vicious place
In public but cannot stop, though watched,
And grubs for easement, he scratched

At the sore of his hunger as if to say
See me, stare at me, see how it is
At the feeding time of the worm in me

And drank the juices off his silver plate and mopped
It clean as a child's brow and drained
A black wine after it and swabbed

His lips with a snowy cloth
And never spoke, only stared at me, and I withdrew
And on the street there in the public view

Vomited and lay
Curled and retching on a point of bile,
The people torn between that spectacle

And Stanhope's flight. My friend
And physician Dr Osterhausen being summoned
Failed to unclench me and I was borne

Rolled like a grub into my sanctuary
That stank of blood and howled
From cellar to attic for the absent child.

Eighth Canto

We never sleep. We have no empty squares.
It would be impossible to deliver him
So he stood out. The wars

Blow children up. Some fall our way.
They know a single sentence. They can say
My father is dead in somewhere in the news,

My mother raped and dead, or thrust it down
In somebody else's lettering
Over our headlines in the underground,

Or howl, just that: a particular girl
Rides the loop, stop by stop,
And holds a stump out and a begging cup

And howls, just that. I have observed her eyes.
They are so absent you would say she hires
Herself as a professional keener in her cause.

And nobody looks at anyone else, we all
Pray there'll be no hold-up for the howl
Cannot be borne beyond its usual

Measure. And much the same
Like wreckage after a catastrophe we have not fathomed yet
Children of our own making squat

Along the concrete walkways and the bridges
We cross to the opera
And hold a cardboard in their laps that says

What their state is. And not long since
At the time of the clear-outs and the big shut-downs
The insane appeared among us in great numbers,

They collected steadily like a bloom
And had to be dispersed. We called them
The big children, the way they lumbered,

Also because they were taking it up again –
Life, I mean –
After a long time hidden

Under the stairs, in cubby-holes, behind the door
Playing hide and seek
And nobody seeking, so three score

Had to be stiched back on to the ten
Or less, which made a shadow
Far too heavy for a child to tow.

Most were as delicate,
Faint and intricate
As snowflakes when they land too soon

On the unhushed concrete or press
At the warm pane of a living room
And with very little fuss

They expired somewhere. Round here
I believe King Billy is the only survivor.
The Pakistanis took him in, to sweep,

And lately they have let him mind the children.
He has a lizard's eyes and a lizard's skin.
It might be several lifetimes

He lived elsewhere before he was returned to us,
The community, his neck cricked
As from a failed hanging, and the head thus cocked

As if he were always listening, which he is
Since everyone coming out had his particular voices
For guidance how to get on

In the increased traffic. But King Billy hears
The languages of all the nations he will rule one day
In peace, from Sans Souci.

Each new one heard he learns
Until his conversation with the voices is word perfect.
He is above dialect.

He learns the mandarin. This purity
Shines out in the children's
English and Hindi. You will say

Town is crawling with men who think they are Jesus
Or Winston Churchill and accost the public
With proofs, in bus stations. King Billy never does

But keeps his council. He has waited so long
There are so many tongues
The grammars of some are hard to get

And the good forms almost forgotten. Hospitals
Were razed and rose again over him like cathedrals
Over an ancient crypt

Where he bowed and studied. He has time on his side.
His eyes are as lasting as diamonds, his bald head
Looks to have lifted clear of the pool of aging.

He says he was put away for safekeeping
Until the fires have passed. It moves me
That he does not think he has come out too early.

He stands at the zebra between
Two bright-as-a-button Paki kids, their hands
Trusting in his, he waits for green

On a street still wearing the black of arson
And will tell you in any language, if you ask,
The time will come. Then I imagine

Caspar entering down the long road
From the upland fields through the plots
Of sunk endeavour and the walled estates

His stride made for him by the man behind with kicks
Like someone carrying a carapace
Already smashed towards a starting place

Under the neon in the whiff of drains
Against an aureole of shattered plate
In the racket of jackpots, the sirens,

The shots, the mirth, the fires
As nightly. But other pairs
Compete. Bone comes in

Pick-a-back
Knotted around the midriff and the neck
Of Dai, his pal, with equal arms and legs

And lately I have watched a mother and son
Put out, invade
Again and again down the same road

Like damp. She wheels him in
Wrapped like her grandfather, they suck the same bottle
Over his shoulder to and fro, their purple

Blustering faces bear
Less a family likeness than the common
Look of matter in decomposition

Wherever it shows
Cakey and fissuring. She vents herself, she slews
Him off the edge, he tips and bleeds.

Hard to be noticed in a town like this,
Even the double acts. Day in, day out
A grown man stands with a bible on the martyrs' spot

And bellows at the traffic. No one hears.
It rains. He wags his book and roars
And no one listens. True,

Anyone dying in a pyre still makes the news
But no one rightly knows
What they should do about him doing it.

Whether to look. The police advise
Against it. Eyes
Often are only waiting for that contact

To strike you dead. Best look away,
Look down, chasten
Your wanton eyesight like a nun

Since any beggar or whore
Whose mouths are asking you to give or buy
Their eyes want more.

Prostitution in a cold climate
Sad, the heels
In dirty puddles

The stockings in a wind
Sharp as cystitis. When the silvery captains land
From taxis, bible-black, the hand,

French or the full supper
Is theirs in the minutes before departure
For next to nothing. All these children

God knows what maladies riding their veins
The way they look at you over their captions
The way they look at you over their mouths

Worse than Christ at the whipping-post who knew
The answers, they ask questions worse
Than what is this and what am I to you,

Stranger, passer-by? They ask
What am I to me? And nobody knows.
They seem to have moved out into their own shadows

And sit watching their bodies round
Over a bowl or tin at the level of our footsteps.
Last night this happened:

I stooped to give a coin, he caught my wrist
As though I thieved, he raised
His look under my guard

And we opened, both, the need, the helplessness,
The infinite requirement of redress,
We admitted them, he appeared

Like the moon in the dish of a telescope
Fetched into perfect focus, near
As the lines of life on my own palm, but deep

In space circling
The warmer life in a cold outer track
Presumably for ever. At my back

My fellow citizens were pounding to and fro
For trains, in the corridors, and he held me out of them
A minute perhaps, he held me to

The sight of him and cocked an ear
To signal me to listen to what it sounds like
Orbiting in the cold, what music they hear

Remote from one another: the whine of the last trains,
Their ghostly doubling in the underground winds,
These are cosy: it sounds

Like falling through eternity,
It is one steady incapable of ceasing,
Diminishing or commingling

Scream. When he was certain I had heard it
A little, and when he knew I knew
A little, he shrugged and let me go.

Tinkle of brass. I should have had him home.
Like Russian dolls, somewhere inside
The last would be the pale curled seed

Of him. Begin again.
He would be still there if I ever went that way.
I don't. He frightens me.

Best never look. I hear the scream
Most nights. I see his bit of card: to whom
It may concern. I read my name.

Ninth Canto

The College congregated
As they were required to when the case was special
All nine, some from a distance. He waited.

They kept him waiting in their coldest antechamber,
The ice house, a low
Tumulus in the snow

Outside the walls. One night, one day, one last night
The people queued to see him without distinction,
The dying wrapped tight,

The newborn and their mothers still unchurched,
Lovers, drunks, cretins, all ranks of these,
They queued to see him in the ice house.

The policeman at the entrance was unnecessary.
Nobody chattered until afterwards.
All stooped and entered with a perfect decency.

For so many years in the dark and the silence
When sleep was the only one who visited
Bringing him water and the carraway bread

After that prelude, after the morsel
Served him next, this coda: the people
Calling on him in their Sunday clothes

Two long nights and a brief winter's day
In the igloo where he lay
On a trestle table among candles

Only to see him with their own eyes
And never a word, a sigh perhaps, the shiver
Lines of verse will give but never

A word on him until they were home again
Somewhere warmer, thawing. Time had slowed
Almost to a halt in him, as when

He lived alone with the wheeled horses
And nothing happened but the kindnesses
Of sleep and all he did was host the nourishment

Through him and pet the horses while he grew
Only because flesh must
And never sleeps so deep it comes to rest.

Now in a sort of hive devised to thwart
The wish of ice in summer to become water
He hesitated and the College would have had him

As fresh as a visible mariner under the Pole
But that the candle tongues, the breaths of his visitors,
Their sighing, the condensation of their prayers

Warmed him a little as we have
The horses at Lascaux. So he had begun
To mottle slightly when the Academy called him in

And he was fetched through the people loath to see him go
To the steps and the doric portico
Where the Nine waited, in black, on high,

Each with his saws and knives in a black bag
Clutched like chastity
Under the paunch, unsmiling, whiskery

And red as diners. They bowed
And a murmur of grief rose from the ignorant crowd
And the beginnings of a mutter of complaint

When the beetle-black frock coats
Of the nine surgeons and the Academy's iron gates
And double iron doors closed on Caspar.

II

In there they got down to it
In shirt sleeves, tutting at
The greenish flecks of the life lived underground

Already advanced over the body of him
Who was as white as bread laid on their board
And scarcely cut. They heard

213

Schinder, the local man, tell yet again
How he was first and had laid an ear
On Caspar's chest and listened in

To the heart plashing like Daumer's rats
And with the middle finger of his right hand
Had gone as far as he could into the wound

And tickled what he thought was a wet lung.
When he was done, allowing
Themselves a pleasantry about this quizzy finger,

They fell to, the Nine, not like hyenas
On a unicorn, nor like
Crabs on a pearly mermaid, but as

Order dictated and the elbow room
Allowed. Off the breastbone
They laid the waistcoat of Caspar's flesh entirely open

And entered the zones of his wound from the right side
Sawing through the bars. He would have died
Four times had he had lives to do so:

Stomach, diaphragm, liver were all mortally hurt
In passing and the long finger of knife,
Its manicured long nail, had touched his heart

Whose sack had filled,
Likewise the thorax, likewise the abdomen,
Their sacks were full and on

Enquiry broke
Their septic waters over the ungloved hands
In pints. The heart was caked a thick

Yellow white
Like a baby and everywhere they went
Was soft and rank, in handfuls. But they lifted out

The spitted liver, rinsed it clean
And laid it for inspection on a silver dish.
It was the largest human liver they had ever seen.

So behind bars
The ape's grows and the bear's
And any wild thing's, out of all proportion, and in this,

Measuring the liver, they had gone beyond
The interrogation of the wound
Whose cause and effect were simple

And pushed their science
Into the enigma itself. Kratz took a leg
To a side table and dug

For the motor oddity. The organs
Of generation fell to Osterhausen
Who botched the job and every important question

Eluded him. The hands
That were quick and careful at drawing fruit and flowers
Did not detain them and they bent their minds

Over Caspar's face. He wore the angel's mark
And the mark of the accident
In Clara's house. Otherwise puzzlement –

That was how he had set and would have faded
Little by little had he been allowed
Time under a shroud –

Puzzlement settling finally into dust,
No bad ending, not a bad expression
To wear into extinction.

But the College, time pressing,
Time stoked by their hot breath accelerating,
Five hours in and the work of their hands stinking,

They wished to see behind the mere appearance
Behind the smile that was not exactly that
Behind the eyes that asked more than they answered.

Open as it always was still Caspar's face
Could not admit them without increase
Of routes. Schlott did a harsh caesarean on

The Child's skull
And proffered them the brain:
More beast than human, or if human

Only a foetus, untimely, the cerebellum
Too large for so ungrown a cerebrum,
The hind lobes scarcely started, the middle

Queerly sunk behind the sphenoid bone
As though reluctant. They sliced
The great brain flat, the smaller down

And there, in the latter, flowering like frost,
The wondrous spread of Caspar's *arbor vitae*,
Astonished them. The rest

Slicing and fingering they could make nothing of
And suddenly wearied. They saw
The stains on one another.

Kratz fetched the leg. Poor Osterhausen put
His parcel back. They shut
The skull over its infant brain and bedded

The liver in its morass. But for
What had run off and the few small
Souvenirs it was traditional

To abstract, they had
The makings of a person on their slab.
Dumb offal, reeking. Wetzel said:

We should have had him the minute he came out.
So much was blurred in the fatal interim
By a social life. We should have had him

Pure. They rang for the baggers and went to wash.
Late afternoon, already dark, more snow.
The men came, masked. One took a toe,

Another an ear, etc. They bagged up what remained.
After the obsequies – his pastor
Lifted the congregation on a swell of grief and terror –

The trade in him began, the entity,
Such as it was, the unsure
First person singular crumbling rapidly

He fed through the academies and the common people
Into the wide world, changing hands
For money one day, love the next, in lands

Only discovered since. Collected up
The crumbs still lodging here and there would make
More bread of life than Caspar ever broke.

SLEEPER

(1995)

for Jim Reed

I

Climbing the last into my narrow billet
I had seen all their faces left outside
The shut lids. When we were lit

Only by a bluish pilot light they played
Over me in the travelling air
Flickering and whispering. Sofia said

Goodnight in the language of where we were
But it was in the tongues of home
Already sleeping everyone answered her.

Anna of the bare white arms with a bone comb
Clutched on the service blanket hoof-shaped
Over her lap lay calm

On tossed hair. And steeped
In weathers, dead beat,
Level with her, but turning away, Jan slept,

Iced on his back with salts of sweat.
I knew he had an orange in his close
Fist, he was breathing it.

Josip faced his daughter's child across
The gap. He held a photograph
Shut like a creature's edible heart in a less

Than adequate shell. His teeth were safe.
They chattered on the hurrying floor
In an aluminium beaker. He was deaf.

The girl slept on a prayer.
I never saw a clearer skin. It showed
Every little branching of the nightmare.

So many veins a face has and are such good
Conductors for the heart and mind
Nobody looking at a face could plead

He did not know. All of a kind
Stacked separately in comfort sideways on
So we passed by as the iron track determined

And I was easy, as though for once
The level discipline of a purpose
Sorted amiably with indulgence

The engine heading for a distant terminus
For sleep's sake dawdled, the country
Lasted, the few booked hours of darkness

Filled with room and the battery
Of sleepers was dissolved and all alone
Let go and drifted only weighted by

Dreams and thoughts so there was always one
At least turning up a shoulder through the surface
Or a puzzled eye or a mouth wide open

As if on a word and sank and from the juice
Deep down where the tongue's pulses
Carry for ever some other speaker rose.

II

The beat and give of sleepers under the rails
Is scored in early but that night because
I was lying on to them I felt the channels

Laid so water will get from the dry snows
To salt, rippling. I was recalling
Some words out of a long disuse

Like rill and freshet when it seemed we were crawling
Across a falls and down the head's side
Sheer and passing under us and falling

Away sheer from the feet such a loud
Body of water fell I was drowned out
And everyone deafened. Jan said:

Sleeping in the mountains every night
By water and all day climbing by it
Something got into me like drought

But not quite that. I sucked ice, wetted
My skin on rainbows, lay face to face
With myself on troughs but wanted

Other faculties. In all forms always
Water had the edge, in a full spate
I thirsted as much as on the screes

Which are only the shards of water. My appetite
Was keener than my means. Falls, for example,
No one can take in, even the height

They start from any one would topple
Leaning back to see it and how they come
Down here through haloes in the smell

Of green in every density of presence from
The kiss of a bubble to the earthquaking
Nobody has the depth of throat to ingest them

Nor the arteries it would need. One thing
I did each day on the day's col as a kind
Of charm or concentration against unravelling

For love of the white flung round
Of water-ridden mountains and the hemisphere
Of blue over the compass on my hand

Was halve the orb of the day's orange and devour
It juice and zest and push it inside out
And lick the empty caps threadbare.

My mouth was sweet then. It smarted. The sweat
Where my pack had been began to freeze. But now
We were over the falls on straight

Track and what he was saying went below
The surface of hearing with the water. We rode
Fast over the clicks of time and how long, how

Far later it was I cannot say, but I had
A feeling of flatness and emptiness
And near the centre of that we pulled aside

And halted. Listen. Trucks were passing by us
Slowly, with a regular limp. I began to count.
Sofia said: Give up. They are endless.

They are the cattle trucks of our continent
This century. They last for ever. Imagine
How many feeders each collection point

Had fastened to it. Over me then
As though my body were the body of Europe
I felt the links of a sort of logic laid down

And riveted. All was connected up,
This to that, a small thing, but that slotted
Into a larger and let a next develop

Larger with spurs each side that split
Into others and the worst was
The certainty that a set mind meant it

To be so eternally and all resource
And all ingenious devising would go to that
One total articulation. Yes,

Sofia said, worse even than hate
In a face is the look of purpose and any network,
Even benign, such as flings out

Spiders of street lights on the dark
And runs the services into every civilised
Home and all the jointing and the fork

Of the syntax of pure reason used
By fixed minds, scares me still.
They had flat land, it raised

Not the least resistance, the trucks could roll
On straight lines easily toward
The bottomless pits that we were meant to fill.

She ceased. The child was whimpering. I heard
That and the trucks. Both were
Final and endless. Each one neared

A while against the continuo of the other
By turns, and lessened back. Silence behind.
All space and time had run together

Level. That was the ground
They limped and whimpered on. Josip hushed
Across to her. But she contained

Already worse than could be wished
Away. The track is laid. The air
Tastes. The ashed

Folk are in the aquifers. Then the unfair
Antiphony of child and iron faded
Against the silence. Nothing was near

Enough to hope for. We waited
Somewhere flat, somewhere black without
A murmur like any cargo sided

Away for now. Anna cried out.
It was the kick of the engine starting up again
Come through to us. She said: Did I skip a beat

Or months? See how I hurry on.
The strange word 'quickening' was quite at home
With me already and the quotation

She felt the babe leap in her womb
Was placed. Now at this start
Surely behind the shield of the bone comb

He gave me it flutters, or my heart
Had fallen into the pit of the future and sends me
Tremors. Sofia said: My thought

Is of the sleepers standing so tightly
Among their dead none could lie down
Coming alive to it at every

Start like that. But now our train
Had got into its rhythm and Anna was jubilant.
Sleep is speedy. Soon

It will have ferried me where I want
To be: down the long long fetch
Of my desire into his present

Tense. I want to match
My half with his over the he or she,
Over the little huddled each

Of us lilting along in me
Asleep. I remember the word 'to raise'
That I never used anywhere else, how he

Raised me and I him, to and fro, it was
Nerve you needed more than luck. And then
'To see', that strange word. His eyes

Were almost hurting mine, looking right in,
And mine (I tried to) looking into him.
But seeing was more than that. Seeing was when

After he said the word I had to show him
The cards I was laying on. I spread
My little anxious fan of them

Shoulder to shoulder until their value showed.
His eyes when he saw me in that sense
Were not exactly kind, he never would

Smile when I tried smiling and more than once
He has looked at me like that while I undress
So that I felt myself weighed in the balance

With a hand he still held close,
And again tried smiling. But this time
I hope his cards are good for I shall be reckless

And raise him higher and higher. This game
I want him following. He must stake
Everything when he sees me and the outcome

Be matching hands, highest and equal. She spoke
All her hope out on a flood tide
Of sleep and no one broke

The surface of it, cautioning. She said:
I will ask at the café for the spare key.
It will be early. He will be in bed.

I have the wish to strip very quietly
And materialise against him like desire
Dreamed. His usual day

Tomorrow will not have time to interfere
And I shall lift him out of his circumstances
As out of a soft earth. For I am more

Compelling now, no other reason has
My force. So she ran on. I knew
Suddenly that the distances

Had swapped, less was to do
Than done. Arrival, with a rising tone,
Had started filling her. She fell into

The repeated utterance of its one line
Collapsing all her future
Into one rapid mantra of reunion

And the heart's beat took it or
The beat of the countless crosses of iron on wood
So that I thought we should have no further

Words, only their rhythm and ride
That in, but there was a speaker still,
The queerest, Josip, he showed

Himself, struggling to be audible
Above the matrix of Anna's love chant
With bare gums, the eyes too full

Of sights were bulging the lids and the lament
Of women filled his mouth. He seemed
Much like Tiresias lent

Out to grief, assumed
By it and where the gap was deepest,
Where the mother wanted, she dreamed

Aloud in him. He quarrelled the best
He could with them, against their chorus
His tongue wagged like a ghost

Of hope alive by accident. Hear this,
He said, and with their syllables
He made a speech of his own. You see us

Travelling as anybody travels
Who has the money to, in comfort decently
With sheets. And how? One of God's angels,

A gentleman in a loden coat, like me
In age, but big, so big, with silver hair
And gold in his teeth, a German, when we

Were in his country and a frontier
And mountains lay between
Us and the abattoir

Our motherland and I had gone
All wrong in my ignorance and deafness
And the little one

Lay flopped over my lap I looked across
The track and saw him look
Across at us as though our troubles were his

And next I knew – perhaps I slept and woke –
There he was, I could not hear but saw
How courteous his hands were as he took

Us up and knew where we were heading for
And found the platform and the train and paid
The difference on a sleeper

And got us settled in with food
And fizzy water and round
The girl's black hair and white white face he made

A gesture like a blessing. Josip opened
His hand to show a picture in a heart
Open on his palm and then like something dinned

Into him till he got it right and fraught
With foreign power he said the address
Again and again like Hail Marys, he brought

The asylum out, his face,
His blind and dreaming face, bowed over mine
For mercy on its hope. I knew the place.

Another week, another shrine
Of sickening flowers against a blackened wall.
We know the street names in that numbered zone,

We learned them on the news. He said: I shall
Be dead before very long and I shan't try
Learning the language but in school

She will and the good manners of the country
Being so quick, and it is well known
That love, if sufficient love comes early

After the thing, although a grown
Man never will be rid of it, a child
If the hands are laid on soon

And often enough the worst is swaled
Away. That said – he ended on the rising note
Of questions – Josip told

His safe address again and set
Between each rapid recitation just
The space for someone to interpolate

Amen, and no one did. The total past
Outweighs the little left. It commandeered
His throat. His voice was lost.

III

I woke. We were running in. The dreams re-entered
The only bodily hope at their disposal:
Us, the particulars, who were being steered

Fast towards onus. Arrival
Lets no one else in. Open-eyed
We fluttered with the dreams that could not settle.

The shrift was ending, we had begun to slide
As water does when it can sense
The edge at last and speed

Assumes the character of a level silence
And everything concentrates. We lay
On and on until the patience

Of daytime waiting outside suddenly
Snapped and the light stood there, with noise,
In the slid door. How guilty

We must have looked, struggling to rise
Like the resurrected in a small confine
With any decency and to keep our eyes

Off Anna easing the bone crown
Home in her hair and off the terrible rictus
Awaiting Josip's dentures. Being seen

Came hard on all of us
Like a shock of shame after the night as though
What the heart had admitted in the darkness

In the light must show
To strangers in the faces and a hurry for separation
Worked among the bodies now

That had been neatly shelved but everyone
Was shoved together by Jan's gear
And Josip's salvage and begged pardon

In different tongues. But I saw
This: Anna's bare hand rest
A moment on the child's black hair

And Jan, the mountaineer, tallest
By far, go down on his knees
And sit back lower and lower till he and the smallest

Were level and eye to eye and house
Her hands in his around
The shining globe of the orange of the snows

There in our midst. We joined
The choked swim down the corridor
To the exits then and by a thousand

Like us we were worked asunder
Without goodbyes. I stood at the engine,
Watching. Jan passed. He needed more

Scope for his stride and so held in
It lifted him like a dancer. Josip, deaf,
Saying his safe address into the din,

Passed with his bags, for dear life
Holding together with his child's child
Who never spoke. Anna was next. As if

The power she had were being annulled
Minute by minute in the ordinary daylight
She ran at gaps. She passed. Sofia was crippled

In both hips, her steps threw out
Her strength to right and left, she looked ahead
For threats. A greater weight

Of harm had gathered in her than ever should
In one small human space. I watched her
The longest, the odd walk she had

Even beyond the barrier
In the vast concourse boiling with arrival
The broken rhythm she made, her queer

Retarding tread in the pellmell,
When she was nothing but a small black
Quaver of effort I could still feel

That walk, it stuck
With me somewhere around the heart. So she,
Sofia, one speck,

One more iota in the daily
Incoming thousands of dreaming sleepers
That silt the openings of the city

Like pollination, with the others
She too passed. That ended it.
My sleepy language left me with theirs.

FROM

THE PELT OF WASPS

(1998)

Piers

A jetty is a brave thought
And a pier a cheerful hubris
Going in deeper and deeper to stay level

It carries the fairground far out. Lovers need a pier
To pace out the new extent of themselves
And learn what they are risking.

At low tide the legs of a pier
Are as shocking as the veined white legs of the fathers.
In the stink, under the decking, in the belly of the whale

You saw the red cigarette-ends of the numbered soldiers
Courting. You see the aged
Wheeling eagerly out to the fishermen and the broken-hearted

Out to the limits of the pier, still pointing.

Returns

Returns: as when
That evening in summer on a sunny breeze
The Atlantic entered

A drop, one silver bead,
Out of it opening a whole water
Out of it flowering and relaxing over the patience of the flats

And the gladness of the salt-loving lives was palpable,
What could was floated, the carcasses
Were at a depth, the veins

Were filled, and we
In a room on a jut of land with a window out,
A captain's window, sea three sides the bed,

Into the chuckling sea we pushed our cries.

The Mirror

Mirror, the window set
On a sharp starlight and the moon ascending
Flat, like a shark. Out of her clothes,

Membra disjecta on their battleground,
All the warmth has gone. He puts his hopes
In cold, expends

His wishes on her glass. Remembering
The silk slide from her shoulders as quickly as mercury
He knows his heart must fall a floor like a lift

And in that loss of heat she will precipitate
As white as flour. The shock,
The sigh, as though his eyes,

Hard on her fingertips, were being put out.

The Apple Tree

Night gone and the dream is stranded
Or this is a bold dream that has stepped some paces forward
The apple tree in a startling frost

Faces the sun in a clothing from elsewhere
Crackles with a freezing fire. There are no proofs
Only these goadings. The frost

Rasped like a cat's tongue at the windowpanes.
She entered suddenly with all her clothes in a bundle
Backing the door to threw the bundle down.

Waking I remember the ha'pennies
I warmed as a child and laid against the frost
To see. I watch the bright grey apple tree

Slowly denuding, slowly vanishing.

Peacock

A man's fist may be very gentle
When he takes a butterfly off the pane
And feels the tickle of her wings like desperate eyes.

She seemed to know what she wanted.
Bodily she made the sign of it against the glass,
Sign of her need, sign of the impediment.

October again. The wind.
The trees gasp and are suddenly naked
And everything whirled in the air is dead or dying.

She had opened like an illumination
Under the wall-lamp above their pillow
Still as a brooch, and the savage wind at the pane.

Eyes in the dark. The man has her in his head.

The Wasps

The apples on the tree are full of wasps;
Red apples, racing like hearts. The summer pushes
Her tongue into the winter's throat.

But at six today, like rain, like the first drops,
The wasps came battering softly at the black glass.
They want the light, the cold is at their backs.

That morning last year when the light had been left on
The strange room terrified the heart in me,
I could not place myself, didn't know my own

Insect scribble: then saw the whole soft
Pelt of wasps, its underbelly, the long black pane
Yellow with visitants, it seethed, the glass sounded.

I bless my life: that so much wants in.

Musicians in the Underground

I was descending early, nobody around
And only the usual noises in the corridors which are
The tremor of departures and the wind
When the music started, there was no evading it
Wherever you might have been that morning underground

The wellspring was so deep and all the shafts and stairs
And the winding tiled runs were rinsed
On every level. How well they know
The acoustics of the system. That girl
Who stood in the rush hour at the mouth of one of the chambers

And showed ten thousand people the countenance of an angel
With closed eyes, singing. It was something
Not in our daily speech but still our language
Older, truer. Then how wrong
And slovenly my tongue felt. They visit the body and soul

Of every love and want and the night's lost dreams
They fetch them home. That boy, that faun
Who jumped us slumbering
And rode the lurching car and into the curves and down
The tunnels shivering under our clothes

We had him as conductor, his black horn
Lifted and moaning. These singers,
These couriers through the labyrinth out of the sight of the sun
They are as free as swallows and they know
What the ghosts felt once, and warn us while we can.

Angels

I know a few girls who might well be angels.
One with a passion for railways. Her most likely.
Show her a branch line vanishing in bluebells
She feels it like a thread. From here, she says,

Give me a week I'll be in Mozdok.
She has the connections at her fingertips.
I have a coward soul. I lie awake
Begging the saints and all the old gods

Whichever had responsibility for wayfarers
Watch her. Intervene on her side. Cancel
Oncoming human error. I see her
Stuck somewhere bad with no train out till Monday

Asking a bed for the night from total strangers.
Must be she wakes an ancient obligation:
This we should do, this we should never do
To strangers. She knows as well as anyone

What terminus the cattletrucks arrived at
But when she speaks of railways I imagine
Land black as space, the night trains
Seeding it through with conversations

To its starry points. Stories, stories.
People with nothing but the gift of tongues
Break that with her who leaves them when she chooses,
Fumble for something she will remember them by.

Angels are like that. Much as we do
They read the newspapers, they watch the news
But cast themselves on the wings of the world
The way not one of us does nowadays.

It is so easy to abuse an angel.
They show their open faces like the blind.
Be courteous. They expect it. That precisely
Is the gift of angels visiting our kind.

Poppies

Poppies have come up in last year's bean trenches.
Nobody tipped in any blood
All we did was back off a yard or so
The ground must be thick with their black roe.

There must be a desperate press under the roots
These two gashes are packed tight
There must be millions of poppies frantic for the light
Perhaps we shall give them another yard next year.

Poppies are what comes when we let the black earth sleep.
It seems they want the room we occupy.
Wake, and lifting the light blood in the lids
More and more poppies crowd against the eye.

The days come up bled white. They need the blood
Wrapped on a dot of black in every bud.
That colour waits in there like music in a score.
The tissue itches. The petals unclenching

Are harder on the cap than is a baby's head
On the tight vagina. So through scabs
And falling bits of scale life crowns.
Under the streaming sky it muscles out red.

Mistletoe

Holly is so robust, the mistletoe was
For kissing under, pale little drops,
I think she would bleed like that
She is so awash. I spend hours at the screen
Appealing, I have nightmares
That in the far north somewhere
On a coast swilled even now with fifty thousand tons of oil
There was a plant like the one the gods called *molu*
Or in a rainforest
Needle in a burned-out haystack the size of Wales
There was. When I implore the web
The word coming down to me most often is mistletoe.
A professor in Arizona bought his wife five years with it,
His beloved wife, and under the Pyrenees
A marvellous boy going white before their eyes
Is now as bright as holly. Day by day
I increase my stack of miracles
All certificated. I have given her the pearls
Necklace and earrings
And nailed a sprig on every lintel in our house.
Mistletoe was in Eden
Sucking the goodness out of Eve's own tree.

On Oxford Station, 15 February 1997

Then everything paused, it all went very quiet,
I watched a small cloud on the blue due north,
Blue that the iron tracks were levelled at,

Such blue, such quiet blue, it troubled me
Like something unimaginable that I could see
And didn't have the word for, I watched the cloud,

One white cloud on the quiet empty blue,
Light as a feather at the lips of life
Testing for breath, feeling for final proof.

Ground Elder

Once since he died I saw him in a dream
Wherever the dead are, he was jovial,
He clapped me hard between his hands and said:
Stay, but I would not and I came back here
Where the living are. Now it is April

And kneeling on the warm earth in a sort of shame,
Dumb, fearful, not fit company
For anything opening I begin again
Pulling the ground elder, its leaves
Show it like flags or floats, the hands go in

After it gently, where it breaks it lives
Like worms, every remnant sprouts, this is
The thing he told me it was like,
This work of crochet through the living ground,
This reproductive act without an end,

A little like, nothing is really like
It, only love perhaps, both strike
And spread. Gathering the long tubers,
Stupidly laying them out in an old bowl
As though they were edible helps, it eases

The grip, the dumbness. Anyone patient
Who kneels half a day in spring and labours
Works wonders here. The summer will live.
You never get it all out, as he said.
No matter here. Here it is different.

'We say the dead depart'

We say the dead depart but can't say where
And can't imagine being nowhere, time
Full-stopped. But absence
Is here and now, we rub along
Shoulder to shoulder with the vacancies
The dead have left, doing the best we can
Less well with poorer means and greater need
In a worsened world, to fill them. This week
Everyone sees the deficit, time running out
Everyone has the dead man's kindness in their view
Everyone needing it, no one
Meeting a friend of his this week
Has had an unkind word. And how alive
The world continues to be with things the dead man loved
Last week, goldfinches, say,
A charm, and how bereft they look, not so well admired, they want
Their due and look to us
The bereaved, his understudies.

Quaker Memorial Meeting

We are facing into a space
And watching roses on the table in a bowl
Dying so slowly it seems like stillness.

We are trying to concentrate. Outside
With the dead limbs buds are coming down
And blossom, weddings of it. Outside

The roses would be gone in a gasp, a heartbeat,
Shape and scent, but here under a roof
It is like the lying down time after giving blood

Or when the tide turns on anxiety and sleep comes,
The images arrive, like clouds
From somewhere inexhaustible, on a still blue sky

The white ghosts passing over. Sunlight blows
On and off and somebody stands
And speaks a memory of the dead man into the space

Or pool, the pool of our silences, and through
The haloes where the memory falls
In the collecting place like water writing

The images rise. In this, somebody says,
Like this he touched my life and since then
Less well, the best I can, I have been trying

To repay him to others, younger. Words
Like water flowers. My signature,
My wedded helix, will unravel in no time, soon.

But life rides on the winds. Love of the light
And creatures under the sun, the love
Like his that lifts our hearts now over the empty space

Is a love of the four winds. Into them
When we have fetched his shivering image to the surface
And remembered the shape he had and recollected

His qualities and the shape they took in deeds
We give him away and ourselves then also
Breaking up the meeting into the four winds.

Bonfires

Eight months dead, the sun low and silvery,
He was seen through the three bare apple trees
In that dirty mackintosh and crumpled hat

At the heap, near the ditch, feeding the fire.
It was himself, content. Now I will believe
There is after all an everlasting bonfire:

One in a sort of heaven. Like the animals
When they dive down very deep for the winter
A bonfire can retract to a small heart,

Keep warm, lie low, suffer the wind and the rain,
Hoarding a decision to come back to life.
The sign is a stiffening of its wisp of breath.

It hurries then, all the bulk, all the material,
Through cloudy white straits of smoke
It comes in a rush to the state of pure flame.

A scent of bonfire entered the house at elevenses,
Hung on his coat among the respectable coats
In the dark for days. Nobody wonders much

That he has been seen in the grey-green lichen light
Behind the trees we stripped this year without him
Making a smoke, bringing on a roar of flame.

Above West Shore, Llandudno

Their seats, before they come, are like
The empty sarcophagi in the Alyscamps
But named, named with the dead, in memory of,
Who loved this place, who often sat here,
Who loved the view from here

Over the red roofs of the homes
To the estuary, who loved the western sea,
Whose heart is here. Bad heart,
Bad in the chest, bad veins, bad bones,
These are the not-so-bads who haul themselves up here

By the handrail, often pausing, one step at a time,
For breath, up here
Where it is level and the many benches are
And the view is famous over the nursing homes
And hospices, to the estuary. They sit

Full in the sun with thyme, harebells,
And the open stars of carline thistles at their backs
And butterflies, the blues
That haunt the limestone, round their heads
And watch the estuary. Nice to go out like that.

There is no agony in the meeting of salt and sweet.
There is some give and take.
Observe how far upstream
The sea extends its life on a flood tide
And how the river lasts. Under the red roofs

Such indignities but here
Where the broompods crack and the gulls
And jackdaws keep on nattering and children
Shout all this way up from the lusty waves
The climbers sit in the airy light

With shades, with better halves
Continuing some talk and watch the waters –
That kind rocking, that cool fusion –
Glad that it was, wishing it had been,
Praying it will be as easy on them as that.

Soldiering On

We need another monument. Everywhere
Has Tommy Atkins with his head bowed down
For all his pals, the alphabetical dead,
And that is sweet and right and every year
We freshen the whited cenotaph with red

But no one seems to have thought of standing her
In all the parishes in bronze or stone
With bags, with heavy bags, with bags of spuds
And flour and tins of peas and clinging kids
Lending the bags their bit of extra weight –

Flat-chested little woman in a hat,
Thin as a rake, tough as old boots, with feet
That ache, ache, ache. I've read
He staggered into battle carrying sixty pounds
Of things for killing with. She looked after the pence,

She made ends meet, she had her ports of call
For things that keep body and soul together
Like sugar, tea, a loaf, spare ribs and lard,
And things the big ship brings that light the ends
Of years, like oranges. On maps of France

I've trailed him down the chalky roads to where
They end and her on the oldest A to Z
Down streets, thin as a wraith, year in, year out
Bidding the youngest put her best foot forward,
Lugging the rations past the war memorial.

Kaluga

Early, alone, before her teeth are in
She opens the morning paper and sees this:
A photo of a man in battledress
Masked so he has no nose or mouth or chin

But eyes, a surgeon's eyes, and bare
Hands. He tilts a skull
On his knee like a ventriloquist to pull
A living from it with pliers. And where

Do they dig like this? What foreign field? A place
She muddled up with Golgotha and said
Over and over when she went to bed

Aloud to nobody. She sees a face,
All of it suddenly, and a glimpse of gold
Top left, in 1940, when he smiled.

'Stuck fast'

Stuck fast, both eyes gone, not long dead –
Only a ewe in lamb, but I suppose
Whatever has a heartbeat and a head
Its terror is much the same. This seems devised

By one of those people (and there must be some)
Whose daydreams on the beach or driving home
Are 'cruel and unusual punishments'
For if they get the chance – but isn't. Is

Mother Nature straight: a slit of mire
In which you fit exactly, the working feet
Nothing to purchase on, you know you are

Desperately visible, but only from the skies.
Nothing will come however loud you bleat
Except the thing that wants your bulging eyes.

'Eyeballs of quartz'

Eyeballs of quartz in the harsh conglomerates
The river rolls them back into the sea.
Up there a creature disarticulates
And tinkles downstream: pretty vertebrae,

A gushing skull, the white bars of the heart.
I fished a length out like a runner's baton
And climbed the waterfalls and found the start
And finish of the clues: a flooding basin,

In it a trap of stones, in that a shank
Caught by the foot, still feeling in the water,
And nothing else: the rest, the weight, the stink,
Was got cleanly away. The piece I brought there

Is fit to lay across the mouth. The remnant
Might wag for ever in its phantom torment.

Lamb

Hats off to the little chap
Eased out like a stool the colour of blood and mustard
On the edge above the sea
And the sea coming in with the wind the colour of steel and charcoal.

Sky like a slaughterhouse. We can't say much about him
But it must be a fact that the field is colder than the womb
And lying curled in there must have been easier
Than trying to stand in the wind on pipecleaners.

Perhaps to be terrified by a sky like this
You need some IQ and to have read the newspapers
And even this field –
Like a battlefield, afterbirths everywhere

And the crows we call the hoodies
The ones with capes of ash
Who are as inclined to mercy as a Kray or a Mengele
And will have your eyes and tongue out if you wander off –

Even a field like this and the corbies treading and tearing at the slung-around
        placentas
Perhaps it only upsets you if you've had an education. Still
The wind, and when I see night coming down
As warm and motherly as the God of Abraham and see him peering out

Through the wire at such a sea
Under a sky more like Cambodia's
Entrails in the jaws of Pol Pot
Than heaven, on his first night among us I say hats off to him.

Endangered Species

No wonder we love the whales. Do they not carry
Our warm blood below and we remember
Falling asleep in a feeling element
And our voices beating a musical way

To a larger kindred, around the world? Mostly
We wake too quickly, the sleep runs off our heads
And we are employed at once in the usual
Coveting and schemes. I was luckier today

And remembered leaving a house in the Dales
Like home for a night, the four under one roof,
I left them sleeping without a moon or stars
And followed my dreaming self along a road.

Daylight augmented in a fine rain.
I had the sensation of dawning on my face.
But for the animals (and they had gathered
The dark standing in fields and now appeared

Replete) the night dissolved, but in the light,
A grey-eyed light, under the draining hills
Some pools of woodland remained and in them owls
And beside my sleepwalking, along the borders

Owls accompanied me, they were echoing
From wood to wood, into the hesitant day
I carried the owls in their surviving wells
Of night-time. The fittest are a fatal breed.

They'd do without sleep if they possibly could
And meter it for the rest of us. I like
Humans who harbour the dark in their open
Eyes all day. They seem more kin, more kind. They are

The ones not listening while the ruling voices
Further impair our hearing. They are away
With the owls, they ride the dreaming hooting hills
Down, down, into an infinite pacific.

Warming

Signs and wonders. We carried an old man
To view his father in the ice.
He is visible in the costume of that day and age

Still ruddy
Like a strapping son. His boy would not come down again
But put on fur

And haunts him, gibbering. I went up higher.
I tell you there is no stillness any more
But groans, chutes and a noise like riddling.

Our little river meanwhile
Continues innocently in the usual voice
But we are remembering the accidents

And murders hereabouts. Who will be called
Each to his own
And lie face down on the clarifying ice

Over a wound in bloom?
At nights I listen to the little river
Prattling as though there were nothing more to say.

But think of the melt behind the teeth of the moraine
And look at the map: up fifty thousand valleys
Ice and gentians

Are ebbing away from us
To a sunny crown.
Has anywhere

For so much backing up
Widened the mouth enough to speak it
And the eyes to weep?

Athens

Dig where you like, you soon hit marble.
We slop our concrete over some wonderful things.
See where we cleared away to start again:
A temple of Aphrodite Ourania shows through.

Another hot night. Bullfrogs. Rats. The drains.

A citizen squats in a greenish light
Hawking videos, all dirty.
Many kinds of bug fall on his head
And a little old mother holds him by the ear for a chinwag.

Deeper, deeper
The electric rides us into the agora.

Master and Man

'Punto bläst Magnifique'

MOZART TO HIS FATHER,
(PARIS, 5 APRIL 1778)

1

Giovanni Punto, born Jan Václav Stich
At Tetschen, now Zehusice, in 1746,
Belonged to Wenzel Joseph, Graf von Thun,
But ran away when he was twenty to have a life of his own.

2

He was a hornplayer, the best in his day,
Best ever perhaps. Mozart wrote him K
297b, the *Sinfonia Concertante*, and Beethoven
The *Horn Sonata*, Opus 17.

3

Count Wenzel Joseph though was furious
For he had put money where Jan's mouth was,
Sent him to masters, the best, in Prague, Munich and Dresden
And wanted a long return on his investment.

4

Now he put money on Giovanni's head.
The ungrateful little swine is mine, he said,
What he produces is my property,
Every silver note. You bring him back to me

5

Or knock his front teeth out. Of this poor man,
Perhaps not one of the best of the von Thun clan
But who for all I know was kind to animals,
Feared God and listening to music in his soul's

6

Best part had once or twice been shown
Love, freedom, joy, nothing is known
Except his dates and in between the two
That thing he sent his bully-boys to do.

7

Easy to imagine Giovanni Punto
On a cloud in heaven playing the silver cor solo
Made for him in Paris by Joseph Raoux, the best,
And poor Graf Wenzel Joseph in distress

8

Sending to Father Abraham for one note
Of the waters of that horn to cool his throat,
Tongue, lips, and being told there is
Between a soul in torment and a soul in bliss

9

A great gulf fixed. I hope instead
He served his time in purgatory before he was dead –
At nights, dreaming it done, the worst, dreaming it carried out,
And woke, and wept for gratitude that it was not.

10

Wenzel was dead. Jan Václav Stich went home
King, through a multitude. His turn come,
He had himself sent off with Mozart's *Requiem*,
Mercy enough in it for both of them.

'Figures on the silver'

Figures on the silver, black;
Their game ending already.
I remember the game: the tide has to be just right.
Cognizance of the sands is also necessary.

Children and a dog. There should always be a dog.
He will not know the rules, he is the game's spirit,
Mad streaker through, mad circler of it.
He runs off the excess, or raises it.

The flat white island is so beautiful.
But the children are not there to be a spectacle,
They want the edge of the tide's exact sickle,
They can hardly wait, they beg the boundary

Come on, come on, come on.
The advance of pleasure over little ridges
And something in you somewhere sobbing make it stop,
Come on, come on. I remember that. It does

Come on, the runners have it warm around their ankles
Like skipping-ropes. The dog
Torpedoes them. This is the real game now:
Full tosses, slosh and slog,

Everything wet and sunny. They are bare shadows,
Substantial, quick, intensely black shadows,
Boys and girls cannot be told apart,
And all their vocables, rising this far,

Are only calls and cries. I should hate to be God
Or one among the dead watching from here.
How they must ache to give up the condition
And join the running on the water.

I know the game. How long will they play?
How deep? Stumps drawn
And floating with the bat, driftwood again.
The pitch is lidded under wrinkled steel.

The breathless dog has climbed this far, to me.
Perhaps I wished it, whistled him maybe,
Inclined myself, and felt his salty snout
Suddenly slobbering my drylander hand,

And the ball in it, the balding mangy ball,
The ball for the game, for more and more of the game.
He grins, he has Ben Gunn's demented eyes.
I scrumped you this from paradise, he says.

Kinder

That feather on the brow a mile away
Is water, the Downfall
Doing its uttermost to get over the edge
But hasn't the body and the wind erects it.

This is a queer place I have brought you.
More like a brain than acres of the open earth.
As complicated as a brain and spongey;
But black, all black. If water had volition

This dome would be its nightmare. The peat
Takes everything: false hopes, false starts,
Every crazy aberration. It rains,
The sky forgets, but where we are

The new arrival of water goes over them all again
And deeper. In the fogs
The thread you were following in these soft ravines
Ends. I never saw so many ends

Loose, sad, dead. Try climbing out –
Something's the matter with gravity
Or with your legs. Go in again,
Go deeper. Then nowhere, nowhere hopeful,

Suddenly you sense a slope, there is a downhill after all,
And you are setting right (how easily
Water can solve a labyrinth
That tilts) and you come clear and the lost tongue

Of water, the purling, the babbling,
Comes back to you and hungry for the edge, grateful,
The body strips – and hits up against that wind
And rises contrary to nature like a ghost

On view. My head is clear today.
I think I can lead you from the plume of water due east.
I seem to remember a cairn on the far edge.
There, in the lee, the water gets off headlong.

Bombscare

But we have bombscares. There was one this spring
The day before my birthday. I went in wanting
The OS map of another island
And sniffed the hush, the hush and a change in the air,
The two together: spring come and a bombscare.

A plastic tape was run all around the centre
Slight and symbolic as a sabbath wire
And nobody transgressed. The sentries
Had nothing much to do, but everyone expelled
From making a living in the centre idled

In shirt sleeves and blouses on the first day warm enough
With those kept out. You feel let off
Idling on the outside if you have to. Inside
It's like a site two thousand years from now
Uncovered clean. A police car like a UFO,

The blue light twirling. You feel absolved
More still when word comes out the thing was shelved
Among the goods a year ago at least.
The thought of it lying where you often came and went,
Its time not yet, is like a present

Coming from where you could not know one might. The tape
Ran to the shop but let me in. Sat on the step
In the sort of respite Sunday mornings used to make
Or overnight deep snow. Sat in the sun
And opened the map of another island there and then.

On the empty blue it floats like an elm-seed.
Seems mostly rock. The thin yellow road,
Run from a steamer route on the east coast,
Includes some tumuli, a standing stone or two,
A ruined oratory in the noose of its lasso.

Fifty tomorrow. From off the west coast
Peninsulas push out. The one pushing the farthest,
I fix on that. Sweet, sitting in the sun
While a man with nifty fingers whose job it is,
Breathing quietly, makes a timebomb harmless.

Don Giovanni and the Women

The notes are there, the dust is always there
And being sorted into arias
And shapes that answer to particular names

Again they feed his everlasting fire
And lapse into the cold with other flames
And cannot tell which ash was ever theirs

The ghostly women coming with a list
Who wanted naming like the glorious dead
They sift among the ashes and the notes

Their mouths are wide, they want his pulsing blood
Among the huddle every listed ghost
Wants her particular music in her throat.

Troubled by the airs of hell the dust assumes
More likenesses than anyone can bear.

A Meeting in the Library

Some good angel should have prevented this
But he is in love and all the angels are against him.
Chances, lots, coincidences
Fall in a way to hurt him, he is too much in love.
So looking up from reading about a courtly world,
Ordeals in hope, rewards for the brave, mercy,
He meets her eyes. Nothing is comparable,
Nothing so serious has been or will be again.
For in a moment of the purest ice
He sees what he cannot live his life without
Withheld. She is small, slight,
There is no blood on her lips, there are no serpents in her hair,
Her wrists are thin, her power is a terrible burden.

Then somebody tilts a window in that gallery
And the sun goes over the portraits of the poets
And the feeling tumbles into him again
After her lightning, and every writing in the library

Clamours to be uttered through his parted lips
And every line of writing has to do with hopeless love.
Nothing is worse, she knows it, she is a yard away,
They stand like statues between the banks of poetry
And for her the tongue in his mouth is a dead letter.

Llyn Conach

Sky bending over a water still hidden;
Track to the lip of it; familiar
Rising feelings; the eyes
Already wide for the moment of inrush. But then

The shock of this lake was peculiar
Like a crack through me. I saw
The ghost of myself passing from right to left
Along the rim, from those low hills

To that black plantation, anxious.
The gulls were clamouring and that tuft
Of an island and the couple of skiffs
Tethered and prancing on the agitated water were witnesses.

I can't date him exactly, couldn't tell you
How many times the skin of his hands has come and gone since then
But he was anxious, one summer evening, late,
Looking for somewhere to shut his eyes out of sight.

The wind is continuous, the serial
Of gulls runs on and on with the same clamour,
You would go into me twice, with a remainder,
But now we have come over the lip to this agitated water

Come closer in. I have the desire
To house you out of the wind under the slant roof
And within the walls of me. The wind
Is dressing your face in your sheer black hair

And I can't see until my hands go looking under. Then
Eastings and northings give a unique place
Time lights it once and you
You rush my heart, love, with the cold draught of a revenant.

Comfort me with Apples

It makes me think of the men of the island of Pitan
Who lived off the scent of apples
And only that. Whenever they travelled
They took wild apples with them, to breathe in.

The sublimation of apples into pure savour,
The spirit of apple, the invisible apple platonic
Was all they ever wanted. Any vapour
Grosser than ghostly apple made them sick.

They were small men, Mandeville says, and had
No mouths. They lived on a river island in the East
Not far from Eden and the eye of God.

We can try, I suppose. It might not be easy
Doing without the flesh of apples and the waters of taste.
The mouth's the problem. Still, we can always try.

'You make the rules'

You make the rules. I rhyme ab ab
And think perhaps two tercets would be best.
They seem less final. So: cd cd
And efg repeated. For the rest

You say, I'll follow on. I scan the stuff
Ti-tum, ti-tum, ti-tum, ti-tum, ti-tum.
Getting the measure right's easy enough
And all the rest, the life of us, must come

To you to know what shape it should be in
And look like, feel like, do. Seems what we had
We haven't now and what we could we can't.

You are too soft for so much discipline.
Seems what seemed good not long since now seems bad.
Seems I must fit my baulked love how you want.

Sleep With

Can't even dream about you. The censors
Squat at the gates of horn and will not let you through
Until last night, incognita. I was sure it was you

And seeing you where you are not allowed to be
I supposed you had changed your mind and I ran headlong
To the one point again. Supposed wrong.

Behaviour is final in the underworld. They say:
I think I shall die of shame. And hear:
You can't, you have, and you will be ashamed for ever.

Sad. But listen. The next thing I knew
From that one point all my desires flew
Slowly, sweetly, they were sent away

Down routes of sleep, travelling to the ends of me
And nowhere touched on you more hungrily
Than your own sleep does and I was sure

This centrifugence suited you, for everywhere
We joined as easily as water, air or fire
And passed in give and take through truce to peace,

Levelling. I am sure it was you
And the way I lent myself to metamorphosis
Is like a gift I never knew I had. But now

The images that come to tell you how we met,
How light it was and how it played from head to toe
Like sunshine, like a warm sea fret,

All without panic, all without fear of doing any ill,
Seem disallowed, seem a touch gross, as though
My absence, finer and finer, would suit you better still.

'That place again'

That place again, the blank seawall,
The fact of the wall, like a wall of death, the sea
Slews off it at an angle calculable
And sickening, can't break, its energy

Gets swallowed back. In daylight, miles inland,
Still mulling over that dumb repetition,
This dawned on me as well: there was no wind,
Not a breath, not a whisper, and there was no moon,

Not a ghost, not a sliver, such unease
Wanting a mover, a sufficient cause,
A cold slant wind, a cold too-close full moon.

The sea in that place troubles me inland
Still heaving at it long after the last
Bright slip of her averted face was lost.

Cycladic Idols

In the night there were owls, so close
One on the chimney pot calling back
As though she had found me and were summoning the others.

The flat white face has visited again.
I warm my hands on coffee in a fired clay.
This bitter morning I am willing to listen.

Grow up, she says.
Your grown-up son was right not to sleep with me.
He has a healthy fear. Grow up yourself.

You will never see me in the flesh
Only in the bone.
Your eyes are incorrigible

As though a nipple in each would cool your migraine
Likewise your hands
Small and ugly and with bitten nails

As though one laid on my pubic bone would warm me through
Will they never learn? Again and again:
Where I belong is never warmer than moonlight

You had no right to fetch me in
I do not belong on your pillow
Your son was right to turn my face to the wall.

Owls are friendlier. I hug myself
For cold and nobody else
And nobody hugs me.

'All night the rain'

All night the rain and the little stream
Hurrying it away off the hill into other streams.
Why can't he sleep? Why can't the water be
For him a sweet accompaniment as it is for me?

And the wind, that I am warm and out of it
How this comforts my sleep and if I wake and listen
To the wind and the rain and the hurrying water
Sleep bides by me, I can turn to my sleep again.

His face in the morning, you would say
This hill and all the great hills east had been
His to run off the water from and the rain
Was him as well and he could only increase.

Why can he not rest? He says when first light came
He dreamed badly. Did I not hear him cry?
In nightmare he thought the wind was me and I
Had crossed the space and swung his hesitant door.

'The lakes, their stepping down'

The lakes, their stepping down
From one small lozenge of water
With skeeters on
And the wild horses come to the lip
With coats the colours of sedge.

I was higher still
Nearly asleep against the megalith
In a bluish mist
And heard the larks above it in the clear
Lifting the origin
Higher still.

From there
To here
Gift upon gift.

Cupping your hands like that reminded me.

'Mid-afternoon in another narrow bed'

Mid-afternoon in another narrow bed
High up in another thin hotel
Now they are watching swifts crossing the snow
And higher, higher, higher criss-crossing the blue.

Freed of their own they think the swifts' hunger
A love of life, and life all play,
All bodying forth some consummate ability
For the love of it, in freedom. Later when they go down

On the choking streets to seek a sharp red wine,
Succulent bitter olives, soft white bread
And oranges, and when they hear
The caged birds hung on balconies as though to test the air

Each in its shaft of sun
Singing as though to burst the heart and the cage
These two seeking their nourishment when they please
By that trapped singing will feel their hunger raised

Higher than the highest floor of their flung-up hotel,
Higher than the ravenous swifts, higher than the snow
Into the blue itself, the keen
Cold infinite and insatiable blue.

Honey from Palaiochora

It is hard to make out where Palaiochora is
    From here. You have to look up, higher up
Than you'd ever think there could have been a town, and find
    The upright that is not a wavy cypress tree
And that's the tower, still standing, lifted like a minestack,
    A pale sign. The rest is above and below
On ledges but even after you've been up there,
    Even with the sun on it and though you find
The Venetian belfry that has stood through earthquakes,
    Still hard to believe from here. On the island
In spring being in or out of the sun is black and white:
    You huddle, out; but in you open up.

When we got down from finding Palaiochora,
    Carrying our heavy honey in a jar,
We made tea in a glass with a wheel of lemon in,
    Golden, and dug at the honey there and then,
Dripping it on broken bread with spoons. The sun rode down
    The line of the hill of Palaiochora
Full in on us. We slid the windows wide, we stripped,
    Every stitch off both of us, I took
The lingering honey and lemon off his tongue
    And had his hand and the sun together
Between my legs, idling, the way I wanted it,
    Slowly, slowly, so that they gave me time

For all the roofless houses of Palaiochora,
    Gone in now under the lee of the sun, back
Into the hill with all their clever paths and steps,
    To appear behind my eyes: flowers, flowers,
White irises and asphodel, poppies and drifts
    And flounces of purple vetch where people slept
And where they cooked and talked and over their wells and walls
    From level to level through their workplaces,
Terrace into terrace ushering through flowers and
    Everyone long since gone, centuries gone,
Except in the unroofed chapels under the sun
    Where it came and went and they were warm or cold

Only the fresco angels, they had stayed, they looked
    Ghostly in the day, ghostly in the flowers,
Being made for the dark and to come out glowing
    Under a roof with candles and now revealed
And fading day by day in the visiting sun:

Angels blessing, angels announcing, but with
Faces of the boy or girl you would wish to have,
   Earthly, pleased, lifted, and showing a pale palm
For a sign where we found them, tall as adolescents,
   In the irises and the purple. Then I
Was in shadow, his, his hot shade, and felt for the sun
   Down the line of his back and as though he were

The sun I pulled him in, in, to ensure in me
   Before the lingering angels faded
Some seed of the flowers of Palaiochora
   Heaped in the standing frames of empty homes
Like quilts and linen, to have them body and soul
   Before the message and the blessing failed
In me while he was doubled by the sun I widened
   Where he reached and gave and met. Then waking,
Opening real eyes on a room replete with sun,
   Sun held on us above black cypress candles,
I saw our jar of honey. It was lit from in,
   From in itself. I saw that first. It shone.

SOMETHING FOR THE GHOSTS

(2002)

Nude

How simple it is: day knocks
And somebody opens, the shutter opens in
And in come light and warmth together as one and the same
And where she stands
Is neither a circle of privacy
Nor the arena of a performance
But only a small round mat for her feet on the cold tiles
While under an empty mirror
She bows to the water lifted in her hands
And sideways on her sunlight comes in from the garden
And on her back there is a man's admiration.

You will say it is only a picture, another nude
But I say it has been that simple:
Jug, basin, washstand, towel and chair
The plain nouns, and a woman at a meeting place
Of warm sunlight and loving admiration
And easy feeling both.

Something for the Ghosts

Here's something for the ghosts who are
No one now and can't come up against
The edge of anyone else: that heavy skirt,
Your bare cold feet come out from under it,
Their print, black wet, on the slabs of slate

For days. Poor ghosts, where they are mine and thine
Flit like snowflakes, drift like mist, not like
My grasp of your black hair, the rain in it,
The smell of the rain that I breathed in after
For days. Poor gibbering ghosts, when they have done

Their best with bits of sound to shape someone
They knew or thought they knew or wished they had
It never amounts to anything more than this
Ghost of a mouth with questions in such as
Who were you and who did you think I was?

Dear Reader

His first morning, theirs together the first,
A white mist filled the deep hospital garden
Even to the lip of her windows
All the arrangement gone in a silent boiling

On and on went the mist into the open country
All the particularities went under it
As far as the hills that she had promised me
And they were all alone like a school of islands

As far away as moons. In that condition
She sank again into the trance of reading
His head had interrupted
One long novel adding upon another

Like a child in winter, perhaps convalescent,
And the shadows of people who loved her came and went
And while he fed and slept and fed
Her eyes were on a page, her fingers left

The soft pulse of his silky fontanelle
To turn another page. She agreed with him
That he must thrive and smiled and winced at his savage focusing
On her and loved him best

When he slipped from her nipple back into the welter
Of nothing belonging yet, no shape, no form,
And she began again in another situation
Somewhere not here, in at the seeding,

Sexing, naming, in at the jostling
Of destinies against their author, she was merciless
On females wistful over roads not taken
And coming to an ending she undid the knot

And slept among the fray of possibilities
The white mist feeling for a slit of warmth
The level solvent going on and on
As far as the hills that lay apart, shining.

The House

You won't forget the house
Will you? I never will.
The south wind rattled the sash
And rain came in on the sill

And the wind denuded the moon
White and the white of the tide
Wheeling into the wind
Lifted, showed and frayed

And the sun came out of the sea
And all that way across
Easily found the house,
The bed, the looking-glass.

Remember the house so well
That somebody else elsewhere
Will say, 'We had a house
The same as where you were

But a hundred miles from the sea
And it was the north that blew
And the sky was as sheer as steel
And everything flared and flew

Stubble went down the wind
The oaks were filled with a voice
And the stars in the Milky Way
Screamed like a slide of ice

And the sun that found our bed
Rose over oaks and a hill
But the house was surely the same
Except for the sash and the sill

And there was a looking-glass
And though they were mine and hers
The faces shown by the sun
Might have been hers and yours

You remember it all so well
That except for the south and the sea
That was surely the house
Except for her and me.'

Sleepwalker

I watched her window from a vantage point.
The sash was pushed up, with the daylight,
Very early, came a steady breeze.
The gap, the blowing through, and her white curtains:
Easy to imagine that she ran towards me
Or that she had flitted for ever
And day and night changing and any weather
Could visit as they liked now and would make no difference.
But I did my level best to think of her asleep
With an open face and open palms
Fast asleep in the summer early daylight
The outdoors streaming coolly over body and soul
Asleep under the inrush of good spirits
Whose shape for entering was the light curtains
Their being raised and flounced and almost steadily laid out
Slant to their quivering limits at her bed. Easy to imagine
Tide-set my way and all
The lovely underwater waking dress and hair
Streaming back. I watched and watched
And I suppose that I was trusting some deep warning
Such as swifts have in their sleeping downward spirals
That I would quit and be gone back into hiding
Before any strangers came.

Man and Wife

He wakes like someone shouted for, she lies
After in the violent lights thinking am I
Invisible, am I already dead?
Trying not to let her ghost go after his
Into the wind and the rain or under the sharp stars
With coughing foxes. He has phoned the police
To say if ever they catch him in their beams
Lopsided, savage and helpless as a badger
To let him be, it's not against the law
To walk the old road between the sea and the marsh
And listen at gaps and holes in the sand dunes
For what it really sounds like, and to get in
As far as he can without sinking, in among
Countless thousand starlings fastened on the reeds
And listen, if that is trespassing, so what?
Who cares? She does, she thinks they should lock him up
For his own good, for hers, for everyone's:
Eavesdropper, voyeur, night after night
Trying to see things as though he were dead and gone,
Trying to be slantways on, trying to get behind,
To be in the deep unease of the marsh and not
Interfere and witness the sea as it used to be
When nothing was watching but the stars. He comes home
A secret way over the old mines, over terrain
Probed and tunnelled and thoroughly gone into
And now for ever liable to sudden appearances
Of wells of water in which the yellow moon
Or a fearful human peers. She draws the curtains
And sees him mounted like a scarecrow on the boundary hedge.
She cannot make him a sign of recognition.
Perhaps he has found how far under their dwelling
The old galleries go, he is watching the tabs
On things, the sounds for house and home, come off
And blow away, he wishes it, traitor, accomplice
He has got beyond the pale and night after night now
Against house and home he will side with the wind.

On the Cliffs, Boscastle

The bulk, thin flora, hunched here like a crow,
Sky red as poppy, black
As the heart of a poppy, some long way below
Slop slop, the constant cuffing of the sea.

Not sensible, too perilous, watching black
Burst slowly from the heart. If fell,
More like a brainless stone, not like a crow.
The red sops up the black. It welcomes it.

Fiddle in a cavity top left with a stalk of last year's thrift,
Meanwhile a black detachment troops away,
Sniff at the stick, gawp at the ghosts, sniff, sniff,
Already its little virtue has gone off it.

Get back, on hands and knees snuffling a track
While there's still blood in the sky, get back
To the B & B and your scented mate
Between silk sheets after her bath, get her on you

To practise, practise, practise the kiss of life.

Monologue

or

The Five Lost Géricaults

*(In the last years of his life Géricault did ten portraits
of monomaniacs. Only five have survived. My four
characters, and their narrator, might be those lost.)*

Commander Olleranshaw at Number 33,
With him it's dogshit, he's out every day
Chalking a ring round every load he finds
And sticking a flag in it, such lovely hands
He has, like a brain surgeon's, poor man
While everyone sensible's watching television
He's in behind his curtains making little flags
And muttering how many tons of dogshit dogs
Do every day. Don't get me wrong: he's right,
I've counted fifty flags just on our street
Between here and the Post Office: times that
By all the streets in Eccles and you'll get
Some idea of the problem and of course
That's only Eccles. No, what I meant was
I'd hate to wake with only one thing on the brain
Every morning, it must be terrible, I mean
There's more to life than your one big idea
However big. That woman's another,
'Sins of the World' I call her, still in bed
Her duty opens like an 'A to Z',
The bits all finish in another bit
And if she ever got to the end of it,
Which she won't, she'd have to start again,
Us being the way we are, she's grown
A special nail for lifting wrappers with
Or bus tickets, for getting underneath
One of their edges when the wet has stuck them flat,
I watched her half an hour clawing like that
On one of my off days, walking, walking, follow
That madman Olleranshaw you hear him bellow
And curse the world to hell but follow her
Just soft tut-tuts, she's like a creature
Only come about because the duty did,
And went by evolution the shape needed –
Humped, with a shoulder up, and swagged with bags,
Tut-tut, pick-pick, scrape-scrape, it plagues
My nights thinking how many bags you'd fill
If you took it seriously after the Council

Has given up, I think of terrible places,
The bus stop where they chuck their takeaways
And outside school and how the winter
Under the hedges shows how bad we are
And think of the graveyard rolling with empties,
Prickly with needles, slippy with condoms – suppose,
I think, she ever thinks of that, dear God
Better by far she got it into her head
Her duty ran to shovelling up the things
With flags in in that madman's rings
Only not what's littering our cemetery.
Now wouldn't you think that any God of Mercy
Worth His salt would send her deepest snow
One early morning, snow on snow on snow,
So she'd see cleanliness on earth for once
Or Jesus give her something for her conscience
In the wine, a worming thing, in the loving cup
Some efficacious dose to make it stop
Whispering through the miles of her insides
She'll never do well enough however hard she tries?
Poor Sins of the World, the world or her
One of us will have to change and it won't be her,
Barring miracles. These people,
They ask a lot of us. For example
That chap who's always smiling at everyone,
His trouble is he wants nothing bad to happen,
Smiling, nodding, bowing at anyone
The bad might come from, which is everyone,
And making little magic jerks, his trouble is
He wants no one to notice him, he says:
'I'm nobody, I'm nothing, I'm not here
To speak of hardly, please don't bother
Your boot with me, don't trouble your fist',
He wants to be like them in with the rest
Where the bad might come from not outside
Where it's coming to. Bright-eyed
Mr Smiley with the very eager face
Some days he has to turn away and practise.
I suppose those are his very fearful days.
I hear him saying 'after you' and 'please,
No, after you' and 'thank you, thank you, thank you'
And 'sorry', the way we do, only more so,
All that rehearsing to sound ordinary
So when he speaks the world won't say 'Who's he?
Who's this queer chap, why don't we tar
And feather him, poor chap, why don't we saw
His head off slowly and stick it on a pole

And why's he wet?' I nod, I bow, I smile,
I roll my hands at him, 'Cheer up,' I say,
'Nothing bad might happen and almost certainly
Not as bad as that and saying please all day
Won't help and practising and anyway
You do it very well.' Funny round here,
When you weigh up, how many folk go queer.
There's that lad living at the yellow door
Though lad's not right, nor living, it's more
Like falling what he does, the way things do
In outer space, comets or angels, falling slow
But falling, surely falling. Anyway
With him it's bicycles. I counted twenty-three
Downstairs, all wrecks except for two,
One ladies' and one kiddies', they're brand new
And bought, he says, the rest he nicked or found,
Frames on the stairs and handlebars around
The toilet and his bed, bikes without wheels
Like little crippled horses. I say it's bicycles
But the other thing he does is fall in love
With girls who'll speak to him and several have
Over the years within a radius
Of fifty miles of his double bed and his
Graveyard of bikes, most recently
In Diggle one in the Public Library,
He rode to see her on a Raleigh Twelve Speed,
One working, high, no brakes, and waited.
Nobody waits like him, I've watched him wait
Hours outside a teashop in Gallowgate
Where another works who spoke to him.
'The trouble is,' I said, 'you frighten them.'
'All I want's some female talking with,' he said.
I thought of the little radio by his bed,
In it more like, and his finger fiddling at
The tiny tuning wheel in hopes he'll get
Some female still awake at 3 a.m.
Who'll speak. Trouble is he frightens them –
Straight limbs, clear skin, long curls – honest to God
The word for him I should have used's not lad
But youth, lost youth, angel
Falling, falling. That's what the women smell:
Pheromones of loneliness, a musk of fear
Of falling further, further, further, further,
That's how he waits outside the library,
Outside the teashop and that's what they see,
The women he loves: the abyss. He'll pull me in
With eyes like that if I speak to him again.

The hands give you away, so do the shoes
But most of all it's in the eyes it shows
What's eating you, some days it seems to me
Half's staring at the other half, very hungry
Even in the café or especially there,
Or perhaps it's only Eccles. That writer,
I call him that though I've never seen him write,
The way he looks and hugs his scribbles tight
In a bundle two feet thick, he's like a bear
The way he growls in his overcoat and hair
And beard that have got so long they've given up.
It makes me itch to look at him, can't stop
Looking across at him, whatever the heat
That hair, that overcoat, however sweet
And light yourself might be he makes you sweat
Only looking at him. Last week, the worst I've had
Lately, I took my tea across, I said:
'For Christ's sake take your coat off, sit and write
Something, here's a pen, here's a clean white sheet,
Sit still, stop scratching, write something,
All you do in here is sit there mumbling
And hugging that.' 'No fucking good,' he said,
'Can't do it, can't speak a word that's good
Next to another word, can't even say,
So that it makes you cry out loud, the way
That girl serving watches the clock and the door
About now when that lad will come in or
He won't, I mean the dread she's in he won't
Or will, her exact way of suffering, I can't
Say even that so that it hurts, that's how
No fucking good I am.' 'Then why, I'd like to know,
Do your hug your bundle like a honeypot?'
'Because,' he said, 'it's all I've fucking got,
It's what I've done, it's what I can't still do,
Not even that, and that was no good too.'
'I see,' I said. 'So you sit and itch instead?'
'Sweat, scratch and itch,' he said, 'until I'm dead.'

Dramatis Personae

1 *Chorus*

Not much of a role, on the sidelines
Moaning over Somebody Else's error
And always worried something worse would happen
Which it always did. Mostly we got things wrong:
Asked the gods (the wrong gods) for a particular mercy
That was the worst imaginable affliction
As it turned out. How they must have laughed.
We were continually amazed. 'Well, I never did!'
And 'Fancy that!' were our catchphrases.
We had less gumption than the Servant
And far less understanding than the Messenger
And never (thank God) saw into the heart of life
The way Somebody Else did. We talked a lot
But it never prevented anything
Or comforted those going to the slaughter
And our summings-up were so laborious
And events in such a hurry
Often, to be honest, we lost the plot.
But we gave the language some memorable sayings:
'Cheer up, it might never happen', for example,
And 'When in doubt, do nowt'.

2 *Servant*

What happened any fool could see it would.
Do this, it will. They did, and so it did
And in they went up to their necks wide-open-eyed
When any blind man could have told them don't.
Always in public too, they had no shame,
Our lords, they thumped their children, laid about
Their wives, swore terrible oaths what they
Would do to every mortal soul if this
Or that, so help them God, amen, which is
Asking for it. Always in front of us
Who stood there like the furniture until
One of our betters said fetch him, kill her,
Clean up. Did no one ever teach them, On
Your own head be it, what you reap you sow,
Don't piss into the wind? Or any manners?
We stood there watching for the Messenger.

280

Then how they roared, always in public too,
And flailed around and tore their hair and stabbed
Their eyes and cut their bollocks off and said
Some god has done this, friends, oh see, some god
Has made me mad. Some god, my arse.

3 *Messenger*

Spare a thought for me. I brought the news
Which was always bad and all the worse in the end
If it ever looked good. From somewhere offstage
Me and my news as fast as possible
Were always getting nearer. Meanwhile onstage
The lords were continuing as though it had not happened
But it already had, the star was dead,
I was the last light, travelling, travelling,
And in the space before the scream began
I got my message into shape, so with decorum
To spill the guts. I was the word that kills
In person. Sometimes on my announcement
Came the sight itself: a lord with the staggers,
Blood in the lovely apples of the eyes,
Dead progeny. Spare a thought for me,
I was there, I was everywhere
Where the worst came true, I saw the lot,
It was my job to bring it home to you,
I have it all by heart still, every line.

Mosaics in the Imperial Palace

Maximianus with eyes of marble oversees
The transportation of the animals out of Africa
Across a sea awash with divinities
And stuff to eat. He stands on the littoral

At an entrance wound into Africa
And the beasts are like a bleeding that will never stop
So long as the vast heart pumps
And it will for ever. In the old world by now

There is less shade for travellers on the highways
And for the beasts less hiding, but Africa
Is an eternal covert and the sea
No human engine will ever sieve it out.

Maximianus has seen everything or enough
To pre-empt the rest. *Nil admirari.*
It is all one: John Dories and the pearly unicorn,
Jackals and spouting tritons. Pitiless

To the Big Top animals trussed, spiked,
And hauled up gangplanks by their tender snouts
And to the monsters pitiless
Who are so encumbered by their heads and horns

And so bewildered by the common daylight
That man the hunter easily presses them
For Rome. Maximianus is not amused
Even by Orpheus and his myriad games

Of mixing: human babes
With wings riding the dolphins; a centaur
Trotting with a gift; a griffin smiling. Orpheus
Playing Cupid between the kinds: a lady

In her mirror showing a white rhinoceros
Their good looks. Watery Orpheus
Practising sympathy and dissolution, shapes
Unshaping, the restless slop and throw

Of drafts and chances, trials of fins and feelers,
The cleft thighs closing in a mermaid,
Leviathan turning with a wink
Into a tippling horn of plenty.

Maximianus Herculius supposes
That Rome's belly and Rome's eyes
Will gorge for ever on the sea and on Africa
And if not there are other Africas

To bleed as many beasts and wonders
As there are sprats in other seas
Or tesserae in the marble mountains
For man the maker to record that it was so.

Dominion

Dear God, if you can imagine us, Man,
Without a chain-saw in our hands or the gun
Or looking away from the prices on the screen
For half a minute, even then in that
Even by you perhaps unimaginable state

The truth is we're not good enough, never were,
Never will be, we're not fit, we don't fit in,
Nothing will live with us except the viruses
And dogs and lice, nothing likes us down here,
Everything else is subtler, finer, fitter than us.

Take a coral reef: we come visiting
It gives up the ghost, it's a boneyard by morning,
Spectral groves. And that's us all over,
The ashes, the fallout, whatever we come near
Even in white, with a gauze over the gob,

We're the kiss of death. Dear God, that day
In Eden when you made Adam boss
What a catastrophe, even you must see it by now,
Anything would have been better than us,
A dodo, for example, a booby, a diplodocus.

The Llandudno Town Band

High water behind them the town band
Give us a tune while the sun goes down
Which it does too soon
Leaving us cold in the lee of the big headland

The old and the very old in stripy deckchairs
Recumbent under wraps like a year ago
And some drawn up alongside in flash new wheelchairs
The same old crowd, minus the passed away,

Huddling together on the big prom
Under the vast sky here we are again:
Sacred on Sundays and the profane
Mondays, Wednesdays and Fridays, always at 8 p.m.

Against the surf, under the cackling gulls
What a brave noise they make, it cheers me up no end:
Fatty the Tuba with the very thick spectacles
Ballooning fast, and his lady friend

(I call her his lady friend) blowing him kisses
The length of her brassy trombone
And two very pretty things, sex unknown,
Winking over their cornets in white blouses.

The gulls jeer and a shrewd wind blows
And but for the plastic clothes pegs in nine bright colours
Away would go the tunes from the shows
Like all the other litter of our yesteryears.

To finish, Dave the conductor promises a solo
But doesn't say it's Sally on the flugelhorn
Or Bob on sax and the regulars know
It's him himself and he'll suddenly turn

And it won't be the twiddling stick he'll hold
But the trumpet and there he'll swell
Facing us all, full frontal
And such a sound will come forth, pure gold

Out of his silver, and not the Last Post
Nor the Last Trump either though I grant you an angel
Recording on the Orme would think it must
Be Jehoshaphat down here – no, our Dave'll

Close his eyes and deliver what he can hear
In his head or his heart or up there in the sky
And give it us neat, give it us proof and pure
On and on, in and in, till every body

And in every body the huddled soul
Shy as an embryo
Hearkens. Then that's it for now,
That's it till Sunday and *Abide With Me* and all

Not stiff for ever get to their feet
And the wheelchair-riders sit up straight
And the team in purple sound and tinkle the tune
For us to hum *Land of My Fathers* and sing *God Save the Queen*

And we do our best but it's not much cop
Against the whole of the Irish Sea
Come very close. The band pack up,
It's cold, the wheelchairs speed away.

Encouragements

One devoted lunatic, I forget who,
Said if he closed his eyes on the right night,
Cloudless of course, every five years or so
And lifted his bare face and kept his eyes shut tight

And said how lucky he was and how grateful
He felt a touch of warmth from her face on his face
Down a quarter of a million miles of empty space
And on these rare surrenders he got by pretty well.

But another, again I forget who,
Said to hell with charity, he lived in hopes of cruelty:
The sudden conviction of a door opening behind you,
Ice down the spine, you turn to look, and she

Is leaning under the lintel with nothing on.
The smile. The 'How about this?' And gone.

Drunk Locked in Music Room Wrecks Grand

The five holes of his sometime face had run.
His voice came up like an experiment,
Gas over phlegm. He wanted out, it said.
A night like this? Moon like a burning glass
Of cold, snow hard as quartz, the wet
Between his legs would set fast like cement.

But still he wanted out. He must have heard.
Why else not lie low in our cubbyhole
Sleeping and thieving biscuits till a door opened?
He had overheard. One lug cocked like a fox's
Had let the spirits in to wriggle through
The labyrinth for his white bit of soul.

He must have woken to the aftermath
The pause after a blessing while it lasts
The silence filling up with pearly light
And under the Masters with their scrolls and quills
Still listening he dragged his body in
And then his howl began. He could still hear

Order in something fleet and sylph as streams,
Reprises, a looping up again, a sweet
Forgiving try again insistence,
A laving clean, a coming back for stragglers,
A lifting up, a carrying to an end
And then beyond an end, I overheard

The howl, the roar, the man tearing apart
Because he felt his bit of soul panic
Like a lad in a flue, that night so cold and still
Across the city you could hear the farthest bell
And sleep, knowing what o'clock, knowing all is well,
And then he ceased and then the worse began,

The appassionato smashing, such a while
It seems to me still hearing it the teeth endured
And chattered, all the breaking teeth and all
The inner booming over his Weep! Weep!
I came in like the jailor with my keys.
Our brass was in his hand. He wanted out.

Catacombs, Paris

Collecting the photos at the counter next to where
She bought the testing kit he sees what he has done,
She has, they have, down there
In the deepest circle by the font that one
Script called the Samaritan Woman's Well
And the other Lethe. She is displayed
Much like a nude against the knobby wall
Of end-on femurs and humeri, arms wide
Along a dado curve of skulls. Boudoir
Or chapel apse in a kraal of bone of some
Few hundred of several millions of dead,
His lens, the flash, her look of centre spread.
The place? Down there. And when? The morning after
One of his several million sperm went home.

Town Centre

Some drunks upset me, it's the way they sit
Placidly vacant in the public place
Or one who puts his hands together in a prayer
And lays his head on it, where does he think he is
With his cherub snout? That boy under the clock

Upsets me too, turning, turning, he is so on show
With his heart on his sleeve and love writ
Large and hopeless over his silly face
Now she won't come. Here where the milling is
And we dance and stamp we don't want stumbling blocks

We don't want drunks and lovers under our feet
And now that widow outside the United Friendly
Puzzling over an absence in her open shopping bag
She makes another hole in the heart of the place
That wants filling in, and what with?

Mel

Mel wants to be an actress.
And be looked at, Mel?
But it wouldn't be me they would be looking at.

Or a beautician:
Ladies' faces under her gentle hands
Making ladies happier with the way they look.

Mel has razored her lashes off.
From wrist to shoulder bone
She has ruled in all the degrees with a razor blade.

Mel with her stripes
Mel with her bald eyes
Her nightmare is a precinct of Saturday people

Suddenly turning from their fun and their purposes
To look at Mel. She has a pet rabbit
And a guardian angel.

Their looks are kind.
Nothing between a rabbit and an angel
Looks kindly enough on Mel.

She has done me a picture in her English book
Of what it feels like being Mel.
She appears as a naked dolorosa

Fuller of daggers than the mother was.
She looks at me
I fear she will show herself in the shopping mall like that

One Saturday afternoon, with lidless eyes.

J

J has been studying the tyranny
The lengths they went:
A tapeworm, for example.

She composes a letter to *Vogue* on behalf of her speechless sisters
Sign this, she commands.

J knows.

J in the mirror without her clothes
Eggshell, x-ray.
She has parted company with the moon
But sideways on
How far she is still from the line of the clean needle
Its minimal eye
How grossly far.

She would teach her belly obedience
But her belly is a ward of court.

She composes a letter to Doctor Fatman
The force-feeder
Who thinks he knows.

Legger

Casting him off from the sympathetic horses
They shoved him gently into the low hole
Telling him the drift, such as it was, would help him
And that the level of the water would not rise or fall.

He went in snug as a shuttle with a lantern in the bows
About as bright as the light on a glow-worm's tail
And lay on his back the way they had said he must
And began to leg his longboat through the hill

Mile after mile, only as fast as Shanks's
And the sun came and went and the same old stars
Shifted their quarters slowly as it is fixed they will
And he continued his course out of sight of theirs

Treading the slimy ceiling in his hobnail boots
Like a living dead as though to slide the lid
He trod and trod and the heavy water
Squeezed past him with a shudder on either side.

I have had a picnic on that sunny hill
And read 'The Lady of Shalott' to a romantic girl
Hoping it would undress her and lay her down
Smiling under my shadow and my smile

And all the while those thousands of fathoms down
Under the severed ends of sinister lodes
His legs even in his dreams, even dead asleep,
Were trudging along the roof of his one and only road

Long since without even a fag end of light
Even the kindness of dumb animals long since gone from mind
Under the weight of millions of years of rock
And twenty hundred of christian humankind.

He will be a wonder when he comes out of the hill
On our side berthing in the orange water
In the old wharfs among the sunken skeletons
Of the ancient narrowboats, strange as Arthur

In his overalls and the soles of his boots and the soles
Of his feet worn through and no light in his eyes
Under the interest of our savants and our developers
Grinning with horror, rictus of the bad old days.

The Immortals of Landevennec

Ripe with years and over-ripe
   The latest breath they took
However thin was never the last
   And when they slept, they woke.

They were under a hole in heaven's floor
   And from it by day and by night
The light of everlasting life
   Fell on them like a blight.

Through the Judas-trap in heaven's floor
   They could see the radiant dead
Like mirrors mounting up and up
   To a light that might be God.

But where they were, on their terrain,
   They could not live or die.
No heart, no muscle, and their poor souls
   Sick for the hole in the sky.

Inching after death they stayed
   Beneath the dead above
Until in pity or disgust
   An angel told them: Move.

Miraculous, the rush of strength
   To unbuild and build again
Their walls and roof and plant their plots
   Out of sight of heaven

A stone's throw west, nearer the sea,
   Under a normal sky
Where they rejoined the way of life
   And they began to die

In turn, always the oldest first,
   You might say courteously,
As though a fitting thing at last
   Was here allowed to be.

For here the earth was debonair
   And blessed and full of grace.
She turned a little stream their way
   To aid the growing place.

Below their walls, above the sea,
  She brought to light a well.
The sweet was bedded on the salt
  And with it rose and fell.

The stag stood at the chapel door,
  The swallows entered in,
All the needy creatures came
  As though to kith and kin.

The sad immortals housing now
  Out of heaven's way
And free to leave, the sweet earth gave
  Them grounds on which to stay.

Like breath on frost they saw her scent
  Above the wetted thorn
In sun the shivering of her heat
  Above the blonde corn

And through their shining majuscules
  The Green Man shoved his head
And down their margins sprouted lines
  On lovers wanting bed.

The Senator

Sleepless, he asks for the car and an exeat
And slides by moonlight to the usual place
Behind the Palace, the Peace Allée,
Statues among the orange trees, halts at the space

He chose for his. From cap to boot he is as white
As orange blossom or a first communion
Except where he has blackened around the eyes
Like the Palace marble when the shells went in.

Sees her: blacker than a bad tooth in the gap
For his white replica, a mother or one
In love who never did become a mother,
Girl as was, one age now with the eternal crone.

He lifts a white glove against the usual photograph
('These sons and lovers lifted up at me
Like permits to beg, who posed them all,
That trash, so they look like Jesus?') But she

'Senator,' she says, 'may you live long,
A long long eventide in the bosom of the nation.'
What does she know? What has she guessed of his days?
Words of a blessing in the voice of malediction.

Daily, after mass, punctilious young men,
Steely young women, the researchers come,
Younger than his many grandchildren,
They want help with the new curriculum

Or they bring maps, the latest printing,
Spotted with icons for a camp, a cellar,
A pit, and, by magnitude, stars for the clusters.
'Senator,' they ask, 'is that where?'

And lists, always the lists, and photographs,
Often they are photographs of before and after.
They hand him a magnifying glass. 'Look closely.
That face, was that a usual procedure?'

The medals he issued return at every post
Mostly anonymously, but he can tell
From his lists and numbers. 'You too?'
A note sometimes: 'Forgive me. It had begun to smell.'

Every day there are hearings, they are polite,
And excursions in the black car
Or mottled helicopter. So beautiful his land
Looked down upon. 'Is that where they are?'

'Live long,' she says, 'with all of an old man's
Usual ailments, and come here often and see
By moonlight in the soft season how sweet
The city is now, if not for you or me

For the young, for your children's children
Fleeing your name by deed poll, live long
In smells of camp, cellar, pit and daily
The dogshit medals coming home, live on

And stand here often when I have vacated it
In the space you chose, all white except your eyes,
Which will be dark and vast and wormy as your many graves,
Senator, live for ever,' the girl-crone says.

The Grief Coming Out

I heard this from the mother of my dead friend:

How she was sitting still among her ornaments
In a vague discomfort among her photographs
In a vague distress so that she couldn't have said
Where about body and soul it troubled her

When suddenly where there had been a little itching
But nowhere very particular from her wrists and arms
But not from any cut or opening, just so
Blood started out, much blood, and how the doctor
Had said this might be from seven years ago

The grief coming out. There are no witnesses
But I believe her, she sounded so incredulous
As though she had travelled to a primitive shrine
And seen among the silvery ex-votos

This strange effusion happen to a statue.

The Porthleven Man

That Porthleven man keeps coming back to me
Who stood a last round, the usual,
And drank his own up slowly as he always did
And said goodnight one and all and from one and all
Got goodnights back, heartfelt as usual,

But in the cold air turned right not left and slowly,
As he was bound to, went the length of the breakwater
As far as you can go, and further,
And never came up, never came back and his zimmer
Stood there lightly on the edge. Remember

Porthleven, that night, that moon
When the sea came in with most of the horizon
Most of the western hemisphere came in on us
To that one point which is as far as you can go
And planed down the length of the granite breakwater

Like all her dolphins, like one continuous
Making of dolphins and how they rolled and showed
Their bellies to the sleeping port and in
Back into the matrix then, into her sea
Under her pulsing moon gave back,

Always to come again, the dream of them
And very idea? There, then:
Edge, salt, hilarity. All Souls
When his loved ones had given him up for lost
They gathered at opening time on the far end and tossed

Four score and two fiery chrysanths on the black
And level sea. These nights when I wake
The Porthleven man keeps coming back to me.
I need icons, I need people to live up to
Because of your horizons, because of your western sea.

Room Facing Cythera

Because she has a horror of lifts I ascended alone
In that twin coffin of one with the bags to a corridor
Lightless, airless, still as a mortuary
Where I was lost and could not tell which numbers
Which side had the sunless yard and which the sea

Only hope, again, for more than the measure
For more than my deserts again and again
And found her there already turning the key
On a room, an afternoon
More shut to light than the corridor, but she

Like the blinded fending something off
Felt to the window, pushed the wooden lids
And light came in, a bay of it,
All the silver sea of light to Cythera and back
Came in on a southerly, a light

To unclothe in and be shown and seen
From under the arc of the sky unceasingly
Landed in waves. What we did, she and I,
In so much indoor daylight
All down the leisurely slope of that long afternoon

I shut, like crystal in an egg of stone,
In the innermost stanza of my heart. But still
At large, and anyone can hear it, is
The measure of those waves in that place shipping in the light
Neither at bloodpace nor with the long arrival

Of rollers down the Atlantic but in a steady haste
And while I slept all night like one of the blessed
That beat insisted against the slowing of my blood
And still in the morning at the window
When I looked out and found her island gone

In a mist, invisible, unimaginable
The waves, that thudding, though the southerly had ceased
Beat like oars in a quick tempo
And against my heart when I descended, again alone,
Like oars they struck in time towards a certain landfall.

Shabbesgoy

Daylight still, a green sky. At lighting-up time
There was already the thin beginning of a moon, and one star
So that from the streets that smelled of the gasworks and coalfires
And gasps of fighting beer and because of the abattoir
Almost rural he went with clenched fists, wishing hard

Over the river that only transfusions from the factories
Kept going. Or it was winter, fog
In which he left her safe by the street lamp nearest home
Shaped and illumined and vanished immediately
Towards the hospital, its thousand smeared windows.

Him, you. You cannot remember, but I say
That on the hill at the big houses waiting for a lamplighter
Or a firemender they never had anyone luckier than you
The boy courting, radiant, burning, for that small service
Out of his trance of vows and wishes accosted courteously

At the gate, passer-by, who lifted his head that wore
The new moon and her star or shone from the drizzled fog
With the aura of apparition. How queer the rules are
High on the slopes above the dead river,
How quick and simple were your offered hands.

The Hoist

The hoist was strange. Going up, the Nurse said,
First floor haberdashery. Stranger than that
Old word haberdashery, the way he dangled
Under the beak of it like a babe arriving,
Mute in a grim patience, his empty mouth
And his eyes tight shut as if he guarded
A fitter idea of himself in a sort of privacy.

A thing to look away from but we gawped
Like clownish witnesses of an ascension
And I thought of an old mad king still gripping
Tatters of divinity around his shoulders
Or one in a tumbril and the old folk crossing themselves
Or a pharaoh, or a lost god, when the Nurse said
Going down, and settled him in the chair and wheeled him off.

Aphasia

He never said much. Less and less in there.
Till nothing. 'But he squoze my hand,' she said,
'And at least he smiled.' His smile! There used to be
A word for it in the childhood of the tongue,
The word 'seely' that came up from the roots
And died but left a ghostly twin, a word
That shifts among the grown-ups still, the word 'silly'.

The stuck for words, I've watched them hit the place
The word should be and find it gone and claw
The air for it and pluck the sheet and close
Their eyes and groan, knowing it's nowhere near
The tip of the tongue but on a piece of once
And no longer terra firma come adrift
Somewhere arctic going mushy in a fog.

Not him. Not then. Come home from being in
Without a word he viewed the garden like
Someone let off, someone let in to where
The things divest. Seely the face
That looks like that, seely the smile on her
Whose talk was lovely rapid like a nymph's become a stream's,
Seely the two in silence like before they knew their names.

Common and Particular

I like these men and women who have to do with death,
Formal, gentle people whose job it is,
They mind their looks, they use words carefully.

I liked that woman in the sunny room
One after the other receiving such as me
Every working day. She asks the things she must

And thanks me for the answers. Then I don't mind
Entering your particulars in little boxes,
I like the feeling she has seen it all before,

There is a form, there is a way. But also
That no one come to speak up for a shade
Is like the last, I see she knows that too.

I'm glad there is a form to put your details in,
Your dates, the cause. Glad as I am of men
Who'll make a trestle of their strong embrace

And in a slot between two other slots
Do what they have to every working day:
Carry another weight for someone else.

It is common. You are particular.

The Anemones

Back here the anemones had died in my big room
Up against the window gaping for daylight
In the long jar scrabbling for drink like children's straws
Like moths the colours of Hades, the crimson, the blue, the black
In rigor mortis sooting the sterile glass
Wide open and raging for water and more light
That is how I found the anemones when I came back.

The Crem

This is a ragged place. Nothing fits.
I suppose the cemetery was put there first
Then someone in Planning, because of the railway
And knowing of the coming of the expressway,
Made it the zone for light industry

With a plot for the crem. The cars arrive
Sighing down the old roads at a decent pace
And leave on the new, unburdened, fast.
Announcements of smoke. This is no place
To come and sit with your trouble in working hours.

The roses mean well but the ashes look ghastly
And the dedicated benches put you on show
On a little hillside, they make you spectators
Of every delivery. But come out of hours
With nobody else to look at it's even worse.

Everything's been tried here and did no good.
There are walls of tablets of stone you can stand and read,
And urns and uprights as though if they could
They'd be next door in the old style, as though
Ash isn't enough. Lately there's cellophane

And dead bouquets on the earth like murdered birds.
They look a mess but the Council lets them lie.
Electrics, remoulds, a couple of scrapyards,
Roar of the living on the expressway,
Lift up your eyes to the hills and the empty sky.

House Clearance

When you were gone, widow in a childless house,
As smoke, as shadow of smoke and thin deposit of ash
Forgive us, we went from room to room under the roofspace
Lagged with woolly dust, under that head of cold
We gathered up your substance, all the leavings
And sorted this for us, this for charity, this for the tip
Breaking and entering on your privacy
We delved for what you might have hoarded among underwear
The orange chocolate biscuits, wallets of photographs
Wads of pension, documentations of a dead baby,
Hardening our hearts, impieties, impieties,
Even against the cards heart-shaped and red and quilted
Addressed to MAM from someone not your flesh
For Christmas, birthday and Mothering Sunday
That being opened down a score of years still chimed
Like mobiles in a wreck, but we
With coats and hats more than in C&A
More dresses than a run of Mothers' Union jumble sales
With orange cardigans and the summer blouses
That crush to nothing like a conjuror's bright scarves
We bloated the first black plastic bags
The grey dust in our hair, and rounded up
From where you had hidden them or they hid themselves
In hide-and-seek and nobody came seeking
The last of your rag and woolly tribe of dolls and animals
Already priced for charity, room by room until
From a wardrobe out flopped
A clown the size of a boy of five or six
Sewn in motley, stuffed and grinning, right as ninepence
And we blessed you for that, for giving us a thing
At once we could give away to the girl next door who asked,
Now you are gone, Was the house haunted? Yes, by love.

Shoes in the Charity Shop

It can't be helped, the way our minds turn
When we see worn shoes in a pile,
It is an evolution of our kind
We shan't grow out of. But this is charity
This widow pairing them along a rack and selecting
The worst for the tip, the better for pricing
And bringing out into the front shop
For the poor still walking
To step into. Noblest
Were those worn shoes of women queuing at the bus-stop
And along the pavement shuffling turn by turn
Nearer the counter and to being served
While above their hands
Gripped by the weight of bags and the worry over every penny
And far above their feet
Killing them in those trodden shoes
Gloriously they were squandering breath on stories
A wealth of natter and tattle
And answering back. Their shoes
Would never have passed from the pile to the front shop
So shaped to them, who never wanted charity,
No feet on earth after theirs would have fitted them.

New Year Behind the Asylum

There was the noise like when the men in droves
Are hurrying to the match only this noise was
Everybody hurrying to see the New Year in
In town under the clock but we, that once,

He said would I come our usual Saturday walk
And see it in out there in the open fields
Behind the asylum. Even on sunny days
How it troubled me more and more the nearer we got

And he went quiet and as if he was ashamed
For what he must always do, which was
Go and grip the bars of the iron gates and stand
Staring into the garden until they saw him.

They were like the animals, so glad and shy
Like overgrown children dressed in things
Handed down too big or small and they came in a crowd
And said hello with funny chunnering noises

And through the bars, looking so serious,
He put his empty hand out. But that night
We crept past quickly and only stopped
In the middle of the empty fields and there

While the clock in the square where the normal people stood
And all the clocks in England were striking twelve
We heard the rejoicings for the New Year
From works and churches and the big ships in the docks

So faint I wished we were hearing nothing at all
We were so far away in our black fields
I felt we might not ever get back again
Where the people were and it was warm, and then

Came up their sort of rejoicing out of the asylum,
Singing or sobbing I don't know what it was
Like nothing on earth, their sort of welcoming in
Another New Year and it was only then

When the bells and the cheerful hooters couldn't be heard
But only the inmates, only the poor mad people
Singing or sobbing their hearts out for the New Year
That he gripped me fast and kissed my hair

And held me in against him and clung on tight to me
Under a terrible number of bare stars
So far from town and the lights and house and home
And shut my ears against the big children crying

But listened himself, listened and listened
That one time. And I've thought since and now
He's dead I'm sure that what he meant was this:
That I should know how much love would be needed.

Ashes and Roses

She is size 10 again like the girl under her banns
But so disconsolate the falling of her hand
I worry the diamond will slip to the grey earth.

These are only the bare bones of roses
This is a garden of little twists of iron
The dressing of ash does not look nourishing.

Let me look away at the sunny hills and you
Look at nothing for a while against my heart.
You feel as breakable as things I have found on the hills

After the weather when their small frames are evident.
You need to put on again
The roses need to flower. Come home

To your empty house. He is more there than here

Visiting

In broad daylight going back again
Under the black poplars to the old way in,
Locus of the dream, naked somnambule
Puzzled at the iron gates, eyeing the pitbull,
Viewing the garden let go to ruin
And shrunk so small how was there room in there
For cricket, the bonfire, the giant snowman,
Flowers and produce and rustic between the two?

All I want to embrace in there I should pass right through
With my closing arms. Better abide
The time of the naked soul and then enter
Easily between the bars and while
The foul dog sleeps come into the multitude
Gathered in the shrunken garden who are as thin

As negatives. But I,
Thinnest letter, is an infinity.

Fine Soil

I've come looking for that unwarlike man
My father, in a khaki blouson
At work riddling soil a yard or so
From where the rowan was and isn't now.

From the terraces settling in a Sunshine Home
On virgin fields with no experience
Only *The Gardener's Enquire Within*
He spoke the words like equals, 'Fine Soil'
With shy authority as though come
Into something homely and holy by amazing chance.

Midnight dreamer, I see him in the sun
And that goodness, that tip of good spoil
Mounding like mole-tilth from a fine rain
So sweet to work and plunge the hands in,
Lovely to seed. It had body, unlike the thin
Ash whose every mote was body once.

Riddling the Strata

Terra nova, so what jigged on the grille
And wasn't let through was mostly alluvial
Rounded pebbles from the old conglomerates
From the old seas and breccia bits,
Undone old makings, and little erratics
Travelled from Cumberland on the boulder clay,
Grits and greywackes, flung on the waste pile.

Now if they'd let me in I'd kneel
Near the scarlet memory of the rowan berries
And riddle our stratum, let the fine soil away
And feel with fingertips for our deposits,
The fuselages of Lancasters,
Limbs and weapons of lead soldiers,
A dinky ambulance, alleys
Of clay, glass, steel, the thin lead sticks
Safely chambered in a propelling-pencil.

Shed

I fixed a good long splinter to a gun of wood
And round the shed's blind corner anticlockwise
Clockwise stuck my brother just beneath the eye.

Inside there hung a gasmask like a trophy head
And the Jack of All Trades, Master of None
(His verdict) stood at the workbench in the sun,
Between his lips bright glints of nails,
Mending the family's shoes. The glue and leather smells,
The leather being pared by a blade gone
Crescent from shaping round the soles and heels
Upended on the last. What ironmongery!
What scores of correct names for all the things you need!
And the Maker and Mender Extraordinary
Eye on the job under the gasmask's insect eyes
Safe in there while round the clock outside
Everything whirls in luck, the bad, the good.

The Dark Room

Black-out and a red light. Safe light
Not light enough to hurt what can't appear
In the light. In it the Trismegist
Amazed the novice and himself in equal measure.
He launched our fortune cards under the surface,
He slipped them under the fluid's skin
With fingertips. He rocked them. As the book said.
My head bowed, his over mine was bowed
And loved ones bodied up, at rest.

Be warned, present occupiers, when I am through the gate
Past the pitbull, the sacred rowan, the million
Million shimmering atoms of the shed
I'll seek the dark room in your living space,
Sackman arriving with an infinite
Capital and compound interest of negatives,
I'll dip and bath to life again my lives.

Streets

Twenty-seven from Waterloo Street
Two from Barlows Road
Five from Blackburn Buildings
Only one each from West Thompson Street
Cranbourne Street, Bright Street, Langshaw Street
And Gun Street.
These are not levels of fervour
Only how many homes
(Unfit for heroes)
Had men and boys to give.
Liverpool Street gave fifty-five
Among them six by the name of Allmark
And my mother's father
8571 Private J.W. Gleave
From number fifty-seven
On the corner with little Healey Street
That gave three:
Private S. Cooper
Private J. Flanagan
Sergeant C.H. Taylor.
Eliza Street likewise gave three, all Molineuxs
Ayr Street gave four, three of them Andersons.
They were all other ranks round here
Nothing bigger than a sergeant.
I counted thirty-seven streets
In a half-mile square
And of them none are left:
Not Ducie Place
Not Brighton Place
Not Willis Street
Not West Joseph Street that gave
Private G. Olive
Corporal F. Cassidy
Sergeant R. Seddon
Private T. McNulty
Nor Albion Street that gave
All three Bowkers.
The bit of Liverpool Street is left
That led to the abattoir
But not a home along it
Nor a church, a mission hall
A corner shop, a stables
Nor any pub but one

The Live and Let Live
Boarded up
And no list anywhere.

I counted two hundred and twenty-one men went from here

To Happy Valley
Nameless Wood
Krab Krawl
Stuff Trench
Hellblast Corner
And Dead Man's Dump.

Fields

On Cruthers, seaward abandoned
So long drenched with salt

Some paper whites
Delicate and plucky as butterflies in rusty wire
Rise every year in the wreckage of bracken and brambles

Three cists on the chine

But on the leeside
High winds can come over
And a man be there
In fields like roofless rooms
Head down quietly
And move up the soft furrows.

Jib Piece, the shape
The sweet curves of the rows
The old man's favourite
He said they could scatter him there but changed his mind
And lies above all the fields with the old lady

Dust and his bits of shrapnel.

Eastard.

Uncle Boss's, the black pine
In red-hot pokers and agapanthus.

John Batty's, a barrow
The cladding robbed for hedges
Strong unctuous earth
Which smelt cadaverous.

The Prison
Four high evergreen walls and so big
Picking or planting seems a long sentence (still
A vast allowance of sky, clouds travelling, sea on the doorstep
There are worse confinements).

The Dry Field.
Ferny Splat.
Enter Hills.

The Homeland
No pain, no death, no grief.

Little Eastard.
Cold Wind.

Adrianople
The wars of the Russians and the Turks.

Spion Kop
That went back long ago under brambles, bracken, gorse
The Christophers broke in
Under the moon
Ridding it of brambles, bracken, gorse
Dry hedging it with the spoil
But split from Cruthers
And dragged on a sledge
Two great orthostats
To be the gateway opening on a risen field
Of sols, avalanches, paper whites
In 1900
For weddings, christenings and funerals
And named it after a battle
In the old tradition
Of native clay and foreign fields
At the opening of the age
Of bulk slaughter.

Eleven little islands
Can be seen from Spion Kop
They have the peace and the patience of animals
That all night under the stars
Are there and in the morning
Still when the mist lightens.

Sols, avalanches, paper whites
Mostly for funerals.

Girls in the East

These girls in their bits of bright skirt
Slung low on the down under their belly buttons
Show me a man in this place who could have fathered them
And among the women
Buttoned up stoutly in old clothes
Any likely mother.

The way they ride the trams of the Republic
The way they stride
They must be a generation of changelings
Such clear skin
You don't get that on a diet of five-hour speeches
Nor queuing round the walls in the acid drizzle of sadness.

Here comes an ancient father with his ageing son.
The father is scaly with medals
The son is trailing a flag
It was a demonstration in memory of the old days
Briefly their eyes shone like the medals
Briefly they stood up stiff as flagstaffs
Now they are going home to the old smells
Trapped on every landing
And matching wives and mothers.

Where did the bare-legged girls blow in from?

They must have seeded themselves
In cracks in the four-square mausoleum
In the clay of the feet of the Shepherds of the People
Or perhaps they were there all along
Under the square and the tanks went over them
And when the perishing of the concrete had begun
At the first tickling of illicit grass
Night after night like white foxgloves
Cool as moonlight
Hard as stars
These daughters of nowhere came up legion.

They have no memory
They have no piety
The dead in this place will have to bury themselves.

School Parties in the Museum

Daily the boroughs, hopeful as a flood tide,
Release some children and Miss and Sir
And several guardian angels conduct them without loss
Through the underground in crocodiles to here,
The Room of the Kings, with questionnaires.

What the Jew Bloom said was no use – force,
Hatred, history, all that – here
There's enough of it to wipe out everything that lives,
Enough Fathers of the People, enough Peace Lords
Among their deeds with a half-life of a million years.

Hurrying through from the Tea Room to the Reading Room
In drifts of children I could make no headway
But a space and a silence came into my mind
Among them crying like birds and flitting and settling
So that for once I saw a thing properly:

A thoughtful dot in socks and a white frock
Under the famous fist on its level length of arm,
Black granite fist, black as the people's blood is
When it has dried on the square in the usual sun,
Fist of some god or president, some wise

Dispenser of plagues of locusts and Agent Orange
And she was under it in pigtails with a clipboard
Pondering up at it in a space all on her own
As serious as the entire Reading Room
And black as a brand new question mark.

Daily for opening time and all day long
Till the last admission the ever hopeful boroughs send
Under the world's colours wave on wave
Of their bright fragments of the New Republic
Future present, with questions, against the Kings.

Jazz on the Charles Bridge

(for Si and Konni)

Go on, go on, I believe you, I believe
The big river, sick of dirt,
Sick of ferrying our murders to the dead sea,
Suddenly feels a kick like quickening
And this is the source come clean again at last

And now she will be well, encore, encore,
I believe it, the unnecessary
Saints and martyrs must pine away
Or raise their instruments like Mr Horn
Or strum like Thimble Fingers on the washboard

Or pluck like that one cuddling the bass, and croak
In Czech, oh, won't you please come home?
All is well now, all is forgiven, the Real
Republic is here, the best we'll ever get
And good, so good, such courtesy

The way they let one another through in turn,
The way they take him up again like the peloton
In a rush of applause of equals,
Go on, go on, no wonder the sun comes out
No wonder the wind kisses up little waves,

Oh, brothers and sisters, this is it
Builded here, Careless Love, and not
The blues but something more like a boy and a girl
Outstretched to one another on the high trapeze, for life
And death, their eyes in one another, laughing.

'Hölderlin'

*('Hölderlin' was the code name used by an East
German poet when she spied for the Stasi.)*

Why? Because after you, what you had said,
What you had put about among humankind,
Even bigger lies were possible and on your highs
That deep came disappointment. After you

We lived like foreigners in our mother country
Among the trades and functions, among the shells
Not one inhabited by a living kind
Of human. There was always a word for us

Because of you, more than a word, the thing,
Your doing, that want, that powerless power
When faces lifted from the text and whispered 'Come
Into the open, friend, oh come, oh make

It true, the spirit quickening through all the veins
Of a republic's life, this very earth,
Ours here – if not now, when?' All that
In a mother country of old men, always

Men and old, the same old men and their
'Not now, not yet'. I sided with the liars
Against the disappointed, I wear your name
Emptily, like grief, like vain revolt.

Hallowe'en

1

Small cluster of our dead
Like a Pleiades, they change
Their quarter season by season
But never go below
For where we are they are.

Apples, lanterns, fire;
On the marsh behind the fire
Soft rollers of mist from the sea.
Come closer, friendly dead
Watch over the waiting house.

2

Little somebody
Eyes shut
You missed the eclipse
But never mind.

Along Mynydd Bach
On every knoll
And some at the trigpoint
And some at the cairns
Where the huddled small
Dead were housed
In good time
Watchers appeared
All innocent
Only watching.

It was like waking
Where you were dreaming
In the queer light
Russet and flickering
And utter silence
Where you were dreaming
Shoals of light
Over Llyn Eiddwen

And just in time
Came a high wind
A quiet commotion
And the sky opened:

Black sun
Black moon
Moon on the sun
And over the rim
Allowed by the moon
And moonshaped
A show of sun
The crowning edge
Of the terror of the rest:

Phenomenon

Little girl or boy
Us waiting know
And you'll soon see
Life here's
Like that
You lattice your eyes
With peeping fingers
And cloud is a mercy
When like that
That bright
Over the rim
The wishing crescent
Of love comes
And hooks the heart
Fast.

Skylight over the Bed

The two stars in the skylight must be Gemini.
Hard to be sure with constellations,
Time of the year, time of the night, and only that
Small window on their travelling, but here
Awake on another middle of a night,
Single the flesh again, single the mind
Again but biding in a patient watchfulness
And only puzzling for the fun of it
What else belongs around that little excerpt
Of silver dots on black, for now
Under the slant look of the loveless sky
As tranquil, almost, as a husband on a marble tomb
No more infringing on your state of sleep
Than little finger crooked in little finger
I'm pretty sure those two stars must be Gemini.

Skylight over the Bath

Starlight is good and a *voyeuse* moon
But daylight is better still and rain
And not a mizzle or a pitter patter
But Aquarius in person astride your ridge tiles
Emptying the urns of heaven down the slopes.

Being in water under water, can you remember
That far back, globule in a swimming mother,
Pod in a swamp somewhere? Or as a tot
Launched all alone in a crib for a boat
Hiding in a quiet pool behind the waterfall?

Full length and single in your snug billet
One thing you can see for yourself up there's
An acceleration of the molecules of glass
Which are slower than a glacier in your usual view.
Under the skim of water watch them come down fast.

That close the sisterhood of hard glass
And water, what hopes of lasting for you
Who are as watery as a lettuce, so they say?
No wonder the easeful Romans let out
Their blood in the bath to unboldly go that way.

Under the grisaille in the agapanthus blue
Voyager feet first in a chaste casket
Announcing yourself to the cold outside with gasps of steam
Leave through the wall like a babe of the *Enterprise*:
Longship, cuttlefish, speck in the salt foam.

Gorse

Keeps with its dead
Shows off by the bare facts of its dead
How hard it was
Living and how it triumphed and all winter
Among its own dead grizzle
Little moist lips of it go on muttering light.

It's the dead I've come for
Put in my naked hand among the spines and feel for
Anything springy I let be
To come on again and add its sparks to the rush of Easter and Whitsun
But the dead snaps off
There and then it can be broken up hearthsize
Lengths straight as flutes
Or curving open like welcomes
Or twirled like dance
For nothing burns like the limbs of gorse
So thoroughly dead
Twisted for breathing space
Drilled and cankered
Host to the hungers of other kinds of life
How they burn
All without fat and flesh and blood
Without dribble or mewling
So much flame in every stub of gorse
Millions of Easters and Whitsuns
The scent and yellow fume under blue skies
All that as flame
With the lights off
Rain and fog over the bit of terra firma
And on the hearthrug
Kneeling
Aquarius and Pisces
Amazed.

Fulmars

I go there most days for a look at mastery
Flat out, eyes over the edge
The warm stink of the ledges up my nose
And the sea far down, never quiet, always mulling over something.

They don't want me there, I make them nervous
But the mastery comes up on the nervousness
So close, light through the ruddering feet
Eyes like coals on a snowman
Breath in a bony housing

I see the wingbeats are a charge of energy
And the glide a sort of freewheeling
That carries to the crest of a long slope of air
And faster down again, but also I see
What else must be there

(Lovely the showing forth
By them
To us
What must be there)

A lift off the lifting sea
Palpable streamers in the empty air
Fender, bias, swing
From under the concave cliff

And the flick, the tilt, the tremor
All the while the eye on me
In a state of total attending
Of utter hearkening to the possibilities
These are continual corrections for best advantage
Of forces not available to me
Airs between the cliff and the sea

They come to the dot
Which is the place in time between thus far and next
And halt on that split second
Then away, sheerly away, for another charging.

All I can ever do is say what things are like
And what they are like is what they remind me of.

Looking down on flight
Or on the shadows of flight over the salt water
Up comes the ancient conviction that I could fly
All I had to do was remember how
Hours of practice off the garden wall
And though the arms were right
Stiff and tilting
And the eye was utterly fixed on the idea
How foolish under the Spitfire
The peddling legs
In the unhelpful air

The gliders my father made did better than that

I can see his hands, his eye on the job
Folding a sheet of paper for the head and wings
A little anxiety watching his own hands
Whether they still remembered how
And the smile when they did

(I thought it would come back to me when the time came
The knack
The man's origami)

Stiff wings, a tight beak
They launched eagerly
Seemed to be able to feel out the best airways
Close my eyes I can see them on a blue sky
Ride and circle
Fail gracefully in spirals

Still nothing like fulmars.

I could lie there for ever they would never get used to me
Always know me for a foreign body
And I could watch for ever and never get the hang of it

That economy
Everything to the point
Grace in the fitness.

By lamplight in the early mornings
I study my hands:
Somewhere between them and the head
And a sheet of ordinary paper
There is an old invention

Ghost wanting blood
Memory wanting precipitation
Thin air a shape
As keen on the heart as an icy lightning.

Close my eyes I can see the fulmars
Head on, coming in fast
Against gravity, silent
Fixed on my attention
As though by force of looking
The pull of love
Every atom hearkening
I could summon them up.

Orangery

1

The trees are coming in down the long aisle
One by one, always the farthest first, on a yellow fork-truck
Lifted as little as need be but like a gift
Or the lares and penates, like the ancestors

Seated, benign, or like the child
Wished for and watched for down the long *allée* to the very end
Arriving now, coming home
Into the warm, the winter house. There must be a music

As slow as a dead march, solemn but not in mourning
For this coming in of orange and oleander,
Lemon and pomegranate on a muffled day,
A pavane, in the slow tempo

Of accustomed transit. What will come. What has to be done.
What will happen if not. Without haste. In good time.
The long forethought. It is early days,
Last week there were swallows still, a long while yet

Till the fountains drop down dead, wood clads them, the lake
Shuts and in minus twenty
Plus windchill the rooted natives aspire
To the only condition for survival: iron.

Slower than a hearse meanwhile
Or a gun-carriage down the gravel mall
Slightly rustling
Into the big house come the delicate exiles.

2

In the terminus, in the grey-clear light
Under the nine windows they have scarcely begun receiving
And these arrivals, the first, from farthest,
When they make an entrance it is still a marvel

How big they are, brought in
And offered by a little yellow fork-lift
Lowered and left, as big as the statues
Brought down from high up under the tympanum. In here

The gardeners are busy barbers
On styles that over the season have reverted to the elemental
A work like grooming the beasts in the big houses
The human voice continuing in conversation

Along the flanks, over the still heads
Of other shapes of life, but softly, not to startle
And not to clash with the colours of the whole interior
The matt greens, the opal, the dull gold. High in the centre

That pair face to face across the apex of a double ladder
Stretching to round the crown of a *laurier-rose*
He has reached her the last bloom
For a lush pink buttonhole in her working blue

And although we can't see her face his is certain
That so much oblation of trimmings from the Greek trees
Has placated death for ever
And her open torch will see them through any winter.

A POETRY PRIMER

(2004)

Pleasure

A poem, like the clitoris, is there
For pleasure and although some experts say
It can't be only pleasure it is there for
But must do something else to pay its way
But what that something else is can't agree
We leave them to their wrangling and say
The pleasure principle will do for you and me:
End in itself, servant to nothing other
Than what it carries (love). Take, for example,
A wanted realisation's long postponement
Over caesuras and line-endings, torment
Of let and rallentando and reversal,
Word upon word, staccato then eliding,
A gathering rising final overriding...
They ask what the syntax of our pleasure does?
Makes with a rush of sense something that *is*.

Simile

By simile we say what things are like.

This morning, love, the wind and the tide are at one
Swinging away north-west, the turn of a big tide
And the wind rising to gale force in a bright sun,
The clouds white, thinning, making a disappearance,
Water into pure air. Yes, the window is open
And the roar you can always hear from the other side
This morning it makes a louder continuo
And on it, against it, the slop, clap, chop, below this window.
There the three boats, two blue and a green, prance,
They kick up, the bows tug, they slew, they fling
Me light here off the cabin windows, they hate tethering
Or the wind does and the tide as they make
For the mouth, the open, the high seas, the bumpy horizon,
Such raising of lovely phenomena in a steady apparition

What is it all like? Love, ask me what love is like.

Metaphor

Gift of our own world of appearances
To all that shivers in the throes of dream
And ghosts along the edge of being seen
And craves a demonstration, proof and sign
And wants a free run of the five senses...

Gods, for example, otherwise unknown
Quantities in space and time, would crash
Our human fancy dress ball in the flesh
Of bull, snake, swan or mighty pigeon, lo
They abhorred not the virgin's womb
So great a need they had to seed and show.
Veiled in flesh, they sang, the godhead see.

Veiled in flesh my love and your love see
Revealed by our unclothing bodily
There present. What our loving bodies do
Is make love metaphors to go into.

Metre and Rhythm

Remember I made us practise? From somewhere,
Perhaps a *Teach Yourself*, I got the dumb idea
That all we had to do was to repeat
In step, you me, me you, the in and out.

Incapable of any steps in time
With someone else, my only dance
Was the satyr's solo, the twirling stomping trance.

Took me a while to couple that with you

And practise what, not from a book, you knew
How to do already. Agree a metre. Play,
As winds do and the currents' understream
Between close islands with the setting tide,
Over, along, below, against and through
What must proceed. So make the thing proceed
In your own good time: thwart, slow, slew, speed
The resolution on its sweet set way.

Form and Content

Become one flesh, engender a little soul
Colouring like a rainbow and as agile
As Thetis, the everchanging slippy nymph.
Without the poem's muscle, blood and lymph

Where would she be? Where thought would be or fear
Or bliss evicted from accommodation in the skull
And brain and rib-caged heart and pubic hill.
Outside the bony housing she is nowhere.

Our feeling, as imprinted as your bite
And tenfold marking by your nails on me,
Our thinking that could lift my appetite
And wet your absent place where it should be

Without a house and home in flesh and blood
Will not impress the sky. But held in good
Black lettering shaped on white may quicken
Like trouble, like delight in lovers then.

Res/Verba

Think of a thing then think what it should wear,
What words, the most becoming words, the best...

Are things not visible until they're dressed?

Seems what they meant by 'res' was an idea;
A thing too immaterial to appear;
Unclad, there was no proof that it was there.

How can you clad an unembodied thing?

So word this poor idea-thing some vim,
Feet to stand on the earth on, cock and quim.

Rule Number One is: Practise bodily clothing.

But – see **Inventio** – another view
Is that the clothes are what you must get through
To find the thing. Find words that will undo
Zips, laces, buttons, bows and do the trick
On the tightest hook-and-eye and quaint elastic,
To see the very thing and show it bare.

Inventio (I)

Make nothing up, it is already there
In the commonplaces. Listen when you come near
They whisper 'Warmer! Getting warm!' Lovely
The old idea that it is there already
And only wants finding out. And how it wants!
All there, always, biding in the commonplaces.
Even the viewing of them brings it out,
Touch much more so and a truffling snout
Or a lick of taste. The inventor invents
Much like the chappie with the twitching fork
The island fetches in to find a spring.
He is in touch through any amount of clothing.
Give him an inch, give him that small place
Between the glove and the sleeve in a cold park,
He knows the rest, or makes you feel he knows.
But the best things it takes two to find, he says.

Inventio (II&III)

The fictions and the figments come from the act
Of forming. And what's done like that is fact.
Adam, dreaming in Eden, when he woke...
But you know all this. I only make...

You make it up, it's in your head
And balls, you visit it on me, in your game
Hider and seeker are one and the same,
And finding's easy what you went and hid.

I only make it show, I swear it's there
To believe or not, and live by, if you dare.
Besides, I invent myself in the light of how
You look at me. Do you not know...

I know I am uneasy, as if I'd been
Visiting somewhere very elsewhere down
Below and like a child the seeds you said you'd found
And offered me I ate them off your hand.

I might have said the same, except the one
Come visiting from elsewhere
Was you and left me viewing your invention
Of me and wondering do I dare,

Then in the grown-up world I wonder what I've done,
What will become of me if this goes on
And look in the mirror with very curious eyes
To see if it's a face I recognise

If you are changing, change, and not to catch
You in your metamorphoses but match
And if it really is there, what you say
You see in me, not visiting, not some stowaway,

How will I live? What is it that you love?
Look at me hard in daylight when I leave.
Them with my own. I do look hard, you prove
The dream true every time you leave.

Periphrasis

Some would never name the name of God
But praised Him through the thousand things He did,
His gifts and grace, and at the centre hid
The unuttered *fons et origo* of all the good.

The poets' way was differently devout.
Saying not saying, spiralling in and out
And in again their wreaths of speech revealed
The pull of nakedness through what they veiled.

We stalk in speech around the thing itself
Because the word's a curse and like a black
Having his gums shown on the auction block
The thing is spread for sale on any shelf.

Taboo. Excite the labyrinth. Then in long
Periphrasis of silent lips and tongue
And signing with the fingers very slowly get
To the crux, the point, the funnelled sum of it.

Poetry and Rhetoric (I)

The expense of spirit (wit) on trying to get
Young women to do things they would rather not
At least seven hundred years of it
In sonnet after sonnet after sonnet
And before that also, either side Jesus Christ,
Centuries of scanning arguments dreamed up
To melt her diamond in a loving cup,
All boiling down to this: Make haste, don't waste
It, girl, we are a long time dead. And then
The expostulation: I ask you!
What virtue is there in your virtue?
I mean, what good does it do? (Dead to
The unhappy possibility it might be
Not virtue at all, just plain antipathy.)
Unbutton, love, let me, unzip, unfasten!
All this in a medium that makes nothing happen.

Poetry and Rhetoric (II)

When I think of persuasion, of the persuasiveness, I see
You that morning on the Circle Line
With a seat for once but squashed in knee to knee
In a thicket of people somewhere on your own
Among them standing, swaying, slumping half asleep
You reading poems through the black tunnels
And chokes of light and – was it suddenly,
Ambushed, or more like rising wells
Little by little but unstoppably – ?
By the sole force of some few signs set out
For absent things in shapes in black on white
The reading clinched you in an absolute
There and then: the truth cold down your spine,
Prickle of love and terror on the nape
And you lift your face to your fellow-travellers
To witness, beyond denying it, your tears.

Personae (I)

These were the masks they sounded through on stage
Saying the lines, somebody else's grief
But got by heart, the jealous love, the rage
With feeling, somebody else's life.
And who they were themselves nobody knew
No more than who he was who wrote the stuff
And gave it them to say with zest enough
For people listening to feel it to be true.

Speaking your tongues after the exchange of breath
I was not hiding, I was striving to appear
So multiply it would be hard for death
To seize and throttle me. My stanzas were
Rooms in which your spirits passing through
As between mirrors might materialise.
The lines and rhymes were latticework to show
A throat that might be yours, a mouth, the eyes.

Personae (II)

In office boxes I am filed away
Under a number that was given me
YB 41 14 40 B.
Or you could swab my gob for DNA.

You say you don't know where you are with me?
Poor thing, try as he will, he cannot be
In two places at once, he only has
One pair of hands et cetera, alas.

I made a grille of syllables, did I not,
To pin him down in truly? Shifty me.
A picture coming like a dot-to-dot
And you appearing with me, to a tee.

But shake the clever casing and we make
A different splintering at every look.
We turn another shape in there, we move
Like smoke in glass still writhing, still alive.

Orphic

Remember what happened: When they were sick of him
Forever harping on the Only One
They pooled their bile and tore him limb from limb,
Manured the scenery with his blood and bone
And tossed his head in the river. This famous head
Being incapable of shutting up
Though all the rest of him was strewn all round the shop
Went on and on, much as it always had,
Rejoicing in the signs of her and him
That lived and moved here, there and everywhere
In common things, in winds and wings of the air,
In the opening sea, the uneasy earth, the fire,
Little tongues of life. Turn every poem I write,
Whatever of, in our peculiar light
Glances of you, glimpses of me will show
In bits of language only those two know.

Mnemosyne

Before there was τέχνη, μηχανή, art and *métier*,
Even before there was spit and breath in the clay
She was there remembering, growing already
The poem's vast memory. Whenever I can say
That reminds me, this puts me in mind
Of a thing that may help me to say it better today
I bless her name, Mother of the Nine,
First Cause, Prime Mover. If I say imagine,
Dream us a dream, where will you go but down
To the wells, to the seabed of memory,
Eyes closed, sleeping and feeling and able again
To breathe underwater? Swim here, breathe
Love in my mouth again, gladden my lungs,
Solace me now with a memory of tongues
Rooting for truth and wagging in a blithe
Airing of love deep down among the drowned.

NEW & UNCOLLECTED POEMS

(2004)

Chapel of Rest

Love, viewing death close up, blushes to see
So poor a likeness. You never knew her
Of course, or for such as she
Was here you have nothing over there
At all like. Look instead
At this photograph taken by her lover in a forest somewhere,
Arden or Brocéliande, where they ran and hid
On earth for a while: it's a shot
At showing what she looked like when happiness lit
On her who had not been lucky, who never quite had her due.
Her lover closing his eyes could give you a thousand more.
I feel ashamed for you, death, so mean, so poor.
Look at her face now to see what she was not.
And look at his. Is that the best you can do?

Before the Lidding

1

The lid stood by discreetly, we could admire
Its fit shape, ready, how it would match the rim
And the screw holes marry up. Oak and brass also
How they were good and well put to their purpose
And the soft quilt was a thoughtfulness, a kindness. All throve,
Even the bone on the cross, they had the virtue
Of use and all in their own colours. The flowers in every degree
From an almost black red to the poles of white
They neighboured one another, they lent one another hints
Of possible other ways of being seen, they bloomed, they breathed
To life in us the fluttering starts of love in dead bracken,
The trespassing in gardens, the pillaging, the armfuls,
The soaked places, the red, the plush, silk, cotton, lace, the webs
And the threads of sorrow drifting on the wind for years.
A stook or a wreath of flowers is a million likenesses
And these faced out and breathed and lived and gave of themselves
To us and faced away from the thing that was their cause that is
Like nothing and the colour of nothing on earth but its own self.

2

Gauche humans that can think and feel and speak and sing
We cluttered in as though we had quit the street
Abruptly for an exhibition, to be out of the rain
And stood around embarrassed
With bags and gloves and hats and crumpled brollies
Bulky and miserable like yokels strangely called
To a levee, who did not know the form.
Some nattered in a little group, averted; one clapped
His phone hard up and spoke away; most looked to be
Not attendant, only waiting, at a loss. But one
Was beautiful and purposeful. She had laid
Her sorrow under ice for the necessary while
And to a man whose office made him witness
Many poor settings for the lights of amethyst
She was handing a bracelet and a necklace. Soon
They rested the head again, they tucked the ornamented pulse
Back under the coverlet to have a kind
Of warmth.

3

The centre froze our hearts. But very late
Before the lidding, in all her scooter gear
Disburdening her head, shaking out her hair
In came a girl who shone from the hard sleet
And looked with candour fearlessly
At you, the cause. She was
An emissary of the ordinary thriving streets who nipped
Through the weather and the traffic, she was agile,
Clever at it, neat, she was the liveliness itself
In its true colours she faced up to you,
Dear friend, the eloquent stopped, the beautiful discoloured
By death, that radiant girl, we saw again what we are fit to be
On the risen wave of life, the lifted face, her face
Come in and shining with the cold and rain, scenting of rain,
Scented with the life outside, come in and risen up,
Made sorrowful, made tearful by the force of love and by that force
Answering for you, answering for us, against
Death's saying forever no, for ever saying yes.

The One Left

Always the one left
Unsleeping
Thinks too much, he lies
Up close
In her shadow feeling
Her heart
For the rhythm of sleep
And breathing
Her hair for the poppies
Thinking
She lies in her shadow
All, but I
Am outside unsleeping
Thinking
I would not wish her
Nor me to be
Ever the one left
Thinking.

Water

I know of a room in a house out of earshot
Of river and stream but sleepers in there
Infallibly dream of a hurrying water. Who died
In that room and bequeathed such a haunting
I imagine him sleeping as I sleep tonight
As close as I dare to the water and mixing
By dreaming her track from a tread in the cwm
By trickle and dash to a spell of reflection
In lakes among hills and over the lip then
Headlong through haloes of irising vapour
And bodily into a falls and escaping
Silver in snakes. I imagine him saying
Love, since tonight you are sleeping without me
Wherever it may be, so long as it must be,
I leave you this dream you will turn to a creature
Of water and enter and live in and thrive in
And fashion a shape in from hoof in the corrie
To mouth on the sea. And however many
The nights you lie waking or sleeping without me
Alone in a room in a house out of earshot
Of river or stream you will listen and mix with
The voice of me running, for ever and ever
Without me without you, in gusto of shadow
And sunlight so long as there's sky
Arched over earth and going between them
Rain, the sweet rain, the falling and rising.

At the Time

Some haunt because of a wrong they did
Or one done them and either way
The dead trail with the living still
Beyond amends. But all you did

Was keep your distance at the time,
Being shy perhaps, and only watched
And never came over, hoping perhaps
I'd notice and I'd be the one who'd cross

And free the talk, for the only gap
Between us then was the living years.
I should have asked more of you at the time
But I kept my distance and never did.

Now you trail me along the river as though
Upstream or down there might be a place,
Beyond being shy, to cross but each
Must always keep his distance now,

Make do with his monologue either side
Like the whispering reeds and the burden still
Is that I should have come over for
Your conversation at the time.

Absence

Absence is easy to imagine lasting
Always in a place
He was. Shall I visit again
Because it is a place I missed him in?

All's a museum now. You can watch a silent film
Of dockers freighting the big ships
Of the five oceans tucked in snug
Thirty-five miles inland. The living image.

But I will remember the flat open fields
And him as a boy – Where was it exactly?
When I visit again I want to miss him more exactly –
At the limit of his furthest bicycle ride,

Stopped dead, gripping the handlebars,
His feet on the earth, his gaze
Thrown open forward and a good long while
Not grasping it: the ship, the biggest, dirty white,

Smoothly inching through the mangolds and the Friesians
A pale leviathan
Passing in silence through the flowered earth
For the estuary, the tide, the grey horizon.

'Go visiting, Memory...'

Go visiting, Memory, take
Him this from me: that early morning waking
High up in another hospital
When nobody said do not and like a sleeper

He walked the ward to a far window
And steadied himself and stood and looked
Not down but away. Remind
Him, Memory, he looked away and beyond

Not down. The air was clean and still,
Every atom bright, and then,
So he told me and looked me in the eyes,
With ease he saw beyond the dominion of evil

And effortlessly as in my picture postcard
There on the mind's eye rose
On blue the stepping up, the pure
White mountains. He had been cleaned again

And bandaged white. Go and visit him now
Back in the filth forgetting, raise
Him a brave glass tower again, persuade him
To look you in the eyes, sweet Memory

Teacher

This child's verdict on
Herself is final. I have
No good in me and hopes of any
None. The cuts
Have reached her throat. Go back
I said, before the fall and grasp
Any scrap of innocence
For a proof and clue. With that
We might begin again. Her look!
Something like pity
As though against her heart
She must enlighten me about the Tooth Fairy
And the apparent blue of heaven.
With that
Something like pity in her look
I tried again.

Photo

They should never have photographed my Uncle Norman
On a background of the Alps. The comparison
Was one he could not win.

Somebody must have said let's have one of Norman
And perhaps we can get the Alps in too.
He would have been better in a dark interior
He could make any room convivial
He could tell stories by the hour
But here he is smiling on an Alpine meadow
Ten years after we buried him
And we say it's a good one of Norman
Now that he has given up what little breath he had.
And so it is a good one, that is how he was:
Short and cocky. Alas
The meadow would have looked better without him
Though the back kitchen in Salford 5 looked worse
And the back parlour at the Live and Let Live.
He was all right in some little habitation
Among the back streets dwarfed
Only by gasometers and All Saints Church, the empyreum
Miles out of sight above the friendly fog.

Legend

There is one story that has run and run
And we fish a meaning from it the best we can
About a wife so pure in heart or steady
And sure of purpose she could carry
The day's water from a running stream
For ablution and refreshment into her home
In her bare hands, in nothing at all –
No bucket, no jug – but as a crystal ball
As shapely hard and rounded as her will,
Pure as her heart, dead still.

I imagine her rising and sleepwalking through
The waking garden delicately as though
She were the vessel and by a deed of mind
Must carry in her a thing always inclined
To slop and spill in a necessary dream
Spellbound every morning from home to stream
Intact through all distraction to where she knelt
Over the water, blue green, ice melt
In it like corpuscles and, going to waste,
On it apples that had an aftertaste
Of nuts. She put in her white hand
And the water meeting with that demand
And feeling no way in between her fingers,
Denied itself, submitted its self to hers,
Hardened against her palm, grew to a sphere,
And rather as some can walk on coals of fire
Barefoot and do the ticklish flesh no injury
As though by force of dreaming she
On her white palms bore the globe of water home
And loosed the spell only in the master bedroom.

Her fall is usually told like this:
She had no inkling, she had dreamed nothing amiss
But went as always to the apple tree and knelt
Over the water, dipped and felt
For obedience but under the fast surface
Began to see things, pale shapes, a face
Not hers but as though at last someone
Had appeared for her in the mirror without question.
And then, only looking, the will gave,
She clouded inside, she felt her hand behave
Like a poacher's, tickling
The water for some warm and kindred thing.

Equally the water and her fingers refused:
It would not harden, they would not be closed
But leaked and spilled and the shaking cup
Of her two white hands could not lift up
Enough of the cold stream for her drought
But she burned in terror and then in delight
That water was water and she was freed
From obeying and having to be obeyed
And could thirst and lap and let the water run
Its way. She walked home woken.

In the old outcome there's a strict husband
Who saw at a glance – her wet dress – what had happened
And did not speak or ask her for a word
But obeyed the law and reached for the old sword
And parted head and heart. One detail:
Blood ran and ran from that bare steel
Long after he had made the sleeping place
Be without spot the pure steel would not cease
Bleeding and bleeding. But this severe
Husband, if I told it now, would be no more
Than herself in waiting, waiting for the fall
That she held off as long as possible
By force of purity and steely will
Carrying playful water as a crystal ball,
No slop or wet, in a diamond hard dream
To an alabaster urn in the master bedroom.

Simile

Like when a peppercorn or bit of one
Gets rammed between two teeth and neither
The conscientious brush nor all night long
The worrying tongue dislodges it but there
With no more savour than a bit of grit
It bides until, next morning in the dark
Outside the sleeping room before you step
Downstairs towards the living rooms, at last
And suddenly in the mouth still harbouring
Faithless dreamtalk by the tip of the tongue
It's winkled out and transplanted into
A bite, and creature, hearth and walls and roof
Of that warm fogou underneath the brain
Flare, they flower, they suffer a thorough feeling
Without a name for it, without a word and then
Saliva wells and bears it in solution till
The throat spasms, demanding it come down
The gullet to the belly pit from where
This whetted memory in the present on the brink
Of more enters and shoots the blood until
You take a step and then another step
Down to the living room and working room
Where with quotidian civility
In all the words you know for all the things
You are refused... It is a bit like that.

'More like today...'

More like today after the wind these days
And last night frost and now the sun
And silence, not a breath, and all that held
Against the wind can't hold out any longer now
Against the nearly level melting sun
But fall and what you fear
You cannot bear is not the violence of the wind
These days nor the hours in darkness bitter cold
But this in daylight now, the trees
Denuding in a silent hurry helplessly
On the level steady earth in a level sun
As clear and steady as the vertical
Midsummer over Paphos... Look
How many subtly brilliant birds are shown
Where even yesterday there was some hiding,
So many and so hungry, and the tips of black
We know is green packed in a tight reserve...
The earth is firm, the veils are falling off
This autumn lasting into winter and if this
Is what you fear you cannot bear, the standing still
In silence while the nakedness comes down
In candour, in a bodying forth in daylight,
Do you think I am safer in St Lucy's level sun
Than you while under this blue sky
The childish lovely colours fall and strip
The bare delight, the bare hunger,
The columns made of rings and rings of life
The tips of branches charged with more and more
All shown? Today it is like that.

Foxgloves

It needed fire
Nothing else would do
On the headland
On the island
We loved the cover
It was familiar
But then it burned
Two days and a night
Don't you feel you were there?
Especially the night
Just above the sea
Fire in the dark
Thrust into the sea

Black earth
When the cover was gone
Between you and the sun
That was the chance
A space in time
For one particular
Life to swarm
Imagine it
Or remember it
You were surely there
That spring, the green
That summer, the red
Just above the sea

A million signals
Run up red
Up masts in the wind
The fingering wind
The wishing wind
Mouths from below
The black in the sun
Nude as a scald
Moist as the weeping
Yes you were there
Just above the sea
Crying in dactyls
It wanted the fire

Asphodels, White Foxgloves, Red Foxgloves

Viewed as absence the colour white
Correctly dresses the flowers the dead are herded through
Knee-deep, waist-deep to the edge and over
Vanishing in the smoky look of asphodels
Which do not harbour in them any little heart
Of red the wind might blow to life
But are the stuff of mist over that lake
The birds can't cross but fall into stone dead. And white
The apparitions in that wood
That looked as though the aghast inside
Nefas, taboo
Turned out were being shown
In daylight and this was
The pause, the white, the staring face to face
In shock before the roaring blood returns.
We should be more like children in our make-believe,
More deadly serious: fit your fingers caps
Of the proper red and maul
Me silky moist with delicate claws. It is
The green leaves slow the heart, the caps
Will quicken it. See if
A hand of fingers hooded red
On your white breast
Makes you believe.

Submerged Site

But the sea will not keep still. Down there
They fixed two lovers in marble tesserae
BC/AD. Peer through the boat's glass floor:
Some days they're as clear as you and me
In the mirror doing what lovers always do
And hope to do again together soon.

In roofless rooms, so long under the sea,
It makes a ceiling painting of us two
Flat out, peering down. They seem to be in the rooms
Of an old sonnet, pinned in place by rhymes
As hard as tesserae, in quatrains, line by line,
Mine and thine, o my beloved, thou and I
Doing what we do and still a while longer will.

But how like us or unlike those two are
In looks today refuses to come clear.
Turbid water. The sea will not keep still.

Wrecking

Sleep hearing the far beginnings of a favourable gale;
Travel the night long on the hope of it and wake
Clear in the head, sniffing the air. Leave home on a sip
And a crust and go to the places that are familiar
With promise. Want all you can but never arrive

Over the bay on the west side of the hill of the tumuli
Or on the north side of the narrow peninsula
Wherever in the favourable night was windward
Wanting any said thing: not planks for the house,
Not a four-poster bed, curtained with fabulous wrack,

Nor even the talk of the drowned. But want
What you know to be missing but haven't been able to say
What it is. Want that, invest the horizon
Body and soul with wanting the loss and watch
The milk of the remembering sea for its return.

Northwesterly

Descried at birth they may be but no invention of ours
Can strangle the winds. And shadowed they may be,
Forecast and warned about, but against

Their landfall, against the face and the front they make,
No science can proof us. The slant this time,
The skew, the sliced stroke of arrival

Differed from last and it flung
Everything oddly on the infinite new woof
Of the waves. I was opened again, breathing. Then she

Wave after wave unveiled her looks and through
This harp of bone, into this
Small bay of a human being delivered up

Line after line the high horizon beached its wreck.

351

Pisces Moon

Full moon, the Pisces moon, after Aquarius
Has tipped the swollen sky into the sea
And called the sea up into the sky again
And tipped it back again, after Aquarius
Comes the Pisces moon, the fishes
Joined at the mouth, hooked through the lips,
Tugging averted, their moon, their spring tide
And down the channel on a westerly gale
The whole bulk of the Atlantic funnels in
Up under the window where the lamp has burned
Since nightfall and will burn till daybreak, day-
Light and the high tide, daylight arriving on a spring tide
Up under the window, the tide of the twin fish:
Peril of a light left on all night, the peril of conjuring
When all the Atlantic is only half a mile away
What foolishness, what lust to wake and watch
All night, the night of the Pisces moon, foolish
The heart's need on a spring tide to encourage the night,
The full moon night, the helpless fastened fishes
Sprats in an ocean raised up by Aquarius
And daylight coming, full moon and the sun
Full on and face to face across the hill of the tumuli,
Which is all there is here still above the sea,
The sun in silver and the moon on blue
Paling, letting the tide go, letting the cold sun view
The wreck, the abundant haul, she pales, she vanishes
After the ninth-wave fling of the year thus ending and beginning.

Not Only But Also

I've seen it here, looked up, looked round or she
Called me to look, to turn and showed it and more than once
On a day when nothing in the weather, nothing in me had signalled
It there: the entire arc, quivering
Substantial light, its makings
Visible, and not only that – the perfection
Held trembling
For a longer space of time than I had powers
To contemplate – but also
Many starts and waftings of it, watery
Airy floatings, the zenith's
Vaguely hovering keystone, the drift, the signs
Of assembling, of will be, of are and the unbearable
Soon will have been, the whitening
Mist of was, and not only that but also
Visiting between the parts of here the boat
Snuffles for, flings off, plies through
The vapours, the gauze, film and tissue of it,
The little boat goes haloed, aureoled, dressed and dishevelled in it,
Forever making and casting because there's no end
In water, air and light of the substance of it
And the knack seems given, the gift of the weaving and sporting
Must come with the job, the craft,
The normal traffic, and not only that but this also
That I am certain here that for somebody else
Out of view over there and seeing
The perfection spring from the sea
And rise in a curve and curve down on a parcel of earth and who wondered
Who stood there in that footing illumined
We did, ignorant of it, those were
Our whereabouts, our eastings and northings, we were
The place it lit upon and not only that but
Its rising.

'There is nothing I can tell you...'

There is nothing I can tell you about the sea.

That it can't keep still and even in daylight
Is under the moon and host
To headlong wanderings and hunger
And that for its appearance it mates with the winds
In all their degrees and every glance of light...

And about islands there is nothing I can tell you.

The rush of landing – Where will we sleep tonight? –
And the selfsame evening, housed,
We climb to another Top Rock or Watch Hill –
Where tomorrow? And the little ferry
Will drag us away with samphire on our fingers...

There is nothing I can tell you about the sea and about the islands.

That they make us liable to the moon
Even to the starving wisp of her in daylight
And nervously alert to every start of water
And our fingers itchy for the herbs that do not grow inland
Night after night, deny it, you told me.

Love Feast

Ripped on bright feathers from their element
The cold, the deep, the delighting
Where they hungered as we do, the three fishes

Under my hands in the shallows bled
When I beheaded them and slit them up
Smearing the gold. I slung their heads and the coils,

The sheaths and the soft bulbs of their insides
To those pure appetites, the gulls. It was not agape
That night between Venus and the full moon

But a love feast all the same on soft white flesh
Under frills of feathery dill
Some peace and quiet and the talk going between us

Easefully as the lapping shallows.

Rowing

The rowing is easy. I was watching you
Like an auctioneer a high bidder,
The coolest, an eyebrow, a little finger,

Yes, another five hundred, yes. I was trusting you
To miss me the moorings and the rocks.
So easy rowing. But if you close your eyes

And offer me your open face and seem
To be gently ridden by the oracle of the sunny water
I suppose it means you trust me to row backwards

And keep your head of hair lined up on Hangman Island
As per your final nod. Much terra firma lately
Has come adrift like icebergs. Easy rowing.

The back of my skull can feel the open Atlantic.

Phenomena

Over the facts the weather blows
Over the sea that ebbs and flows
And sometimes hides and sometimes shows

A fact of rocks whose floating hair
Signals sailors to beware
They have no depth, the facts are there

And over them the fictions go
Over the archipelago
Set in the sea so long ago

It seems a certain fixity
In all the mutability
Of shadowy and watery

Appearances under the moon
And sun and crepuscules between
And in the mix of rain and shine

That irises our open eyes
And in the race of nights and days
That show us truly weatherwise

In fictions we have made as fair
As any mermaid's floating hair
That shows a fact of rock is there.

'So slim you are...'

So slim you are, stand there
You just about cover the Pennines but over there
Against Siberia you are barely a finger post.
Strait the gate
To where you go from me
The infinite land
The railways running to a vanishing point
The foreign speech in golden hieroglyphs
Visible very briefly on the cold
Then from the screen
Falling like the Leonids.

Earrings in the Forest

Pearl dots on the lobes no bigger than sleepers
That keep the flesh open, but pearl
And never before. Remember
Hylonome? All lady
Above the waist except that her ears
Whose lobes were clasped and slung with fine gold
Ran to points and split like forks of flame
Against her bound-up braided hair. Like that
As at the Lord Mayor's Banquet
From under a white hem
The private showing of a cleft and hairy foot
In our tame forest well within the peripheral
I read your oyster drops.

Dreamer

I swear – my hand was on your heart –
It lasted only a little while. Your whimpering
And shuddering and the racing of your heart
Was ten or twenty seconds. But you tell me
You were in an extensive city
With such a weight of grief in your arms
Hurrying at a loss down the hard streets
For help, for mercy on the agony
For an ambulance, for charity from strangers
And all in vain on the neverending streets
Such haste, such distances
And such a burden of grief you had to show to strangers
No help in sight, no end
Of need and little sallies down the unpeopled streets. But I
Can swear to you the passage was of a short duration
No more than twenty seconds
And all that everlasting city
No bigger than this bed.

Crossing

I am under the water
Surely. That loud sign of life
Must be my heart. Where I embarked
The name of it was Chaos
And no idea where for. I never wanted
To be in anybody else's hands
But this between is snug. Head first
Or feet first, I have no idea
And even in daylight through myopic glass
What landmarks will there be
Or proof of any progress? Only the roaring
Of engines underwater
And in it me
My thought bubbles
And thudding heart
Meanwhile.

How It Is

Under the leads
Where it is always noon
And the ceiling melts
She envies me my frozen bulb
Of midnight in the wellshaft.

We are a mechanism. She
Ascends me when she sinks.
We cross, we swap
Horrors. The poets were right:
Love is an icy fire.

Inquisitor and Sinner

Pity the Inquisitor. Lying in the dark
Nothing his head and heart can breed
But questions.When the Sinner comes
Letter by spitting letter
The questions brand his tongue. Her answers are
A martyrdom by single needles. Pity
The Inquisitor. The Sinner weeps
Salt on the bloody pores. Listen:
I have remembered something else.

At the Frost Fair

There was hot spicy wine
And fiery sweets that might have cheered us
Body and soul. But all I bought her
Was an image of our love
In ice, and mittens to hold it with
And stop her warmth from coming out.
How she cherished the image!
We agreed there must be no kissing
And soon she whispered not to talk too closely either
For fear of the melting power
In our ghosts of breath. At the Frost Fair
In all the quaffing and feasting
And skaters dashing hand in hand
Among the fires to the broken limits of the freeze
We emulated certain small animals
Whose way of getting through winter
Is to almost stop the heart
In absence, absence
So cold and constant the image will survive.

Lover

Eros unarming, what will be left
Of him? Listen:
That end of music was the soul
Already flitting. Through the winter now
He must shift and work his limbs and make a sound
Of life. But in the spring
Like that apple tree that saddened us
Among the greening things he will be shown up grey.

Epstein's Lazarus

We are the dead and must attract
Like a buried north
To slew his head
That great muscular man, his head
Our way, gawping like a moon
Eyes craterous. We,
The inert, so strong. But he is leaving,
Swaddled and hobbled, mincing like a tight lady
Things stronger than us dead are dragging him out
And the body, unwilling as a yew tree
To rot just yet, says yes by creeping,
Inching, shuffling lightwards whatever the head
Slung like a sack, like a goitre of cowardice
Flung over on his neck backwards and mooning at dissolution
Whatever his brainy head or his traitorous
Pineal gland wants – wants nothing, wants to be nothing,
Wants to stop thinking and wanting –
His body's one idea is
Creep, shuffle, inch it back into the daylight
And in that tug of war we on our knees in a sunk nave
Lose, he will escape us,
A small rain falling will open his eyes.

Porlock

The high moor, such a catchment; a trapped marsh; the sea.
But the sea's invisible down there
Behind the dam of pebbles and against them
The moderate river stops. So between
Keeping an eye on the skies
And knowing the tide-tables and the time of the month
They to'd and fro'd, noting
The salty carapaces half a mile inland
And a cast of silt over the plank bridges
And the greens that look sour and undecided
Whether or not to die and come again
Adapted. The growling sea with every pulse

Accumulates its own prevention
And weight of rage. The river, become a sump,
Is still in touch with the high springs.
They were walking to and fro
Betwixt and between, below the lowest contour
And whatever the conversation was
I know they were thrilling the back of the mind
With thoughts of double drowning. Up here
On the airy headland
All's as clear as hindsight.

The Second Mrs Hardy

The second Mrs Hardy found married life
Full. Yet with the first
How he had pined, how they had thinned away
To nothing and passed
Through one another on the landing and the stairs
Like cold draughts. Like hunger artists
They could not find an appetite for any food
Till death. Then how they binged
The pair of them
They bulked so large the second Mrs Hardy
Set for three and over her plate of crumbs
She watched them sup the blood and cram the flesh
Of early life. Server
Upon this sacrament she waned
To the bare bones of a bright-eyed mind
And the neat hand
Of a copyist.

Off Lerici

Shelley at Lynmouth launching little flagships
Well-keeled and -rosined, with a brave sail
And a freight of rights; above Lechlade
Pushing towards the spring, halted
In toils of weed, an audience
Of placid paddling cattle. Shelley
In his last notebook doodling boats,
Airy little craft. He wrote: We breeze along
This quiet bay at dusk
Under the summer moon, earth seems
Another country, the airs
Of Jane's guitar accompany
Our harmless wake. Cease thinking
Back and futurewards and I could say
To now: You are so beautiful
Abide with us.

Keats at Lulworth

Everything contrary, omens, tempest,
As though he should not go. Two weeks
From Tower Dock to here, all sick
To death, the choking waters in the little living space.
Then respite, terra firma, life as it had been
When I was in health. He showed the after-image
In joy to his survivor. Then the wind turned favourable
For death. Look there love
From this white face of beauty out past Portland
Lessening away. Eternally
I see her figure eternally vanishing. He made a difference
Between his dying – this was bearable –
And never seeing her again – this not.

Under the Gunnery

Lush and sweet
The prize for flowering will be ours again this year;
Our morris men
Leap and jangle and wave their handkerchiefs
Mildly delightfully. No one here
Is alarmed by sudden firing.
We mind our own business
And the guns mind theirs. Above us –
We call it by an old name: the Demesne –
The flora is said to be out of this world
And creatures thrive
That can't get on with us down here and a very old
Evacuated house of God
Has in the moon. Under the gunnery
We are as safe as houses;
We toast and grill and circulate among our kind.
Over our heads meanwhile
Young men from elsewhere
Practise, practise.

Enclave

Our shape on the map is
Gynaecological, a bad drawing
Of the tight way in to a bulb
Of living space. How do we live?
Dumbly in our speech bubble.
We listen to the guard dogs and the warning shots.
The searchlights feel around our bedroom walls.
Our remaining romantics
Creep to the entrance on summer nights,
Lie in the close there, it is an ancient thicket,
And weep deliciously for the final nightingales.
But most we wife-swap, hose the lawn,
Flick like fleas all over the world
For breaking stories. Hard to believe
We are the temptation. Pity the poor brutes if they still think us
The womb of better times.

Treptow. Deserted Funfair.

A year and a day; then came an innocent
And pushed at the iron gates which were not tight after all.
Their loop of chains eased like a serpent,
Allowing a slit, and in she went.

Kennel on the left, empty; and on the right
In the ticket office nobody glaring out,
Only a roll of tickets unrolling through the glass
Like a pious initial quietly running riot.

Slow uprising; this is not the rainforest,
It is the dull north and the cold east.
But the ways of asphalt, thin as humanity,
Are converting to the earth which they suppressed.

Wreckage is good: the storms last year,
Wounds unattended have flourished here,
Rottenness, weakness, whatever couldn't bear
Another winter fodders up this spring,

This second May month since the desertion,
This heave of seeding, leafing, fluting, building.
There was some catastrophe, the boss has gone,
And left a future: the old viridian.

The trespasser smiles, and no wonder: see
A tyranosaurus rex felled by a snapping tree
And a diplodocus spared and grazing on the new shoots
And the Swan Lake, set for a finale,

Miring from the edges, has huddled the whole tribe close
Like a Soviet fleet abandoned in black ice
To rot. They filled with autumn. Now
Some ugly ducklings have boarded them and set up house.

The Dipper stuck aloft like a caterpillar;
The Dodgems sad as cast-off heavy-duty boots;
The Big Wheel already a monument like winding-gear;
Standstill at the Carousel; shutdown at the Hoop-la.

Even if power were suddenly restored
Nothing would obey: the neon is in flower,
Cables have mated with bindweed and ground elder,
Mice are in the guts of the photocopier.

Through tunnels under the wire
Or flying, gliding, drifting on the free air
More immigrants are arriving every hour
Than Ellis Island processed in half a century.

In this little township about as large
As the one the Americans built against the Wall
To practise streetfighting, in this local
Involuntary park twinned with Chernobyl

(Where creation without us is doing fine)
What did this fairy-story's heroine
Eat and drink all day? Not known.
Manna? Her packed lunch? But one thing I do know

She slept that night in the ruinous Haunted House
Listening to the owls. She wanted advice
By owls or a dream or a friendly ghost
Who she should tell, if anyone, about Paradise.

Corpse

Like a shell
A small one, dumb
And in much blood,
Her mother's, steeped
And with many tears,
Her father's, salt–
Watered and now
Muffled tight
For the dark she is
A black hole all
The aid of the earth
Sucked in by her
Won't fill, a pod
Of wrong, a seed
Of death, a time–
Capsule for eternity
To read us true:
The ill we were
The deed we did.
Little implant
Ache for ever.

Body Parts and the Rapture

Good question. The President
Has been to the Top on this one and the Word is:
So long as none of your parts was ever a terrorist
And never in all its born days
Possessed a vibrator or did the unclean solo
And just so long as all the parts of you when they saw it coming
(Alas and I'm very sorry if they did not see it coming)
Abjured the tribe of the false gods and turned
Beaming to Jesus and even being disassembled
Not for a split second in any atom's atom
Had a bad feeling about America
Rest assured
Come the Rapture your parts will whizz together
On your hopeful soul, their individual magnet,
And you will jig and carol with the rest of us
And be with the President in Eternal Felicity
For with the right God all things are possible.

Deer on the Street

And I wished we were only a clearing
And had tended the small space
Neatly, with tact
So we should have been fit to be visited in the hard cold
By the beasts in need
Hungry, finding no greenery, one of them lame
Trekking on a hopeful instinct to a little heart of warmth
To a small surplus. Like setting
An extra place at table for a possible guest.
I wished we were a homely and frugal clearing.

Outlook

Some warmer days.
The drunks come out from under the bridge, to dry.
But the more feeling earth

Looks to have had it too hard, too cold, too long
And the waters also
Look fearful of appearing.

The snow was beautiful
The snow and the ice together made a lovely covering
But now it shows: the harm but not the cure.

Come more such days
And a soft rain at nightfall hurry it on
Melt the frail lozenge of ice in the soiled mouth

Hurry us through to knowing will we leaf.

Remembrance Sunday

In come the town band down the long prom
And all the services with their lifted standards,
Veterans, new blood and a hopeful shambles,
A long long tail of mothers and children

In at the opening we have left for them
Into the space we are the shaping of
On this cold day, the cold wind makes her weep,
So cold a day I can feel her shake

Frail as a sparrow when I hold her shoulders
I feel her shudder like the ancient priestess
Who had to drink snow water before she could speak
But on Remembrance Sunday she can't remember

The word 'poppies', she hits on 'red things'
And tries again till she lights on 'badges',
So there we are in our black and badges
All present and correct for the incoming

That packs us to the heart for eleven o'clock
For the reserve of silence in the filled-up space
And while the town band murmured hymns
And red things heaped the cenotaph

I couldn't say what was shaking her
Who can't remember: the cold day
Or the cold that is the heart's flinching away
From the heap of presence in time stopped still

In her one tense, in the vessel of her,
And none were missing, all were there
Without a word on Remembrance Day?
I am her son and I still can't say.

Stroke

'You're lovely,' he says, touching her face.
So much is true
So much is well said
But for the rest, like sixty years ago
She seems to have tongue-tied him.

He was never much of a talker
And won't make up for it now
But once he remembered a thing from Lorna Doone
And said it out suddenly to his boy
In love: when Jan Ridd
Climbs the stream
Into the upper valley and sees her there
'And all the world was lovelier for that sight.'

It wasn't in his own words
But he had it by heart
And it was fit for the heart's affections.

On Conwy Mountain

Of the earth's breath, the dumb stormwind,
Up here on the long hill
Long before daylight I have swallowed enough for two

For both of us
To inflate the lungs and to erect the clay
Already wetted with tears and the rain, the old god's spit.

Must be that sorrow is another energy. Down there
On the wards under the long hill
He can't see anything exactly, it is neither dark nor light,

The voice won't run, the hands
Puzzle at one another like a baby's or one rises
Lost to the left side of the head and rubs there, rubs

As though for a genie with saving wishes. This has sharpened
My hunger for clarities, for the bright points
Of stars if I tear the clouds.

But now day breaks like the worst of shepherd's warnings,
Rears up like a face in the mirror
Appalled at the bruising, shows

On the waters of the estuary a soft pink
Like blood through lather. Here
Is the last step down from the Welsh Three Thousanders

Or the first step up to their shining ridges,
The kestrel trembling steadily
And the cleanliness of the picked white bones. Go little soul

Ease out and away this morning when the tide turns
And the river makes its donation of sweet water
Out of a clamorous mouth

Go babbling of the untouched fields behind the housing,
Of walking out
Among the grasses we called the silverspoons

That filled with a rose and a dewy light, oh now
At tide-turn dying under the long mountain
Go gentle, leave me raging.

Visiting

Visiting her lately, once or twice
She has seemed to think I am my father's ghost
On leave. I do miss you, she says
More wife in her looks than mother
Her voice confessional. Asked the questions
When do you have to go? How far is it home?
I don't know who I should answer for.

Estuarine

Big river giving up what made it
It. No fighting visible
But all the colossal loss of self
Flat silent under a hemisphere
Of stillness. Then I'd only been
Three or four years on the dry land
Still wrapped in native wonder. I recall
This much: a level the lowest possible above
The sea and it
Was greening gold, sheep safely grazed, the lark
And curlew signed it differently, water
Holed and threaded it so that it blinked between
More dry than wet, more wet than dry,
An earth dissolving into steppingtufts and mud, the water
Salting. How I loved
My game of pondering a route
Dryfoot and intricate to the farthest out. I thought myself
Out there where the wavering decided on
The sea, the river,
Biggest imaginable, lapsed without any trace
And on the brink of guessing at a place
Of nowhere, nothing, no one evermore
I reached up for love's
Always waiting to be reached for hand.

Cave Dale

I was dreaming about the place you told me about
And woke continuing. All the darkness long
The cave dale, as you said, entered the town
Between two ordinary shops and there I lay
Like a figure in a frontispiece
Of visions and that dark tunnel off the uplands
Entered my labyrinth and all
The mysteries of water in the limestone country
Were given me, the caves, the swallow holes, the sudden vanishings
And fresh resurgences many miles away. But best
Last night I saw the high bare places after rain when for a while
On the green grass lying in hollows shaped for it
Between the drystone walls transfigured from grey to white
Under the sun, under the blue sky
The silver waters shine. Dreaming with my ear
To the place of entry of the long cave dale
I felt I could go in under the hazels and begin the climb
And rest on handholds soft and damp with moss, ferns on my face,
An owl preceding me and one of the rivers of paradise
Under my feet under the scooped and polished bed. I felt I would arrive
Where you said you had stood and wept to see
The waters and a children's sky
Dancing with lapwing. We will go, won't we
While there's time, we'll wake
Before the sleepers in this ordinary town
And I will show you what I've learned which is
The limestone secret climbing out of here?
I sleep badly. I want more of the dark
That has the light in it like Blue John. But now in daylight
I must lick up my dream like a placenta
Before the crows get it.

Head of a Kore in a Marble Mine on Paros

As though I had dreamed and woke
In the locus of dreaming, that in my lap,
And like a blind man feeling

Assured myself of her smile. Now I must fag
That weight and my own
Up the steep diagonal. I could remember

Swifts over pools of lupins and see
On the small square of blue daylight
The clean silver dip and lift of one bare fig branch.

More galleries went down behind my back
Like bad thoughts to their hell
And I must fag up the infinite diagonal,

The girl's head heavier and heavier on my heart.

Mother and Child

Upsurge for a while around Hallowe'en
Not only of the dead, the unborn too
Desire a surface of life to flower on
Like frost. Over the child
The settled elders are content with a likeness of the known
And a glimpse of ancestry. But the mother
Sunk in the pose of adoration
Still in the radiance before she closes again
Mists her vision breathing warmly on
The unseeded flowers.

Trilobite in the Wenlock Shales

When the kingfisher flitted
Under the hazels I entered again into boyhood
Over a hurrying water.

The church clock dropped the quarters nearby
And from a little school
Children hallooed like enchanted animals

But I was watching a water that shipped the wild apples
With all the time in the world
Patient as a fisher bird

In the hazel light to learn to be a finder
Of life, its mark, on a black stone
Opened like a butterfly, a soul that water,

Swaling and swaling, had let be seen.

Obolus

That newborn on the Morrison
Is me. He looks flung down
From elsewhere. All's familiar:
The woman, a bowl of oranges, the galleon.
I'll say she brought the oranges through Musso's Lake
I'll say she brought my father safely home
I'll say the trade winds never wafted in
A fuller hold of love. Asleep
Before I had a single English word
I look to be dreaming all my life to come
I look like one under Vesuvius
Set for as long as there'll be eyes to look
Fending it off. Or look
To be beckoning it in:
The home, the native land, all the warring world
In, in. Charon
My obolus will be a good luck ship ha'penny
Of 1944. What galaxies
Hades must have for housing if on every
Arriving dot
Rides such a swarm.

374

INDEX

Index of titles and first lines

Poem titles are shown in italics, collections in bold italics, first lines (some abbreviated) in roman type.